A FOUR-EYED WORLD

A FOUR-EYED WORLD

How Glasses Changed the Way We See

DAVID KING DUNAWAY

BLOOMSBURY ACADEMIC
NEW YORK • LONDON • OXFORD • NEW DELHI • SYDNEY

BLOOMSBURY ACADEMIC

Bloomsbury Publishing Inc, 1359 Broadway, New York, NY 10018, USA
Bloomsbury Publishing Plc, 50 Bedford Square, London, WC1B 3DP, UK
Bloomsbury Publishing Ireland, 29 Earlsfort Terrace, Dublin 2, D02 AY28, Ireland

BLOOMSBURY, BLOOMSBURY ACADEMIC and the Diana logo are trademarks
of Bloomsbury Publishing Plc

First published in the United States of America 2026

Copyright © David K. Dunaway, 2026

Cover image © iStock.com/ Nuthawut Somsuk
Cover design by Diana Nuhn

All rights reserved. No part of this publication may be: i) reproduced or transmitted in any form, electronic or mechanical, including photocopying, recording or by means of any information storage or retrieval system without prior permission in writing from the publishers; or ii) used or reproduced in any way for the training, development or operation of artificial intelligence (AI) technologies, including generative AI technologies. The rights holders expressly reserve this publication from the text and data mining exception as per Article 4(3) of the Digital Single Market Directive (EU) 2019/790.

Bloomsbury Publishing Inc does not have any control over, or responsibility for, any third-party websites referred to or in this book. All internet addresses given in this book were correct at the time of going to press. The author and publisher regret any inconvenience caused if addresses have changed or sites have ceased to exist, but can accept no responsibility for any such changes.

A catalog record for this book is available from the Library of Congress.

ISBN: HB: 979-8-8818-0482-4
ePDF: 979-8-8818-6786-7
eBook: 979-8-8818-0483-1

Typeset by Deanta Global Publishing Services, Chennai, India
Printed and bound in the United States of America

For product safety related questions contact productsafety@bloomsbury.com.

To find out more about our authors and books visit www.bloomsbury.com and sign up for our newsletters.

CONTENTS

Preface: Glassers vii

Introduction   The Struggle for Sight 1

   Sunday 9
1 The Beginning of Assisted Vision 19

   Monday 37
2 Living with Lenses 45

   Tuesday 61
3 The Glasses Stigma 71

   Wednesday 85
4 Fashions in Glasses 93

   Thursday 107
5 Glasses Turn Literary 113

   Friday 131
6 Glasses Go Hollywood 135

   Saturday 153
7 What People Think of Those Wearing Glasses 157

Sunday 167
8 What People Say about Their Own Glasses 171

Monday 183
9 Glasses Today 185
10 Glasses Tomorrow: AR, VR, and Beyond 205
Epilogue: Three Years Later 225

Acknowledgments 231
Notes 232
Index 258
About the Author 270

PREFACE: GLASSERS

Before glasses, the world was fuzzy unless I brought objects up close. Back then, I couldn't quite figure out what to do with glasses. I remember turning them over and peering intently at the long side pieces—they looked like something from the kitchen drawer used to slide onions into a pan. My first pair was a miniature of my dad's—thick black rectangles editors favored in the 1950s. Over time, I got used to this new way of seeing things.

And then, between the ages of ten and thirteen, I lost half my vision, going from 20:400 to 20:600. I couldn't make out the big "E" on the eye chart. Today, as I write this, my eyes are slowly failing. I'm grateful glasses let me see as well as I can, but I wish for more.

Billions of humans have shared the experience of wearing lenses to see better. Today, whether we see sharply or blurrily, in focus or out, most of us eventually come to view the world through corrective lenses because of aging. Although we make up about two-thirds of the US population, we don't think of ourselves as a distinct community; there is no National Association of Glasses Wearers conference in Las Vegas. The dictionary lacks a word for those wearing lenses, so I'll call us "glassers": anyone who walks around, sometimes or always, with a lens between them and the world. (Hey, it's better than "four-eyes.")

Some might think there's nothing particularly interesting about glasses: You put them on and they work, or not. But particularly for those whose lenses have framed their sight, there's more to be learned about these essential tools. For people who must rely on glasses at all times to see, they might be the device kept closest, more so than even that modern appendage, the smartphone—kept no more than an arm's reach away, if not already riding the nose. Shakespeare said eyes are the portals to the soul, but some of us need discs of plastic to see through them.

I have no training in medicine, optometry, or opticianry; but my lifelong struggles to see made me reflect on how critical glasses are to those of us who rely on them. I wondered how people survived before they were invented. If you wear glasses at times, consider this: How would you manage without them? Could you drive or work? Do you remove your glasses for selfies to "look your best," and slip them on again afterward? Move the restaurant menu toward the light to avoid putting them on? When you misplace them, do you need glasses to find your glasses?

Questions like these, in turn, led me to ask what would happen if I gave up my glasses for a while. Most people who see as poorly as I do wouldn't take the plunge, and for good reason! They could trip and fall, burn themselves on the stove, or tumble down the stairs. The rest of the time, they wouldn't see straight.

* * *

In the 750 years since the invention of spectacles, society's stake in vision correction has only grown. Visual aids have influenced the history of the world's commerce, transportation, and education by allowing people to see and work productively into and past middle age.

Unfortunately, today, we live amid a largely unknown but startling world epidemic of myopia: In the United States and Europe, the number of nearsighted young adults has more than doubled over half-century.[1] (Fortunately, steps can help prevent or lessen myopia in children.)

Now that glasses are a tool more and more rely on, readers might want answers to key questions: Why do they cost so much? How can we choose the right pair? Will the glasses of the future reshape privacy, as computer-enabled smart glasses allow people to stream everything they see? And if such devices become widely adopted, will kids unable to afford them be taunted as "two-eyes"?

This book is a journey into sight and how the world is seen, from the biological basis of vision to the technology of its correction. It combines the history and sociology of glasses, explored through interviews, far-flung journeys, hundreds of articles and books, and a weeklong personal challenge to live without them.

This work attempts an explanation as to why eyeglasses have cut such a wide swath through American and world culture. For those readers who already wear glasses, I hope to offer an engaging history and provoke curiosity about a device we sometimes take for granted. For those who don't wear lenses, perhaps this book offers a window through which to see the world as we glassers do—a book for anyone who wears glasses or who has friends and families who do.

Introduction
The Struggle for Sight

The greatest thing a human soul ever does in this world is to see something, and tell what it saw in a plain way ... To see clearly is poetry, prophecy, and religion, all in one.

—ART CRITIC JOHN RUSKIN, 1856

President John F. Kennedy inaugurated the race to put humans on the moon in 1962. After their first trip, early astronauts decided that its most important moment was seeing the world in perspective. As they gazed down at the Earth sparkling like a diamond in a black velvet sky, their experience was unique not just in human history but in the history of sight itself. Seen in its entirety in a single glance, the earth seemed fragile. "I looked away for a moment and poof, Earth was gone," wrote Apollo 11 astronaut Michael Collins. "I couldn't find it again without looking closely."[1]

"As we went further and further, the Earth diminished in size. Finally, it shrank to the size of a marble," astronaut James Irwin commented. "The most beautiful you can imagine. Seeing this has to change a man."[2] Indeed, it changed humanity to see our home in the cosmos, a small and vulnerable foothold in the universe that humans must learn to share and care for together.

The search for Earth from the cosmos mirrors humans' timeless quest for sight against all obstacles. Since the beginning of our time on earth, humanity has relentlessly sought to see more clearly. Our need for visual clarity is codified in our language. In discussion, we "see the point" and assess the evidence to "see if someone's right." We try to "see what they mean." (That is, unless we've "lost sight" of what they're saying.) We're always "looking ahead," "looking forward" to something. In parting, "we see someone off," knowing we'll "see them later." If we're concerned, we "look out for someone." Dozens more such metaphors underlie our daily consciousness, as we connect visually by looking people straight in the eye to see where they're coming from.

The quest to see more clearly started with salves and herbal tonics applied directly to the eyes, and then lenses. The invention of lenses led in turn to telescopes, microscopes, and every kind of visual device from the slit-eyed, lensless sunglasses developed by native peoples of the Arctic to magnifying glasses, and finally to that wonderful, portable, almost magical device, eyeglasses. To develop this technology, scientists struggled to understand vision, light, and how to offer clear sight to those who happened not to be born with it.

One of the thinkers leading this effort was a controversial thirteenth-century Oxford scholar, Roger Bacon. Bacon was a Renaissance man in medieval times; his career suggests a time traveler flying backward from the twentieth century to the thirteenth to predict automobiles, submarines, and helicopters. Long before Galileo, he realized how Earth's position in the universe could be calculated by observing the sky. Bacon believed that everything important on heaven and earth comes to us through our visual apparatus. Devising eyeglasses was his ambition—and for this ambition and his resultant experiments, he ran afoul of authority and ended up in shackles. Sometimes called the world's first scientist, Roger Bacon is the man who *almost* invented glasses.

I remember reading about Bacon in a high school science class. It wasn't just his exploration of lenses that fascinated me, but his passionate belief in how experiments alone justify scientific theory. His work exemplified the struggle of scientists to understand vision; Aristotle, for example, called sight "the soul of any animal," pointing out that after death, an eye no longer functions as an eye, but as a symbol, like the eye of a statue or a painted figure.[3]

As critic John Berger points out, sight establishes our place not just in the cosmos but in the surrounding world.[4] For most of us, sight is our dominant sense—yet it's been a long time since seeing was believing. In today's world of deep fakery and AI memes, what we see is often *not* what we get; what we see on a screen might not even exist. With AI video-generation tools like Sora or Movie Gen becoming steadily more precise, it's a wonder we trust our eyes at all. A picture may no longer be worth a thousand words.

Just as Galileo struggled through a primitive telescope to place us in the solar system, or a surveyor today measures property lines with a high-tech scope, accurate sight is something everyone seeks. Yet despite our burning need, the invention of corrective lenses proved surprisingly controversial in human history. A stigma against wearing glasses has trickled down even to the present day, rooted in a reactionary attitude toward their once-revolutionary potential. That potential remains incompletely explored, as eyeglasses take on startling new roles in augmented and virtual reality applications. Already, smart glasses allow us to surf the internet, blink our way through emails, generate images for the blind, pay bills, and play out fantasies. Glasses aren't just glasses any more.

* * *

In antiquity, people believed that objects emitted rays of light, which were thought to be received by the eyes and the brain. Around 330 BC, Aristotle punctured this idea by asking a simple question: If objects emit light, why don't we see them in the dark? Rather, light from the sun or a fire, he concluded, is *reflected* by objects and passes through a transparent medium such as air to travel to the eye. (Since there is no sight without light, in absolute darkness, images cannot form.)

As they studied light and vision, researchers had a lot to figure out: How do images reach our brains? Where does color come from—is it something innate, plastered to an object, or a trick of how light falls? How does a three-dimensional image become two-dimensional on paper, or if one eye is damaged?

The Roman scholar Ptolemy divided the field of optics into light, color, and stereopsis (the depth-giving difference between what each eye sees). Later, researchers added motion and form to this list, and for centuries, those studying sight divided it into physical (genetic and environmental) and spiritual (informed by faith) dimensions. Early experiments with light used a pinhole in a light box, known as a camera obscura, to focus images. The narrower the hole (the aperture), the more detail observed. That same pinhole principle works for us when we squint. (Kids sometimes discover this by closing their fist around an eye to sharpen detail.)

When we see, light is being reflected to the eye. The eye's cornea and lens focus this light onto the retina. From there, it passes through the optic nerve to the visual cortex of the brain, which processes patterns of light into information that's useful to us. This process puzzled researchers for centuries: Exactly how do percepts—raw visual data—make their way to the brain and form images?[5] For centuries, scientists could only guess at our visual pathway. (In AD 77, Pliny the Elder suggested that visual decoding comes through the stomach, giving new meaning to the expression, "Your eyes are bigger than your stomach.")

At the time people guessed how images form, they inhabited a spirit-filled world, so it was inevitable that in explaining vision, another Roman scientist, Galen, believed that animal spirits connected with visual spirits to allow sight.[6] For almost a thousand years, this connection was called "spiritual vision," as opposed to physical vision derived from physiology.

Eventually, scientists came to realize that understanding vision also required knowing how the eye focuses. In the seventeenth century, German astronomer Johannes Kepler and French philosopher-scientist Réné Descartes separately figured out how images are inverted and focused on the retina, a curtain in the back of the eye having rods and cones sensitive to light and color. This process was partly discovered by shining rays of light backward through the eyes of the recently deceased.

The eye's accommodation system—how it shifts from near to distant focus and how it selects among objects—was not easy to understand. In the beginning, scientists thought that to focus light on the retina, the whole eye alternatively elongated and shrank. It was Descartes who suggested that it wasn't the whole eye that changed but only its lens. He was close—actually, it is the cornea's curvature that flexes and focuses, shaped by the eye's ciliary muscles. Recognizing this, one scientist called these muscles "The Most Wise Omnipotent Frame of the Eye."[7]

Johannes Kepler thought nearsightedness was determined by environmental factors, convinced that all his reading had weakened his eyes. Other scientists figured out that the physical shape of the eyeball determines visual correction—nearsighted eyes are elongated like a football, while farsighted eyes are compressed, like a doorknob. Scientists such as Isaac Newton discovered how vision works (or doesn't), correcting vision before they knew what caused the problem.

Newton, of course, is the seventeenth-century English scientist who supposedly theorized gravity after an apple fell on his head. He also broke new ground in understanding how we perceive color. Earlier theories turned out to be right: Objects do possess innate colors, but we only see them according to how light falls on them. Color proved quite subjective. Everyone had an opinion: Green, Descartes decided, is the most universally liked color. Newton, on the other hand, considered yellow and orange most affecting. Goethe, the brilliant author, once called "absurd" the idea that all colors mixed together produced white.[8] Yet Newton had already proved this, by using a prism to separate white light, containing all the colors of the spectrum, the palette schoolchildren learn: Red, orange, yellow, green, blue, indigo, and violet (ROY G BIV). He could have refined his experiments further if he'd opted to pay more than a shilling for a not-very-clear prism.[9]

* * *

Over time, people have explored different ways of seeing. Painters, for example, have always colored their vision by imagination. A quote attributed to Oliver Sacks is, "Looking at what's invisible? That's what we call imagination!"[10] Though eyeglasses don't appear in paintings until the fifteenth century, in a portrait of a saint, artists have long tested ways of directing our sight through shading, perspective, and other techniques. They play with light and shadow and experiment with color. Thus, the story of art is connected to the story of vision, and of visions. Take William Blake's engravings: "He did everything he could to make his figures lose substance," John Berger wrote, "to become transparent and indeterminate . . . present but intangible."[11] In presenting the world around us in new ways, artists unlock unseen doors.

Visual art and vision are inalterably joined, relying on the elaborate process of turning raw information about light and color into images—or, as a scientist might put it, into electromagnetic radiation to which the retinal nerve cells can respond. When that process is interrupted—when weakness or disease alters visual input—the artist no longer has a normal view of the world.[12] Are they accurately painting what they see, or rather, how they want us to see?

Critics have long speculated on how painters' sight influenced their work. According to Drs. Michael Marmor and James Ravin in their book, *The Artist's Eyes*, those whose art has been considered distorted because of eye problems include Botticelli, Titian, Matisse, Modigliani, and Degas. Scholars wonder, for example, if the long and thin images produced by Spanish genius El Greco were caused by astigmatism. (No, Marmor and Raven conclude, because other of the artist's canvases from the same time were perfectly proportioned.) Some wonder if Van Gogh's loose and wavy skies came from myopia (probably not, but many painters paint more freely in their older years).

The nineteenth-century English painter J. M. W. Turner has been considered color-deficient because the hazy skies in his paintings—particularly the later ones—are yellow-dominated. (He used this color throughout his career and mentioned its use in his writings.)[13] His yellow-white skies seem to float off the canvas, an effect that caused one critic to suggest his brush was dipped in sunshine. In 1845, when he was seventy, Turner painted a series of blurry, hazy oils. They look just like the images I see without my glasses. Though the Tate Britain museum doesn't suggest this in its literature, that haziness probably resulted from cataracts. For Turner, visual limitation became visual transcendence.

One problem with discerning the association between artists' visual acuity and their painted images is the lack of vision records concerning pre-nineteenth-century artists. Because of this lack of evidence, diagnosing eye problems from finished artworks is speculative. However, some famous artists are known to have been myopic, like Paul Cézanne, who nevertheless disdained help from lenses: "Take those vulgar things away," he reportedly said.[14]

In paintings and drawings, artists routinely brave the physical paradoxes of vision that researchers discovered over time. Binocular vision, for example, creates our depth perception. The brain codes depth into a scene by assessing relative motion, which is why objects at a great distance hardly seem to move at all, the way the moon appears still when viewed from a moving car.

Depth perception is created by perspective, where mathematics and art meet. In linear perspective, lines intersect in the background of an image, creating the illusion of three-dimensionality from the contrast of objects near and in the distance. The rules of perspective are geometrical, for eyes see receding lines as convergent. In the Renaissance, the laws of perspective were subtly practiced and understood: how image size changes with distance, and how this effect is enhanced by shading. Painters use this technique to direct our gaze, to turn contours into straight lines separated by color, and to detail items using high contrast. They turn to luminance, the physical, measurable intensity of light, to gauge the effect of colors: the blue end of a spectrum appears dimmer than the red-yellow end, even when the same light hits both colors.

The painter's way of seeing is translated by the marks he or she makes on paper or canvas such that when we see a landscape, we situate ourselves in it.[15] Prior to the advent of eyeglasses, landscape drawing was challenging for myopes; portraits and finely wrought jewelry difficult for the farsighted. In the twentieth century, the Russian futurist filmmaker Dziga Vertov claimed his artistic vision created a fresh perception of the world, one previously unknown to the viewer. Eyeglasses offered similar promise.

Deciphering our complex visual apparatus (and how it could be corrected) took scientists a millennium. The long, bumpy road to visual clarity contained potholes and detours. But it's a good thing scientists finally figured this out, for people spend more time looking—at screens large and small, surveying the world around us—than they do tasting, feeling, smelling, or hearing. The average American spends more than four hours a day staring at their phone for work and pleasure. For some, screen time takes up the majority of their waking hours. Sight fully occupies our time: driving, reading, watching, playing. So, I decided that, in order to better understand what glasses bring to our lives, I was going to give up all of it for a week.

Sunday

I bumped into things as a child. Before glasses, my forehead looked like a golf course, full of hollows and knolls. I thought this was normal—I had no idea others saw differently. The world's just full of bruises, I thought.

My near-sighted eyes needed a correction, it turned out, of −10 diopters. (A diopter measures corrective power in a lens; −5 diopters is highly myopic.) Even with glasses, life didn't become less chaotic all at once: I was just thigh-high to adults and in summer, all I saw were hairy legs. Running for a ball, or after a friend, I had to watch out. Bump into anything with hands full, and down I went. Glasses flew off my nose, ice cream off the cone. Things got sticky.

Perhaps because I was so young when I had them, I never paid them much attention. If glasses worked, fine. For me, they were an appendage, like my foot. Even so, the fact that my sight was weak left me with the feeling that *I* was not right, or whole—a visual loser.

The idea came to me one summer, not long before my classes began at the University of New Mexico. Chained to me as a child after I lost too many pairs, over time, glasses had become a plastic shackle I couldn't resist trying to drop: what would it be like to live for a week without them. I had to understand, after so many years of living with them, where they ended and I began—or whether they had become an undivorceable part of me.

Of course, *really* learning about life before glasses would necessarily catapult me back to the thirteenth century, a time of religious crusades, the Holy Roman Empire, and courtly love. It's one thing to speculate on how someone with little vision would have managed long ago and quite another to try and live that way today.

When I first started reading about the history of glasses, I quickly learned that eyeglasses had been invented in the thirteenth century, a dozen or so years before Dante's *Divine Comedy*. Et voilà! One of the most welcome inventions in the world.

* * *

Let me start at the beginning, in the silent bake of a New Mexico summer. One evening as the sun streaked purple and copper across the sky, I was sitting with some former students under the cottonwood trees by the Rio Grande. On a limb above us, I could see a hawk blinking sleepily before dinner. Past him, in the lion-colored dust, heat rippled over the banks by the river. Nothing moved. The hundred-degree temperature stretched me as thin as the skin of a drum. The only sound was the cicadas singing in the heat.

We were discussing eyeglasses—the curious habit many of us have of sometimes not wearing them, even when we need them a lot.

"Not wearing my glasses? I haven't done that since second grade," said Nora, a slim, brown-eyed twenty something with long brown hair and enviably thin lenses. She swiveled her head left and right nervously, her glasses sliding down her nose in the heat. She looked as if she'd seen a phantom at the edge of her frames.

"*I* couldn't do it," chimed in her friend Cynthia, an MFA student with red hair that matched her frames. She plucked her glasses on and off teasingly.

Pulling off my glasses, the world abruptly blurred. Shapes melted. "I'm addicted to my glasses," I said. "I never take them off except to bathe, sleep, or kiss. Every morning I slide them on without a thought. Yet without them, I couldn't cross the street." An idea rose inside me, like Albuquerque's famous hot air balloons. I had that odd feeling you get when you realize what you're going to say before you say it. "I could try leaving my glasses off for a week," I said suddenly. "How bad could that be?"

Lately, I'd been reconsidering my sight. Over the past few years, my vision had clouded due to posterior-vitreous detachments (PVDs)—"floaters"—a condition that occurs when the vitreous humor (the jelly inside the eyeball) thins, shrinks, and separates from the retina in the back of the eye. Strands of connective tissue floated before me as specks, dots, or spider webs across my vision.[1] Severely near-sighted people like me are prone to PVDs; the longer the eyeball, as in myopia, the more bits detach with age. Those bits were caught against my retina like leaves in a car's windshield wipers. Short of vacuuming out the vitreous humor inside the eyeball and replacing it with sterilized saline, there's only new, high-tech laser treatment.

None of this was the fault of my glasses, but without them, floaters sometimes faded into the blur. Normally, they cruised the dusky horizon of my eyes like tiny battleships. My optometrist told me the brain grows accustomed to blocking floaters after a year or so; but then others arrive. Before long, it would be as crowded inside my eye as New York's Coney Island boardwalk on Labor Day.

"Well; if you're going to try that, you better do it soon, before school starts," Cynthia said as she too pulled off her glasses to examine an out-of-focus world she seldom noticed. "But you must be crazy," she said, half smiling, half daring me.

"Let me get this straight, David: You're ditching your glasses? No peeking?" Nora asked.

"I'll give it a try."

For a moment, silence hung around us. Two doves settled in a tree in the dusk. A horse clopped by, trailing dust like a shiny brown mist.

Why experience life without glasses? I didn't fully know at the time, but I imagine now that with my vision fading, it felt like the right time to refocus, to step away from that routine of slipping on glasses without a thought. Would there be any value in uncorrected sight? Could I, in effect, develop more than one way of seeing? That thought felt heretical. Doing so would mean accepting sight as individual, subjective, and imprecise—not like the eye chart at the optometrist. Perhaps it was time to find out whether the lifelong quest for clarity my eye doctors had encouraged was really mine, or something imposed from outside myself.

Without glasses, I was leaving behind an in-focus, well-lit world for a dark wood. Yet the idea forced itself on me, bit by bit. There would be pitfalls, and perhaps real falls, but this week might offer a prize: visual autonomy. I could hardly wait, I told my students.

The women departed with the fading light. The ground was hot to the touch, and the air smelled stormy. In the distance, lightning tore the firmament in two, pale yellow bolts against gray clouds. All this I saw sharply outlined against the sky.

* * *

Like many who grew up wearing thick lenses, I was teased at school. It stung like a half-pulled splinter. Teachers tsked but never seemed to be there when it happened. Sometimes the teasing left me shaken, stealing into my dreams where the encounters repeated themselves. Why was this happening: What's wrong with wearing glasses?

The bullying robbed me of control over my psychic surroundings. Grasping for that was like trying to catch a fly ball but missing, my glove coming down empty. My identity as a four-eyes reminded me of that line from George Orwell: "You wear a mask and your face grows to fit it." I needed to drop my four-eyed mask, embrace a lack of visual control, and make it mine. This coming week I wanted to force my eyes to see without help, to turn—I hoped—limited visual capacity from an enemy to a strength.

Growing up, I learned to appreciate when glasses did their job well. Every six months I needed a stronger prescription for thicker and heavier lenses. With each new pair, I'd walk outside and stop in my tracks: Leaves flickered distinctly in the wind. Pigeons flew by on sharply dappled wings. Even the animals in the zoo looked less menacing. Visiting the optician became fun. Like medicine to reduce a fever, new glasses brought relief, reclaiming a world which had slipped into obscurity in the intervening months.

Germans have a word, *Brillenbrillanz*, for the sudden, enervating clarity afforded by new glasses. In a way, glasses were my first drug: They provided a mechanically induced, mind-altering clarity. But then the drug wore off, and I had to return to the optician for another fix. And then another. I became a "glassaholic."

Today, few notice the weakness of my eyes. With thin, high-index lenses, I pass for normal and ace the driver's test. But especially when I was a child, affording good pairs of glasses wasn't easy. I knew this from the grimace on my mother's face each time the optician told her how much the new pair cost. To save money, we traveled to New York City's Lower East Side to visit an optical factory with half-off specials. Half the time, I had to return for a redo after their pairs caused eye aches, as if someone had poured hot wax on my head. The company once handed me a pair with someone else's prescription. I remember asking Mom if there wasn't a law against this. (Parents should listen carefully if their children say their glasses aren't working.)

Yet despite the trouble, the pain, and the expense, I had no choice but to keep coming back. Without glasses, I was staring through the wrong end of a telescope. An accidental blow, a fall that dashed my glasses to the ground, would mean I couldn't find my way home. I never wanted anyone to know this fear.

* * *

If you're reading this with glass or plastic between you and the page or screen, you're a member of a community. "Four Eyes" is a name commonly thrown at people with weak ones. According to Merriam-Webster, the term "expresses contempt or dislike for the person wearing glasses," someone "physically weak, unlikely to engage in physical activity." This disdain for glassers is nothing new: Prejudice against those needing visual correction began as soon as glasses were invented and continues to this day, albeit in different forms. Many who wore glasses growing up have never considered how this bias affected their development and personality.

Some take glasses for granted, until they've sat on them, dropped them, or just plain lost them. When that happens, they've suddenly lost a part of themselves. Glasses are deeply personal: like a toothbrush, they're ours alone—keepers of sight, appreciated but sometimes damned. Some of us need them only for driving. The unlucky cannot function without them. Thus, the visual aids which provide sight also leave wearers vulnerable. In an instant, they can be lost, sinking their wearer into a world where focus dissolves. These shared experiences constitute a community. If you too have had trouble wearing glasses or contacts—it's been a problem—at least you're not alone.

I've wondered what eyeglass-wearers share, beyond the trivialities of daily wear? To answer that, I'd have to comprehensively swim through statistics and dive into demographics—because the shared experience of glassers may come down to understanding how they're viewed by others. Later, I'll look at what the research says about how someone's identity changes when they choose or have to don glasses. Times have changed since a debutante's pair was her ticket to spinsterhood. But how much and in what ways has this change occurred?

* * *

What I remember most is the infernal popping, like the sound of corncobs tossed into a pan the size of a living room. The popping and crackling give way to a crash that sounds like a hundred light bulbs thrown from a roof. Black smoke creeps into the room on the second floor of a friend's house, where I am sleeping next to my girlfriend. Jane and I, both twenty-one, have been lovers only a week, while she accompanies me on a cross-country journey to graduate school at Berkeley.

First thing, I grab my glasses off the end table and run into the hall to find out what's happened. Someone downstairs is passed out, leaving a cigarette burning on the couch. People are shouting at me to get out the door. Too late. The flames cover the living-room floor and are halfway up the stairs. If we were to dash down, we wouldn't make the door. What started as a cool place to crash in Berkeley is now hot as hell.

Jane's screaming. "Shit! What are we going to do?" Flames are now ten feet away, and the thickening smoke prevented me from seeing clearly. Everybody's out of the house but us. The flames below crackle loudly.

On the second floor, we're about twenty feet above the ground. There's a window in our bedroom, and another in the small sitting room next to us. I remember you aren't supposed to open a window during a fire. So, when Jane tries unsuccessfully to pull open the bedroom window, I run to stop her. Instead, she must think I'm running to join her; because right at that moment, she dives headfirst through the glass. I can't see where she lands, but I hear a scream below.

Now fed with a renewed supply of oxygen from the open window, the fire surges up the stairs. I run to the window in the other room and look down at the thick black swirls behind the pane. Making out a structure below, I push open the window and jump. My glasses fly off, and I land on my back on the hot roof of the garage. Jumping the next eight feet to the ground is instinctive. I hear a woman's cry from the other side of the building, but in the dark, without glasses, I have no way to reach her.

It's just past midnight. I need to look for Jane, but I can barely stand. An acrid smell hangs like fog. Fire trucks pull up, their pumps roaring and clanging. I can't see more than a few feet, but holding my arms out in front of me, I start moving. A bystander (whose name I never learn) leads me around the house to where Jane is being loaded into an ambulance. She's receiving an injection for pain as she moves her head slowly from one side to the other. In my underwear and a blanket the medics give me, I sit next to her in the ambulance.

"You can't take it with you," Aldous Huxley wrote after a fire destroyed his books and manuscripts. "I'm evidently to learn [this] in advance of the final denudation."[2]

The ambulance drives us to the nearest hospital. Because we have no money on us, they pack us off to the county hospital, eight miles away. There, I sort out the forms with a social worker—slowly, because she has to read me the questions. Without my glasses, I see only corridors without end and white oblongs of people. Their faces are blank, like the crowds losing their memories as they cross the River Lethe in the *Inferno*. Jane sleeps, my hands in hers. What can I do?

"Where are my glasses?" I ask. But I can guess where they are: melted into a coagulated pool of ash and plastic, next to a still-burning building. My spare pair was tossed at the last minute into the moving van.

In the best of circumstances, the inside of a hospital is a soundtrack to a nightmare: beeps, alarms, sirens. Without glasses, I see only corridors without end. Tears blur my vision.

Finally, a friend picks me up. Jane has fractured her vertebrae and will go from a hospital to her home to recover; though she will eventually heal. My heart aches: it's the end of things between us. The next day, an optometrist sends out for new glasses for me. I will never be found without two pairs of glasses in my possession again—except this week.

* * *

These days, despite the floaters, I rely on glasses more and more. I asked my optometrist what she thought of the idea of going without them for a week: "I'd be afraid to even jog without glasses." It's wild here at the edge of Albuquerque, the city of *Breaking Bad*, where I live in an adobe house by the Rio Grande. My neighbors are lizards, bats, coyotes, snakes, foxes. Something's always hopping or slithering by. There are no shops unless I drive or hike. Delivery vans rarely find my unmarked road.

So maybe this experiment *was* crazy. Even staying at home, I'd still be taking risks—cooking on a stove I couldn't see clearly, for example. Yet, the very near-sighted can see at least a little without glasses. We notice the handle on the cup and which side of the knife is sharp. We're not likely to mistake the pantry door for the garage and end up with a motor-oil omelet. I would still be able to read a book or newspaper or tablet held inches away from my face, listen to the radio, play with my phone. I'd be me, lost in a blur.

As I prepped for the week ahead, I remembered how Thoreau decided what he'd need when he decamped to Walden Pond: "Whatever is so essential to life that few," he wrote, "ever attempt to do without it."[3] He kept careful accounts—so much for flour, for sugar, for tea. I wasn't as organized: I gathered a cell phone and charger, apples, half-bottles of wine (screw top), and snacks in a backpack—as if going on a picnic. But this was no picnic. At best, I would be learning how to function on my own two eyes. At worst, it'd be hell without Virgil.

I didn't kid myself: I knew I would put my lenses on again. But I hoped when that happened, I'd know more about why I use glasses constantly and unconsciously. I was taking an opportunity to look at glasses with new eyes and learn something of their meaning.

1

The Beginning of Assisted Vision

Tis much better and more useful that one leaves spectacles alone. For naturally a person sees and recognizes something better when he has nothing in front of his eyes than when he has something there. It is much better that one should preserve his two eyes than that he should have four.

—DR. GEORG BARTISCH, 1583

Today, glass is everywhere we look. On our laptops, tablets, and phones, glass is in our faces most of the day. Glass is also the perfect building material where natural light is required, resistant to heat, sun, and moisture. Without glass, our lives would be profoundly different: We'd live without windows. We'd be ignorant of what we have learned about the universe through telescopes and computers. We'd read less and have no television or film. And we'd travel less and slower, having no windshields, mirrors, or fiberglass for cars, trucks, or airplanes.[1] We would phone less, for long, thin fiber-optic cables are what connect the globe. Nations would be vastly more separated, trade stunted. All this from glass—which is made largely of sand, one of the Earth's most common materials.

Though today's lenses are mostly plastic or polycarbonate, the history of glass is where our story begins. The discovery of glass was accidental—perhaps someone noticed shiny pebbles in the ashes of a bonfire on an Eastern Mediterranean beach. About five thousand years ago, Phoenicians discovered how limestone, sand, and niter (sodium nitrate) combine to make glass; initially, it was not transparent.[2] Later, Egyptians created prized "Alexandrian" glass, still clear after thousands of years. Later, glass manufacturers filled furnaces with sand to make twenty-ton slabs, then broke them down for lens makers.

About two millennia ago, the first lenses were called "burning glass," able to focus sunlight because, as children often discover, a magnifying lens can start a fire.[3] Archimedes is said to have created a large burning glass or mirror to defend Greek harbors against the Trojans by igniting the sails of their wooden ships—an early death ray. People in this era would have carried pocket-sized versions to start fires for their meals. Primitive lenses also served as magnifiers. Scribes of Mesopotamia worked with tiny cuneiforms on small clay tablets; such microscopic writing could not have been written or read without magnification.[4] Rock-crystal magnifying lenses have been found in Crete that date from 1200 BCE.

Starting in the Han Dynasty, about the seventh century BCE, the Chinese wore rock crystal as sunglasses and eye protection, with frames made from tortoise shell.[5] These, however, offered spiritual protection, not visual correction. They were hung in position by silk ribbons tied around the head or weighted strings dangling from ears. (The legend that Marco Polo brought back eyeglasses from Asia to Europe appears to be false; he brought reading stones (magnifiers) to China after their invention in Europe.)

Romans in the era of Christ had tiny glass globes that enlarged letters when filled with water. Around 60 AD, Roman emperor Nero watched sports through a green stone, perhaps an emerald. Seneca the Younger, his tutor, understood refraction, how lenses bend light: "Letters, however small and indistinct, are seen enlarged and more clearly through a globe or glass filled with water."[6] Reading through a glass of water proved impractical, but the practice led in turn to transparent "reading stones," made from rock crystal, quartz, or beryl. Reading stones were flat on one side and plano-convex (dome-shaped, like a snow globe) on the other. Laid on a page to enlarge letters, the devices worked well, though because they only magnified a word or two at a time, they had to be shuttled across a page.[7]

Ancient societies, however, didn't much need glasses. They assigned the farsighted to hunting and the nearsighted to work as artisans, weavers, or cooks. Only when humans began to need more precise vision for work and art did glasses arrive. Civilization expanded behind this invention: printing, education, industrialization. And the longer people lived, the more they needed lenses, particularly after Gutenberg repurposed his wine press for printing in the fifteenth century.

* * *

The English word "lens" derives from the Latin word for the common lentil: *lens culinaris*. Like an aspirin tablet, a lentil's symmetrical curves resemble a convex lens for magnification. Roger Bacon's lens designs came from Arabic and Persian science of the ninth through eleventh centuries. Abbas Ibn-Firnas wrote a treatise about how mirrors and lenses bent and focused light; he calculated how a semi-hemispherical lens could best magnify images on a page. Ibn Al-Hayem (Al-Hazen, 959–1037) is known as the father of modern optics. His *De Optica* (Treasury of Optics) and *De Luce* (On Light) laid the foundation for optical science in the West.

Though no one can tell where glass was first used to help humans see, we know how precious were the secrets of blowing clear glass from medieval laws on the island of Murano, near Venice, where glass production was moved in the late thirteenth century by Venetian lawmakers worried about glassblowers' fires. To persuade them to resettle from Venice, glassmakers were awarded titles of nobility—but they faced death if they moved off the island with the secret of clear glass, called "cristallo." (Cristallo was prepared by burning saltwort, an herb from Syria or Egypt, then adding Italian manganese dioxide to the ashes to clarify molten glass.)[8] Yet even with this technology to clarify glass and Italy's monks already using reading stones, it still took a long time to devise a pair of what we would recognize today as glasses.

Before the invention of eyeglasses, those with weak eyes depended on a strange mix of concoctions and salves. Galen and other Greco-Roman scientists tried zinc oxide, saffron, opium—even beaver's testicles and crocodile excrement.[9] As late as the eighteenth century, eye doctors were recommending "Bleeding and Blistering in the Neck," writes optometrist-historian Dr. David Baker.[10] Anyone prone today to cursing at fogged-up or scratched lenses might consider the alternatives of that time: hanging a cow's eye around one's neck, or drinking the powdered head of a bat, the blood of a turtle, or hog-grease. For eyestrain, "tie in unwrought flax as many knots as there are letters in your name, pronouncing them as you go, and tie it around your neck." Or "apply eight to ten leeches to the temples, also taking a wineglass of Sherry, a tablespoon or two of castor oil every night."[11] Another remedy for weak eyes was this: "Pint of Cold Spring Water, tablespoon of White Wine Vinegar, Tablespoon of cognac brandy, applied with a sponge." Whether this mixture helped, no one knows, but the user might have been better off drinking it.[12]

For a truly bizarre approach, nothing tops this cruel, ancient formula for weak vision: "Catch a fox live, cut his tongue out; let him go; dry his tongue and tie it up in a red rag and hang it around the man's neck."[13] For better vision without this violence, Elizabeth I's royal physician suggested poor sight might be remedied by the position in which we sleep. "Best to begin the sleep upon the right side and then turn on the left side," he advised.[14] For aging eyes, another remedy: "The eyes of an old man are not sharp of sight; and then shall he wake up his eyes with rubbings . . . use little and careful meats and comb their heads and drink wormwood before they take food. Then shall a salve be wrought for unsharp-sighted eyes; take pepper and beat it, beetle nut and a somewhat of salt and wine; that will be good salve."[15] This sounds more like a marinade than a visual aid.

There had to be a better way to see. And there was, though it came at a bitter cost to its early inventors.

* * *

Born around 1214, Roger Bacon was the first person imprisoned for inventing glasses (or trying to). Raised in a well-off family in Ilchester, England, Bacon started Oxford at thirteen with a thirst for knowledge. After graduation and after his family lost its land and house, he ran out of money for research; his only way forward was to join the recently established Order of Franciscans. Like their patron, Saint Francis, Franciscan friars gave up their property (including the little left to Bacon) but were allowed intellectual pursuits—only up to a point, it turned out.

A gaunt figure with long, thin hands, an aquiline nose, and wide-open eyes, the young friar unfortunately had a flaw worthy of Greek tragedy. He was proud, a genius with a heart of thorns—Bacon did not suffer fools gladly, as the saying goes. At Oxford, he once interrupted a rival's lecture to denounce his logic in front of students. That scholar would later be named his superior, with predictable results.

Through his research, Bacon vowed to discover how vision worked. To this end, he learned French, German, Greek, and Latin. Yet after mouthing off one too many times—declaring a fellow academic "renowned for having the greatest reputation in that stupid crowd"—Bacon was exiled to Paris by his order for discipline through menial tasks. Despite this drudgery, by night he explored the theory and practice of optics and studied Arabic, making him among the first Europeans to read the writings of tenth-century Persian and Arab optics scholars. He could also grind lenses.

Unfortunately, Bacon's fellow friars resented his scientific gifts.[16] If he'd had a lower profile and a less abrasive personality, he might have placated them; but Bacon was naïve . "If you called someone an idiot, he thought they should be grateful and learn from that,"[17] biographer Brian Clegg comments dryly. In Paris, he taught optics, "perspectiva," and defeated—to his later disadvantage—Albertus Magnus, the leading scholar there. In the moment, it might have seemed like glory, but soon this would turn into one of those win-the-battle-and-lose-the-war episodes.

* * *

Part of Bacon's misfortune was to be caught up in an upheaval then shaking the foundations of the medieval church. The Franciscans had become divided into two camps: the spirituals, who felt their order should remain poor, and the traditionals, who were loyal to the well-off church hierarchy in Rome. A new Minister-General was instructed to rein in spirituals like Bacon, and he soon issued a crushing edict: Henceforth, books or pamphlets could not be published or studied without permission.[18] Without a dispensation, Bacon couldn't even read a book.

Censored, spending his days cleaning pots, Bacon and his writing were silenced—an "exile of the mind," one author called it.[19] His fragile health broke down. Then, one fateful afternoon in 1266, he received a letter he must have thought would liberate him. It was from Cardinal Guy de Foulques, declaring how appreciative he was of Bacon's scientific pursuits and encouraging him to continue them despite Francisans' new rules of his order—but to do so in secret. De Foulques had heard that Bacon had completed a book on science; he wanted a copy. But not only was the book not yet written, the cardinal hadn't provided funds to have it copied, in those days before the printing press. Here was a bind Bacon had neither sought nor deserved: An immensely powerful church figure awaited a book he did not have permission or funds to write. Further, he was under scrutiny by his superiors. Then, matters became even more complicated: Cardinal de Foulques was elected Pope, Clement IV.

One might assume this would have caused Bacon elation and sped him back to research on optics. Instead, he must have panicked: he still had no access to books, nor money to buy them. On top of that, he'd broken the Franciscan rule forbidding friars to have direct contact with the pope. There were, however, grounds for hope. After all, the most powerful man in Christianity—a patron with uncountable wealth and power—believed in him, even if Bacon couldn't let anyone know.[20] Bacon's research, however, relied on funding. But without explaining why, how could he raise funds? The way out of his bind, he decided, was to instead write the pope a massive proposal for his work—540 hand-lettered pages, his *Opus Majus*. He wrote and wrote. He kept at it long into the night. He begged his friends for support.

By 1268, Bacon's application to the Pope extended to a million words, a stupendous literary feat. His optical work was so crucial to him that of the seven sciences he explored in the work, his first treatise was on optics.[21] Visual correction, he insisted, could help people through lenses arranged "in such a way . . . that the rays will be refracted and bent in any direction that we desire [to] . . . see the object at near or at a distance."[22] This was a broadside in humanity's struggle for sight: "If anyone examined letters or other minute objects through the medium of crystal or glass . . . with the convex side towards the eye, he will see the letters far better and they will appear larger."[23]

There it was, scratched right on the surface of the rough parchment: a new way to see! (And please, sainted excellency, send a basket of cash to get this book written.) As a closer, he sent the pope a matched pair of magnifiers, the closest thing to glasses yet developed.

* * *

But still another tragedy awaited Bacon. His patron, Clement IV, died suddenly in office, likely not having read a single page of what he'd commissioned. Bacon was now in serious trouble. His abrasive personality trumped his brilliant discoveries. Bacon might have seen his fate coming; he'd once written, if "truth falls to [the crowd's] notice, it seizes upon it and abuses it . . . to the manifold disadvantage of persons and of the community."[24] Was Bacon putting man above God's own words? His superiors thought so. Alongside other dissident monks, he was locked up in a musty cell in Ancona, Italy, for thirteen years.[25]

Imprisoned for "Suspected Novelties," unable to exercise or to talk, held in a cell with a tiny slot for admitting water, gruel, and light, Bacon's even worse punishment awaited: He was forbidden to take communion, meaning he would be forever in a state of sin and damnation. Bacon wrote nothing for more than a decade. In 1290, after the appointment of yet another Minister General, he was finally released. Though prison was better than its alternative for heretics—burning at the stake—the ordeal cost Bacon his health, and cost humanity all his science could have offered. Disbelieved and shunned, he was a victim of scientific curiosity and an antisocial personality.

They could chain Bacon's body, but not his brain. He'd already figured out that the world must be a sphere, rather than a flat disc, an idea that centuries later inspired Christopher Columbus to consider that by going West from Spain, he would arrive in spice-rich India. The man who almost invented glasses is thus indirectly responsible for the colonization of the New World.

Over the centuries that followed, his reputation as The Friar of Science spread. Bacon became a figure of folklore. In Oxford, they whispered he had created two mirrors: "By one of them he could light a candle at any hour, day or night, anywhere; in the other, he could see what people were doing anywhere in the world."[26] People also claimed he'd built a head of bronze that talked and prophesied. Its message: "Time is. Time was. Time is past." Damned as a magician but later redeemed as a penitent, the stooped futurist with a long white beard achieved much by working all night and sleeping little. A sufferer of insomnia, he left his dreaming for the daytime. And what dreams they were. In the end, Bacon was a man so far beyond his age that it's difficult to imagine how he could have existed.

After gaining his freedom, Bacon lived barely two years. "As he lay on his hard straw pallet in the friary at Oxford, Bacon might have mused that he who had always been so certain of the benefits of science had gained little from it personally," biographer Brian Clegg concluded. By the time Bacon died, someone in Italy was already wearing a pair of pristine glasses. His last words reportedly were, "I repent of having given myself so much trouble to destroy ignorance!"[27]

* * *

It's easy to overlook just how long and tricky a process it was to devise lenses that could actually be worn. Bacon's research was a milestone along humanity's path to clear sight. The next step on that path would be inventing the contrivance that eventually unlocked vision for so many: eyeglasses. After hearing Bacon's fate, early tinkerers with lenses must have hesitated: Who'd take on the church for another try? The mystery of who invented spectacles isn't the kind of question that keeps people up at night, but clues exist: There was a friar who said he knew who did the job; but he wouldn't say who. There was a family *sure* that their son was the inventor—but somehow no one noticed, and the plaque attesting to his achievement showed up only hundreds of years later.

Though the story of the inventor is a who-dun-it, the evolution of eyeglasses is clear: a painstakingly slow progression from discovering "burning stones" for starting fire and then "reading stones" for magnification; to quizzing glasses and monocles, single-lens vision aids on a string; to glasses on a stick, the lorgnette; to the day someone managed to hang two of those magnifiers before eyes—eyeglasses; followed by pairs for the nearsighted and astigmatic; to bifocals popularized by Ben Franklin and frames made comfortable with sidepieces; finally to our time, where machines carve lenses driven by sophisticated software: a visual pageantry.

In this evolution, poorly made lenses and frames were driven out of circulation by better designs. Inventors pursued quality lenses with determination. Optical science attracted some of the best minds in history; those who wrote about the pursuit of clear sight include scientists so prominent they are sometimes known by last names only: Da Vinci, Descartes, Kepler, Newton, Spinoza (a lens grinder).

The technological development of visual correction had a corresponding echo in culture. Glasses eventually brought widespread literacy by allowing people, and particularly seniors, to read books, newspapers, and magazines. Any occupation, from accounting to zoology, owes a debt to visual correction. Glasses opened up possibilities for trade, travel, commerce, education, sports, to name just a few. At the same time, beliefs about glasses reflected the cultural norms of many eras, from the medieval church's outrage at the provocation they posed to patriarchal and religious hierarchy all the way to modern Japanese customs which had women fired for wearing glasses at work. (Among their alleged disadvantages were challenges with makeup and a suggestion that glasses don't go well with a kimono.)

After centuries of struggling to invent corrective lenses and position them on a face, one would hope societies would be more accepting of this handy device.

* * *

One day in the thirteenth century, a monk's eyes must have grown tired from a long day of copying manuscripts. Ready for his supper, he picked up his burning glass to start a fire and noticed how large the letters appeared. Was he thinking of wearing these orbs of glass on his head? Probably not.

Eyeglasses must have been invented somewhere between heaven and hell. For those of us who depend on them, they're a bit of both. Multiple nations claim the invention: Scandinavians ground lenses out of rock crystal, but perhaps only for decoration. The Dutch, who later invented both the microscope and telescope, have a claim. Germanic countries enter the fray because pairs of early glasses have been found there; Germans trace this invention to a thirteenth-century minnesinger (minstrel) in 1280, six years before anyone else claimed it. Italy's claim is likely to be the strongest, despite rivalries between its city-states that pitted Pisa, Florence, and Venice against one another in this race for clarity.

Eventually, though, someone must have held two reading stones together in just the right position to discover binocular vision. Whenever this happened, the discovery brought together refraction, eye protection, and, later, fashion in a device that revolutionized how our species sees.

The first spectacles were reading glasses to compensate for presbyopia, age-related farsightedness. As one thirteenth-century monk wrote, "I am so debilitated by age that without the glasses known as spectacles, I would no longer be able to read or write. These have recently been invented for the benefit of poor old people whose sight has become weak."[28] (These poor monks, bent over parchment, forced to squint as they copied manuscripts in dusty, poorly lit rooms!) He was mum as to where his pair came from, but his enthusiasm came despite having to hold these riveted-together glasses in one hand and his reading material in the other.

The first published mention of spectacles is found in a document produced in Venice on April 2, 1300. Venice's spectacle makers' guild, the document notes, allowed artisans to make "discs for the eye" only if the maker specified whether they used glass or a rock crystal (quartz or beryl), the latter being harder and more costly.

It was in Florence, on February 23, 1305, that spectacles were first widely announced to the world. A Dominican friar from Pisa, Giordano da Rivalto, revealed the secret in a sermon: "It is not yet twenty years [so, after about 1285] since there was found the art of making spectacles, which secure better sight, one of the most useful arts on earth. I myself have seen and conversed with the man who first invented and created it."[29] Rivalto didn't identify the inventor—but, he told the Florentines, the man was surely from Pisa. A year later, another Italian friar claimed to have met the first man to invent them, again with no names or place given.[30]

Perhaps the inventor of eyeglasses kept the work under wraps because he (or she) had heard of Roger Bacon's plight and the church's position against tampering with nature—or its fear that reading via glasses would threaten the church's monopoly as keeper of esoteric knowledge (though of course sacred texts were written in Latin, which was not widely read).

Pisa shows up again in an archive in a monastery that held an oft-quoted diary entry: "Brother Alessandro Della Spina, a modest and good man, learned all industrial products of which he saw or heard. Spectacles were made first by someone else," he said, "who did not want to communicate anything about them."[31]

Did the Pisan invent a pair himself but shy away from announcing this? Or was he covering for an inventor hesitant to accept the honor? Somebody from Florence, maybe?

An odd and hotly contested epitaph is found on a tomb in Florence: "Here lies Salvino D'Armati of the Florentine Armati, inventor of glasses. May God forgive his sins. A.D. 1317." This might be the most famous line in optometry, but it begs the question: What exactly was his sin: inventing spectacles? In doing so, D'Armati, like Bacon, likely would have been seen as defying a God who gave us the eyes we deserved, and who are we to defy God?[32] A second source also credits D'Armati: An ambassador created a sensation at the marriage of the grand duke's sister by appearing with a pair of spectacles on his nose, "these being a recent invention of Salvino, called Armati."[33] But if this is true, why doesn't D'armati's name appear in books on optics until 1684, about 350 years after his likely death?

To straighten out the record, in 1956 Professor Edward Rosen wrote a headspinningly dense treatise in the *Journal of the History of Medicine*—more like a Talmudic commentary or a law review article. His inquest is considered definitive, based on more than a hundred sources written in Latin, Greek, German, French, and Italian. Among the many rumors Rosen debunked was one speculating that Roger Bacon was actually a Belgian who secretly delivered glasses to Italy. (This concoction was traced to the Belgian journalist who cooked it up.)[34] All this fabrication shows the immense pride tied up with the invention of this device, despite its once controversial nature.

And what of Salvino D'Armati? He's honored in a book about noble Florentines in the seventeenth century by a now-discredited author, Leopoldo Del Migliore. After checking church and birth records, Dr. Rosen did discover a Salvino D'Armati, but the man had no apparent connection to the creation of glasses. Furthermore, Del Migliore's evidence was rooted in a street plaque no one else recalled, and records he cited conveniently disappeared.[35] Dr. Rosen concluded D'Armati's claim was a hoax perpetrated by a family longing for retrospective prestige and a chronicler "who loved truth less and Florence more."

So, what, in the end, do we know about who invented glasses? He was probably Italian, probably not Venetian or Florentine but Pisan; and very likely a craftsman rather than a cleric.

* * *

Regardless of their controversy, the invention of spectacles helped usher in Europe's Industrial Age. Naturally, once sharper vision became available, people expected it—and the mass production of lenses and frames required industrial devices for precision measurement and quality control. As Europe's trade routes developed, the technology for assembling spectacles moved from Italy to the industrial North, particularly the Netherlands and Germany. Despite their dubious status with the church, glasses found advocates. Painters started adding them to favorite saints, even those born long before glasses were invented; one artist even put glasses on baby Jesus.[36] (The name of His optician is unknown.)

The more glasses were made, the more were sold, bringing prices down further. Fitting spectacles consisted of plucking reading glasses out of boxes of stock, marked with the age of wearers. Street vending gradually eroded the church's spiritual-optical guilt trips. "Power and wealth comes to those wearing spectacles," the peddlers cried. Enthusiasm for glasses grew, as did the list of claims of their benefits: In China, spectacles were said to be curative, bringing health and mystic power; in Spain, to bring gravitas and poise; in Germany, to cure nervous dyspepsia and headaches. Other benefits included a claim that sun-gazing through green glasses straightened narrow, arthritic backs. Glasses tinted red might cause a housewife's corns to go away; scolding wives and wife beaters would be rendered gentle.[37]

The notion of glasses as a remedy for ills besides poor vision continued to modern times. A doctor suggested that alcoholism, an "abnormal appetite satisfied by intoxicants," could be cured by glasses, which would somehow decrease a patient's thirst for liquor; he provided the example of a man who gave up drinking (for a month) upon getting his first spectacles. Another researcher suggested that putting glasses on criminals—particularly teenage delinquents—could cure truancy and crime. He fitted glasses to twenty inmates, and off they went, all receiving jobs. Releasing two hundred more, he predicted that if they didn't lose their glasses, they'd become desirable citizens (or at least better grifters).[38]

* * *

Once the concept of glasses became firmly established, keeping lenses positioned in front of the eyes became the major challenge of glasses inventors who tried loops, hooks, and attachments to hats or wigs. Early spectacles have been called "one of technology's best examples of poor engineering."[39] Rivet glasses were stiff, heavy, and prone to tumble and break. They had to be held in hand or carefully balanced on the nose, as if the wearer were a seal spinning a ball. (The unsteady had to wait for frames to be invented.) Their geography on the head was tricky, because people's noses vary in size and shape, and ears differ in symmetry. Their center of gravity had to be far forward, to prevent them from sliding off—and wearers had better not sneeze.

In the continuing struggle to keep spectacles upright, mass-produced lens frames of much lighter flattened copper wire were a big step forward, allowing for interchangeable lenses as clients' vision changed. Glasses-making remained a skilled craft protected by guilds; by the 1670s, inspection teams of the Worshipful Company of Spectacle Makers roamed London shops to ferret out pairs considered defective, snatching them up to be broken with a hammer.[40] The improvement in lens frames was important because earlier attempts were cumbersome. One could tie them to one's hat—troublesome in church, for if the two were taken off together, one might not read the hymnal.

Or one could hold them on one's nose while walking down the street, hoping not to stumble.

By the eighteenth century, "temples," the sidepieces used today on glasses frames, replaced hooks, straps, and ribbons. The first ones that could be worn comfortably, advertised by Edward Scarlett around 1717, had metal pads that lay flat against the head (like headphones). Then, in 1783, English optician Addison Smith offered for sale a frame with not only sidepieces but also two additional lenses that pulled down to further magnify images. These looked odd, as if the wearer had four eyes.

In colonial America, pastors were the first people seen reading in public, and so spectacles were initially called "pulpit glasses." Thus, the first stereotypes of eyeglass wearers in the United States were clerical. Still, their popularity inevitably grew: George Washington bought a pair of glasses costing $75, or more than $2,000 today. "You will permit me to put on my spectacles," he said to a room of Continental Army officers in 1783, "for I have grown not only gray, but almost blind in the service of my country."[41] In Philadelphia, in 1799, John McAllister hammered up a sign offering spectacles to a broader clientele. His fame as an optician spread, and in time, presidents Jefferson, Madison, Monroe, and Jackson all got their spectacles from him.

In the nineteenth century, temples that curved around the ear finally crossed the Atlantic. Initially, frames and lenses came from Holland and England, but the naval blockades of the War of 1812 put an end to that. Without imports, Americans had to make their own vision aids and, slowly, an industry emerged. In 1833, a jeweler named William Beecher moved to Southbridge, Massachusetts, and added spectacles to his business as a sideline. Beecher may have been the first American to make lighter, less expensive steel frames. Cheaper frames, in turn, stimulated both the American steel industry and those professions that relied on literacy, such as law, authorship, and higher education. The new spectacles industry therefore helped create a knowledge economy and American university culture. Clearer vision also opened the door to domestic literary craft, which blossomed in the nineteenth century: Nathaniel Hawthorne, Ralph Waldo Emerson, and Henry James all wore glasses.

Still, as we shall see, these eyeball fixer-uppers faced continued social resistance. In 1893, the *Atlantic Monthly* reported misgivings over the constantly increasing use of spectacles: "It is not without sadness that the uninitiated see innocent schoolgirls and sturdy schoolboys disfigured with these appendages."[42] Furthermore, the wholesale manufacturing of spectacles had technical problems. The cheapest pairs were sometimes ineffective; complaints poured in from wearers about spectacles ground from wavy window glass, or lenses that were mis-centered, badly polished, and full of specks and imperfections.[43] It's a wonder people wore them at all.

* * *

When eyes age, reading glasses become essential. Yet one must be able to see not just what's directly in front of one's nose but all that's farther away: items located on a shelf, street signs, and approaching people. Before the eighteenth century, this would have meant carrying two pairs of glasses, one for near and another for distance viewing. This is where that shining example of what was called "Yankee ingenuity," Benjamin Franklin, helped out.[44]

The idea behind bifocal lenses is simple: The older a person is, the harder it is to see accurately at both near and far distances. Starting at about age forty, the eyes' crystalline lens stiffens and the ciliary muscles surrounding the eyes weaken, making close focusing challenging. Franklin faced this degradation while representing the American colonies before the court of Louis XVI. Though best known today for flying a kite to attract lightning, Franklin was a polymath who had been a printer, publisher, editor, author, postmaster, and educator. He traveled in the highest scientific circles. At the top of his game in his seventies, with diplomatic status, he still carried the urge to invent.

While traveling in France in 1784, Franklin found he disliked exchanging his reading and distance glasses. "I formerly had two pairs of spectacles which

I shifted occasionally to read and often wanted to regard the prospect."[45] And so that famous mind began to churn. "What a man sees clearest and best at the distance proper for reading is not the best for greater distances," he decided.[46] Franklin found a solution: he had two pairs of glasses cut and pasted together. Lo and behold: bifocals! He had pairs made in London and passed them around. He wore them everywhere and had a side business sending them to the states.

Franklin was actually not the first person to create bifocals; German inventors had worked on the idea as early as 1716. His design, though, was both wearable and optically excellent. Even today, "executive style" bifocals, split across the middle, are popularly known as "Ben Franklins." The popularity of the man himself further augmented the popularity of the visual aid he designed: "Whereas eyeglasses had long been the mark of a learned man," one researcher wrote, "many in the eighteenth century shied away from them for personal and other reasons. The fact that Franklin wore eyeglasses and had them on when he entered Paris set an example for others to follow."[47] Franklin's bifocals had another advantage that he himself understood: As he wooed the French, seeking support against Britain, clear sight showed him nonverbal cues he might otherwise have missed. "I understand French better," Franklin wrote, "by the help of my spectacles."

If Franklin's vision (and his French) improved with bifocals, he was certainly not alone in needing them. Improvements in lenses rapidly opened doors, bringing students into the classrooms and libraries Franklin loved. In the United States, domestic lenses became more affordable. This new availability stoked an accompanying rise in literacy and developed the market for mass-circulation magazines, newspapers, and "dime novels" by allowing people to read them into their senior years.

Despite Franklin's success in popularizing bifocals, spectacles were still largely considered unsightly, particularly for women. Sometimes, to help their sight, women carried a single lens, called a "quizzer," on chains around their necks, in handbags, or hidden in their clothing. Alternatively, the lorgnette, lenses on a handle, became popular because it could be folded out of sight when not in use. Though the accusations of witchcraft and sin had long since faded in the face of their utility, the social stigma of wearing glasses never fully disappeared, despite the availability of cheap, effective, face-worn eyeglasses for users of all ages.

Looking back over the 750 years humanity took to invent and improve a device to transcend our visual limitations is an amazing experience. The inventors of spectacles could not have dreamed that one day two-thirds of the world's population would wear them, or that some of us would put on a boxy version plugged into a computer that lets them share someone else's eyes, as if inside another's head. In our time, glasses represent the future as much as the past, in augmented and virtual reality—all descended from shiny pebbles of beach sand.

But then something odd happened amid this technical development. Whereas in the thirteenth century, wearing glasses could have one accused of heresy, by the nineteenth century the struggle for the right to see took new forms, meeting prejudice and ageism against those needing help to read fine print, like me.

My out-of-focus experiment ahead? Nothing heroic. It wasn't as if I'd lost my glasses climbing up to help someone stranded. And if I was preoccupied with going visual cold turkey, what glasser wouldn't be? I set aside glasses for my weeklong experiment, in a world ever more dependent on vision. How did wearing glasses become a stigma? This was one of the many questions I planned to answer as I navigated my twenty-first-century life with twelfth-century eyesight.

Monday

"He took off his glasses. Deprived of their six and a half diopters of correction, his eyes were instantly reduced to a state of psychological despair," wrote Aldous Huxley. "Unspectacled, they were like a pair of jellied sea creatures, suddenly taken out of water. Then the light went out; and it was as though the poor things had been mercifully dropped, for safe keeping, into an aquarium."

This passage became swimmingly clear as I got out of bed this morning. I reached for my glasses. I couldn't stop myself.

The morning was warming and brightening, but I drifted in a purgatory between sleep and consciousness. My first day without lenses refused to come into focus.

Glasses were hijacking my dreams. When I first began wearing glasses, I fantasized about not needing them—or if I had to wear them, maybe they'd come with a superpower, like X-ray vision. Last night I dreamt just that: I was ten, shopping with my mother for school clothes. I looked down at a display case and suddenly saw through to the shelves below. I looked down at my mother's toes through her espadrilles. In front of me stood a tall man with hard, flat eyes in a flat face. He looked exasperated, as if someone had filled his pockets with gold that vanished when he reached for it.

Past him, I lifted my gaze to a wall safe that held dollar bills inside, rubber-banded. I couldn't believe it. I took off my glasses and rubbed my face. I put my glasses back on and looked at the gears of my little watch ticking.

"I see," I said to myself in my dream. "*This* is why I wear glasses. With them on, I see better than others, like Superman. Four eyes? Most people only have two!"

Why do some people require glasses or contacts, while others don't? No human attribute is evenly distributed—not athletic prowess, intelligence, or good looks. Some write a symphony at age eight; others are still making mud pies. Why should the struggle to see be any different, I muttered to myself, staring in the direction of a tree out back. Without glasses, it wasn't that I didn't see well; I really didn't see much at all.

Like most who wear glasses daily, I have two different visual states: in-focus and functioning; or out-of-focus, and not. With vision on standby, I needed to find advantages in uncorrected vision. My spirit had divided between ambition and hope and fear. I was excited to test my limits, to try something new, rather than regret what I currently couldn't see. "Calm down," I told myself. "Make your way down the hallway to the john as you do at night."

* * *

If you've worn glasses or contacts since childhood, you've probably never been without them. Fine. I'm not suggesting you stop wearing yours. Exploring visual individuality is not for everyone. Still, if you need glasses, you might try this experiment: Doff them for a minute—first making sure you'll be in no harm and know where you put them down—then look around. For a moment, you're lost. If you're as poorly sighted as I am, you may find yourself alone even in a crowd, the world a crazy quilt of color and indistinct form.

Wait a few minutes more, though, and you're found in a blurry creation all your own—one subtly, indescribably different. For those living at the liminal edge of vision, laying aside glasses can offer a magic garden where fantastic shapes loom and pass. Removing glasses can even be a pleasant break, like pulling off a hearing aid. Glassers see through a poor set of eyes, but our own.

Despite the inconvenience of poor vision, new techniques to restore sight may not be embraced as quickly or universally as their inventors imagine. As we'll read, glassers' self-identities are tied in with their mechanical aids. If *cogito ergo sum* (I think therefore I am), then this is *video peor ergo sum differendum* (I see less well, therefore I am different). On its first day, this experiment has already inspired in me respect for those living with far greater physical disabilities. If uncorrected sight has anything to offer, a difference model is more useful than a deficit one.

My admittedly minor disability parallels those of other writers avoiding spectacles. Jonathan Swift cast them aside, despite how badly he needed them: "I make nothing of mistaking 'untoward' for Howard . . . monster for minister; in writing I put N for P; and a hundred such blunders cannot be helped."[1] He too accepted not seeing clearly. Perhaps we try too hard to make the half-sighted full-fledged members of the majority.

Still, many glassers are ambivalent about the devices that make their difference into sameness. Among the many who hid their glasses-wearing while growing up was my spouse, N. Only today I discovered her secret, which she mentioned off-handedly, as she packed to San Francisco for a half-week of consulting. "Between eighth grade and tenth grade, I wouldn't wear glasses, except for taking notes off the blackboard at Redwood High. I didn't put them on outside." Later in life, she went with contacts.

I'll miss her, but what's ahead needs to be done alone. "You need to be alone when you change; when you know that you are going to change you seek loneliness," wrote Jan Myrdal, a strange, privileged Swede who wrote a book I'm reading, *Confessions of a Disloyal*

European, about questioning the Western tradition's claims to progress and reason. "With contact your sight is blurred, you will get lost in illusions, lose your capability to look outwards, and behave foolishly."[2]

* * *

"With contact your sight is blurred." Wasn't that backward? Sight puts you in touch with people. It lets you notice the lift of an eyebrow or a sweet smile. Myrdal, however, describes the advantages of *not* wearing glasses for a child: "Unpleasant grownups, teachers or police, would disappear in fog," he reflected, "if one only focused the eyes in such a manner that they floated away."

For me, the first changes were colors becoming more vivid and shapes blending. My yellow writing pads vibrated with color, and their formerly sharp edges dissolved. The rowing machine had a handsome tan housing I'd never noticed. Exploring new ways of looking at the world, I found these hidden in plain sight.

What could I see? In a circle of two feet around me, things were mostly clear. At ten feet, shapes assembled oddly, like an early Cubist painting. At twenty feet, clouds and everything else grew indistinct. Colors washed across objects without edges. I saw a tree trunk, but not the ridges of its bark; the glow of a TV screen, but not its image—a world more translucent than transparent.

Everything around me needed more light. Using a tape measure (found by virtue of its bright yellow color), I measured the distance my eyes needed to read: four inches to a newspaper, five for a book. In public, I had always tried not to take off my glasses to read; I had to hold a book like I was going to bite it. People stared, and I looked like a scientist eyeing a small bug.

Semi-sight ended multitasking. My feet reached cautiously for a step. The loss of depth perception particularly irked me, for being out of focus made objects disorientingly two-dimensional. Eating neatly was impossible; food improperly speared by a fork fell back to the plate. I couldn't make out letters on the computer keyboard unless I bent my head down. Sometimes I had to laugh: reaching for a pencil, I'd find a pen in hand. Forced to slow down drastically, time stretched ahead like a plane that never leaves the runway. When could I sleep again? When could I eat?

My long, out-of-focus day passed like an errant diet. I knew what was allowed and what was forbidden. I wondered how long before the urge to cheat would hit me, like an alcoholic who knows there's a bottle left somewhere in the house. Yet living without glasses was not just a visual diet; it oddly resembled a drug trip. In college, I had joined fellow students in experimenting with psychedelics: colors pulsed madly; walls undulated. But that was a hallucination. What I was seeing now was just the way life was before someone invented glasses.

* * *

Reading history about the discovery of the science of optics and glasses, I'm struck by the monumental stamina of humankind's efforts to see. Some of us arrive in the world with perfect vision; others need help. And from the time of antiquity to the age of the internet, from orbs of glass in pockets to today's fashion frames, people avidly sought equipment for visual enhancement. There's a fascinating but outdated theory in biology, asserting that as human embryos develop, they repeat each stage in humans' development through our entire evolutionary process: "ontogeny recapitulates phylogeny." Darwin discredited this notion, but I still like to imagine each of us, however briefly, becoming earlier creatures as our cells multiply, divide, and develop: lungfish, reptile, mammal. Likewise, glassers today benefit from early experiments in visual correction that preceded the tools of today, despite pinched noses, sore spots on our heads, etc.

The closest I've come to finding a writer who shares my current situation was while preparing the life of Aldous Huxley, a man whose vision problems started while he was still in school at Eton:

> At sixteen I had a violent attack of *keratitis punctata*, which left me (after eighteen months of near blindness, during which I had to depend on Braille for my reading and a guide for my walking) with one eye just capable of light perception, and the other with enough vision to permit my detecting the two-hundred-foot letter on the Snellen chart at ten feet.

Afterward, for Huxley it was night all day long and night again in the evening; later, he would call it a "kind of death." Eventually, eye injections at the Institute for Tropical Medicine in London cleared the infection but left his corneas virtually opaque, two tiny bluish clouds. He got used to drinking tea with both hands and learned, over time, not to stray near the stove. (Significantly, he blamed his lost vision for propelling him from a medical career into writing fiction.) And even with spectacles, strain and fatigue were always present. "There were occasions when I was overcome by that sense of complete physical and mental exhaustion which only eye-strain can produce. Still, I was grateful to be able to see as well as I could." That's where I, too, found myself on the evening of my first day, wondering how to cope after leaving my glasses in their penalty corner. (Why Huxley also gave up his glasses, I'll get to later.)

My interest in Aldous Huxley had begun with a tattered copy of *Brave New World*, which was required reading in my high school. I rooted for *Brave New World*'s "savages," in these same mountains of New Mexico where I now write—oddballs of the future who mated for love, not eugenics. I knew little of Huxley's life then beyond his birth to a distinguished family of authors. One of Britain's angry young men after the First World War, he soon ranked among the world's foremost authors himself, translated into twenty-eight languages.

By the 1960s, Huxley had become fashionable on college campuses. His last novel, *Island*, circulated in dorm rooms on account of its sex scenes and psychedelics. His memoir *The Doors of Perception* was all the rage (and inspired the name of an immensely popular rock band, the Doors). Huxley was hip.

In the 1970s, Huxley's memoir of using the put-glasses-aside Bates method, entitled *The Art of Seeing*, was republished. That book swayed me in my current direction. My own eyes had kept me out of the army, perhaps sparing my life, but had already begun to weaken. I tried the eye exercises Huxley used in the book, but they gave me a headache as bad as listening to an out-of-tune marching band.

* * *

When I was young, a hunger for sight obsessed me; what I could see with glasses never satisfied. I could never reach 20/20, no matter how I tried. Putting aside the sight glasses offered, I find myself wondering about what would happen if I lowered my visual expectations. With glasses, I saw the world's sharp edges. Without them, a comforting vagueness settled in. Would I come to prefer this out-of-focus world? Something positive was here, if I could only grasp it. Could I live this way? Could there be a slow-seeing movement, like the advocacy for slow food, slow cities, and so on? My newly imperfect sight was a poor translation of my former sight—and as humorist James Thurber commented about translations, "my work loses something in the original."[3]

Overhead somewhere, a woodpecker tapped a tree limb. I couldn't see it. Yet, I could still tell a cat from a coyote, a woman from a hat. I missed, though, the mountains sharply cutting the horizon at sunset. I tried to imagine what it would feel like to never see the expression on the face of my best friend. To never mean it, when I tell someone, "You're looking good." To miss the gleam in my son's eye after opening a present, or to watch the blush rise in my spouse's cheeks at a naughty remark. All this made me feel unbrave today, a fool on a fool's errand.

In pursuit of perfect vision, I had overlooked much in the visual matrix surrounding me every day. An ordinary chair and table now had a dynamism of interesting shapes and bright splashes of color. The boughs of the old cottonwood out back rose up to the sky like the beanstalk Jack climbed. I didn't have to see its top to appreciate it; I can still see with the eyes of the mind. This week I'm looking to find the "extraordinary in the ordinary," as philosopher Stanley Cavell wrote. Still, this self-calming strategy didn't always work. You know the expression "to find one's bearings"? Mine had rolled out of sight, and I was back to where I'd started in life, out of visual control.

2

Living with Lenses

For any man with half an eye . . . optics sharp it needs to see what is not to be seen.

—POET JOHN TRUMBULL, 1782

As I newly navigated the world, I learned immediately how important visual correction has always been to me. Eyeglasses offer us so many things: A medical necessity, a fashion statement, an aid to help with ocular disease, a tool for safety or protection, functional art, a requirement for workplaces, a collectible, a symbol of intelligence and wisdom, or, most commonly, simply a sign of getting older. Once we know how amazingly good glasses and contacts are at letting us see, and how they work, we may all take them less for granted.

Imagine a world without eyeglasses and contacts. Picture the chaos of drivers not seeing clearly and colliding, people slipping off sidewalks and bumping into objects and each other, accidents at work and home. Poor sight is linked to 59 percent of road accidents worldwide. Poor vision is also tied to a decline in cognitive abilities.[1]

Yet, living with lenses has never been particularly easy, either; people hate and love them. They can be treacherous: Lenses fog in wet weather or when wearing a face mask. Frames roast in summer heat, as anyone knows who's put on a pair after they've sat in the sun.

Lenses can shatter. Broken glasses lenses are so hideously dangerous that long ago, impact-resistant lenses were made mandatory in the United States and Europe. Despite this, prescription lenses still chip and crack, costing bother and hundreds of dollars for a moment's fault—and potentially days or weeks of delay. Merely scratched, the streak in the lens catches and reflects the sun. Then, look where we might, a thin line stays before us, more clinging than our shadow (which at least rests at night). Some pairs of glasses get so scratched that their lenses become translucent shields, through which only light passes. That scratched lens becomes a record of mishandlings, the way Oscar Wilde's portrait of Dorian Gray reflected Gray's misdeeds.

Even new and undefaced, glasses soil and get dirty. Gnats crawl their inner curve, amidst the soot of the city, sebum and eyelashes, spots of moisture, and dust. Cleaning is often overlooked or unfeasible on a moment's notice. Washed with what's at hand, they're often worse off. Rub and wipe, rub and wipe—what other device requires such constant cleaning?

Glasses and contacts are the keepers of our sight, which makes it all the more urgent not to lose them. But honestly, they're worse than keys: They hide under beds, or in bathrooms when retired for a wash or shower. On crowded desks, they burrow in among papers. In cars, they're clever at finding cracks between seats, out of range for those ill-equipped to find them.

If not lost, they periodically vanish. Unlike clothes hangers, which seem to reproduce quietly in closets until little room remains for coats, glasses disappear into thin air. They take off at sporting events, ride away on buses and trains, and drop neatly into the crannies of sofas or airplane seats. They like a good day at the beach and like better to stay behind in the sun-warmed sand. They can be as frustrating as a winning ticket lost at the races.

When best-selling British author Laura Barnett had her first eye exam and learned she'd need to wear glasses, she burst into tears. "I was ten years old—gawky, bookish, rubbish at sports—and the chalk-marks on the school blackboard were looking increasingly blurry. Now, the optician said, I'd be able to see again—but only by attaching to my head what looked like an instrument of torture designed to extract the maximum potential for teasing."[2]

If Laura's parents had better understood how traumatic receiving glasses can be for kids—and how parents and grandparents can protect their kids from myopia— her glasses might have been more welcomed.

* * *

Vision is our most dominant sense, taking up nearly half the brain's resources. With such a complex system, misinformation about its workings is inevitable. If a child's eyes are crossed, for example, some imagine that if we simply leave them alone, they'll outgrow the problem. This is false: the earlier misaligned eyes—strabismus—are diagnosed and treated, the sooner eyesight improves. Some are afraid to wear contact lenses—if a lens is lost behind their eye, they think, they're in trouble. But this fear is misplaced; contact lenses normally can't slide behind the eye. Such folklore is full of fears about what could go wrong, and superstitions about how to prevent that. Take carrots: Eating them helps night vision, supposedly. The truth is more complex: Eating carrots is good for your eyes, but so is eating *anything* rich in vitamin A; a sweet potato contains 50 percent more vitamin A than carrots by volume.[3] And saying something is good for eye health isn't the same as saying it can improve your vision.

The legend that carrots improve night vision is actually a ruse perpetrated during the Second World War by the British propaganda ministry to fool the German forces. In an attempt to hide the development of a new radar technology that improved the Royal Air Force's ability to shoot down Nazi bombers, they claimed massive consumption of carrots had improved their pilots' night vision.[4]

Can reading under the covers make you nearsighted? No, doing so doesn't change the shape of your eye, and thus your focal point on the retina—but this may cause eyestrain, or what the American Optometric Association calls "pseudo myopia," where "after long periods of near work, the eyes are unable to relax to see clearly in the distance... Constant visual stress may lead to a more *permanent change* in distance vision." (Italics added.) A frightening thought, but in short, experts agree a few sessions under the blanket causes little harm. (The answer to whether reading in dim light causes myopia appears soon in our discussion of the physical basis of poor vision.)

When we see, light rays strike the eye's transparent cornea and travel through the cornea and crystalline lens to focus on the macula of the retina, light-sensitive tissue lining the back of the eye. There, light rays are converted by rods and cones, photoreceptors, to electrical impulses (neurons) and transferred by neural fibers carrying photons to the optical nerve and to the primary visual cortex at the back of the brain.

Think of the eyeball as an old-time box camera: There's a lens near the front for focusing on the film in the back. In the eye, light rays focus clearly on the retina by the combined power of the cornea and lens. The retina converts rays of light into electrical impulses and sends these along the optic nerve to the brain's visual cortex, where they are reversed and recognized as images. Corrective lenses bend (refract) light rays before they pass through the cornea and lens, to shift the focal point forward for farsightedness (hyperopia or hypermetropia) or backward (for myopia) to the fovea, the spot on the retina offering the greatest resolution.

When eyeballs lengthen, images form in front of the retina, resulting in a blur, myopia, that can be corrected by the use of a concave lens that is thinner at the center. If a nearsighted eyeball grows too long, so that it's shaped like a football rather than a sphere, its cornea and lens must try to flex and accommodate to move the focal point backward to the retina's surface.

Lenses aren't fitted into a frame at random by good opticians. They will study the frame fit, including its vertex tilt and wrap: how glasses frames interact with a face. Another important factor is pantascopic tilt, the angle of the lens to the eye's axis. "Eyeglass lenses work best when the frame bottom is tilted toward the cheek about 8–10 degrees and wrapped around the head 6–7 degrees," according to a knowledgeable optician.[5]

* * *

Farsightedness (hyperopia) results from an eyeball shorter than needed, mirroring rays converge behind the retina. To correct this condition, optometrists use convex lenses that are thicker at the center, like a magnifying glass. Among the differences in effect is that the nearsighted may see the color red better; for the farsighted, blue may be more intense.

Astigmatism (twisted-perspective vision) can accompany either of the above conditions, adding distortion. It's caused by an irregularly shaped cornea, lens, or both, which create multiple focal points. It's resolved by adding a cylindrical curve to either lens, or even to lenses without far or nearsighted refraction.

Presbyopia (age-related farsightedness) happens to almost everyone over forty or so, leading to a need for reading glasses. "There are three things we can't avoid: death, taxes, and presbyopia: The gradual loss of the ability to read up close," said one professor of ophthalmology.[6]

As we age, our crystalline lens hardens, and the ciliary muscles of the eye lose their flexibility, reducing their power to reshape the lens to focus. At thirty-five, the lens in most human eyes focuses over a range of nearly 5.2 diopters; at fifty-five, the eye's flexibility has commonly fallen to a mere 1.7 diopters. By sixty-five, most people's focusing capacity has shrunk to a tenth of what it once was.[7] Presbyopia means that those who have worn glasses since childhood will eventually also need reading glasses or multifocal lenses to clarify near objects.

Contact lenses work differently. Soft plastic lenses adapt to the surface of the eye, placing a miniature plastic version of a concave or convex lens between cornea and eyelid. (Gas permeable lenses are more rigid.) Contacts float before the cornea yet hold their position.

Originally cut from the ends of test tubes, modern hard and soft contact lenses are sophisticated and even come in multifocal versions. Not having frames, contacts offer a wider angle of vision and, for some, sharper images. These benefits, however, may be offset for some by the squeamishness of putting a finger to their eyeballs and by other discomforts, such as dirt trapped under the lens or irritation when a contact dries out (as contacts are mostly water). Users must also be on guard against damage to the cornea from infections, which eye professionals can diagnose.

Three different professions service our eyes. The optician has specialized, licensed training in fitting lenses, frames, coatings, and other treatments. The optometrist has four years of postgraduate work (OD, or doctorate in Optometry) and examines the health of the eyes and write prescriptions for refraction. They often dispense eyeglasses, frames, and contact lenses. The ophthalmologist has either an MD or DO (Doctor of Osteopathy), treats diseases of the eye, and performs surgery. Discussions about medical problems of the eye are outside the scope of this book, but they explain why a routine visit to an optometrist might reveal something more urgent than a simple need for glasses.

It's human nature to seek out the best, whether pizza or medical care. So some hunt the best optometrists and opticians the way they might look for the best schools or jobs. They try one frame after the other, hoping for clearer sight or a more economical pair: This one looks more durable, this one costs less. All of this is based on hopes, not so much for a better pair as for better eyes. It's an increasingly important urge in this four-eyed world where more people need visual help.

* * *

"Why Is There an Epidemic of Short-Sightedness?" is the title of Laura Barnett's screed on glasses.[8] It's an important question. Today, more folks are wearing glasses earlier in life and for longer than ever; nearly half of young adults in the United States and Europe are nearsighted—double the percentage half a century ago. According to the National Eye Institute, European myopia has increased a whopping 66 percent in thirty years, from 1972. In the United States, 41.6 percent of African-Americans have this problem.[9] *Nature* notes that sixty years ago, the percentage of Chinese youth who wore glasses was

10–20 percent; today it's up to 90 percent.[10] Unfortunately, 30 percent of the world's children lack corrective lenses, according to the PBS documentary *Sight*.[11] Today, the progression of myopia and the need for glasses and contacts can be somewhat controlled.[12] Early diagnosis, built with a profile of parental genetics and measuring time spent on near-focus tasks, can help optometrists create a treatment plan.[13]

What's causing this epidemic of myopia, and what can be done to control it? Why aren't our kids seeing clearly? The answer to the causes of myopia raises questions of nature vs. nurture, genetic inheritance vs. home environment.

For centuries, people assumed nearsightedness was wholly genetic. "If both your parents are shortsighted," one BBC article notes, "there is a 40 percent chance that you are too"; this is four times the rate of myopia among children of two parents with normal eyesight.[14] It took a trip by scientists to remote Northern Alaska to document that genes alone cannot be responsible for intergenerational increases in myopia. Among an isolated Inuit community studied in 2003, only 2 out of 131 adults had myopia. Yet one generation later, among their children and grandchildren, *half* were nearsighted. Genetics alone could not account for this sudden increase, though researchers have identified more than one hundred associated genes affecting vision, including a gene specific to myopia.[15,16] Neither can genetics explain how, in Seoul, South Korea, an astounding 96.5 percent of nineteen-year-old men are shortsighted.

As the *Freakonomics* podcast wrote, "If there's a drastic change in disease prevalence, this cannot be explained by human genetics, because genetic make-up simply does not mutate at this rate."[17] Only gradually, using studies with identical twins and factoring in ethnicity and education levels, did scientists begin to make out a surprising pattern.

Besides family genetics, the long-suspected cause of myopia has always been reading excessively or under poor light in childhood. This idea was set forth four hundred years ago by the great astronomer Johannes Kepler. Kepler blamed his shortsightedness on all his study of optics, and "the idea took root," according to *Nature*.[18] In 1824, William Kitchener, a doctor, noted how needleworkers were losing their sight from close work.[19] Bookishness and nearsightedness are widely associated. It turns out there *is* a relationship between myopia and long days spent inside on screens when young—but it's not what people expect.

In a myopic eye, the contrast between black words on a white page decreases. Naturally, one pulls the book or phone closer, which forces the eye to accommodate to this near work. Dim light further strains the eyes to maintain focus on something close. Normally, sight recovers quickly from this kind of strain. This led some scientists to doubt the effects of reading in diminished light or overusing phones: "It's an old tale, a ploy used by moms to get kids to go to sleep when they wanted them to," said Dr. Jim Shelby of Oregon's Pacific University.[20] Some epidemiologists found "no association between time spent using digital media and the development of myopia."[21] Yet, if that's true, how are children of fully sighted parents, whose children should normally have less chance of myopia, becoming myopic so dramatically fast? One study showed that in the pandemic, for instance, many children's eyes deteriorated from online schooling and increased amounts of indoor activity.[22]

The relationship among light levels, close work (such as reading or staring at small screens) and myopia is complex. Severe myopia has been observed to be highest among people with a postgraduate education in occupations requiring a great deal of reading, like lawyers, editors, engineers, and doctors.[23] Education level—more so than genetics, but less so than home environment—is consistently associated with myopia. The *Guardian* reported on a 2014 study that found that among 4,658 university graduates, half had myopia; among nongraduates, the rate was only a third. Each additional degree a mother earned greatly increased the likelihood of her teenager's developing myopia, by a remarkable 33 percent. (It's a wonder the children of two PhD holders see at all!) Interestingly, once education is controlled for, European and African Americans have same incidence of myopia.[24]

Researchers are actively investigating whether reading or close work on digital devices is harmful. But one factor on which they agree is this: The more sunlight a child's developing eyes receive, the better. The Sydney Myopia Study was one of the leading studies on the development of childhood myopia. Starting in 2007, Australian researchers found a simple, free way to retard myopia: "The more time children spent playing outdoors, the less likely they were to have short-sightedness."[25] (Time with screens indoors is time not spent under bright daylight.)

Before their eyes attain adult size, infants are born farsighted. Because young children's eyes grow rapidly, they can develop myopia faster than those of teenagers.[26] In children, a hormone stimulated by daylight, retinal dopamine, inhibits excessive eye growth. And even on a cloudy day, light outside is ten to twenty times as intense as light inside a home. Thus, the more time a child spends outside during the day, the more retinal dopamine is released into the bloodstream, thereby inhibiting the elongation of the eyeball that causes myopia. The vitamin D children receive from solar exposure also slows eye globe growth. These statements are not theory but researched fact; an article entitled "The Sun Is the Best Optometrist" summarized this research in *The New York Times* more than a decade ago.[27] Children of myopic parents are more affected by lack of outdoor time than others.[28]

We should care about preventing myopia for more than its effect on visual clarity: A longer eyeball is also more subject to glaucoma and to retinal detachments and tears that could lead to blindness. And the younger myopia begins, the longer the time the eyeballs have to stretch and the greater the burden to correct these problems. Special glasses and contacts exist that alter eye growth by focusing light across the entire field of vision rather than just at the center. Another new device for myopia control is "novel spectacles," lenses patterned with micro dots which diffuse light as it strikes the eye. Brands like the Stellist are popular in China, but as of this writing, not approved in the United States. Preventative myopia is why countries like the UK, China, and Singapore are passing laws mandating schools to provide more hours of outdoor time. The simplest activity parents can do is to encourage children to read outdoors, under natural light. Reading in the sun on a bench or patch of grass educates, entertains, and reduces myopic growth. Unfortunately, more time outdoors can't help eyes that are already myopic.[29] For adults, though, visual training for myopia may improve visual acuity by stimulating the brain to deblur images, the way a computer can by manipulating contrast.[30]

How much time outside is enough for kids? About two to three hours per day.[31] For each weekly hour spent outside, there's a 24 percent decline in myopia among children.[32] Besides lack of outdoor time, other factors may enter into the dramatic increase in myopia: artificial light and possibly having nightlights in a child's room (though here the evidence is inconclusive).[33] Even being born in the summer may double a child's risk, because such students commonly start school, and with that close work, earlier than those born at other times of year. The answer to "Are our children seeing clearly?" is another question: "Are kids spending enough time outdoors?"[34]

Certainly no one was making efforts to control my myopia; and since all my parents' friends wore glasses, I assumed this was inevitable. Though I was the first in my elementary class to wear glasses and suffered for that privilege, lots of kids later wore glasses. To edit his anthologies, my father spent nights behind his only pair of glasses—reading, selecting passages, and annotating them. By the time I put on glasses, my mother had them too, for reading. And even if we had known about the connection between outdoor time and a weakening eye, Manhattan is not known as a place where the sun shines brightly. The many options discussed below for slowing myopic growth were unheard of, not yet invented, and probably would have been unaffordable had they existed. So I took glasses for granted and hoped fervently they would work better. Or at least that I would misplace them less often, a habit which has plagued me.

* * *

1956, Greenwich Village. I'm lying in bed. In the pale twilight, I make out only fuzzy circles and strips of color; my glasses are nowhere to be found. Sounds, though, are distinct: high heels clacking by on the sidewalk above my room, strollers hauling groceries home to what shelter New York City offers on Thanksgiving. Across America, kids are giving up on homework; mothers are battling oversized birds into ovens. The smell of roasting chestnuts drifts in, and I wake up hungry.

In the 1950s, the Village is a small town in the world's largest city, its streets too curvy and eccentric for delivery vans, so the bourgeoisie wouldn't live there. Rents are low, making it an artist's hang-out. School days, I dawdle on my way home from school. I gaze up at the dark brown hams and waxy yellow cheeses hanging like pawnbrokers' balls in the windows. Gazing back at me I see a kid with unruly dirty-blonde hair and a hungry look.

Now, light filters down from the street through tired, bone-white curtains, the used light of autumn in the big city. In the growing dusk, I listen to the high-pitched whine of a bicycle tire, the low, dull rumble of trucks leaving their warehouses on Houston Street. A foghorn sounds in the distance, followed by the thwack of the evening paper against the front door.

I am an ear-witness. Hearing is my favorite game. I can tell which bus is passing by its unique acceleration and its gear changes as it turns. The rain's intensity I gauge by its drip into the sewer: a trickle means a raincoat; an uneven plop means the storm has passed. I recognize the clip-clop, clip-clop of the vegetable cart's horse before it turns the corner and I run out to buy the first apple. Right now, I'm listening for help.

I can't find my glasses, but I can't afford lose them. Thick lenses cost so much we can't afford a back-up pair. My mother is off directing a play, my father ill and absent. Closing my eyes, I taste the crusted tears on my lips. The faint scrape of the curtains against the window rasps like a paper cut.

After school, I'd lain down for a nap. My mother believes in naps the way some trust patent medicine. Her Shakespeare is dog-eared at numerous passages: "Sleep, that sometimes shadows sorrow's eye"; "Sleep, nature's sweet nurse." Sleepy, I'd tossed my glasses off to one side. A half hour later, I'm in a panic. I can't cross the busy street to my neighbor's house, or pick out food in the refrigerator. I go back and search again. Nothing I can see.

The world of the severely shortsighted is rarely described in detail. Our culture so privileges sight that one size is supposed to fit all. Those who can't see are corrected. Those who don't need glasses or contacts—well, just wait.

Finally, the bell on the front door tinkles as it swings open. I hear a quick, high-heeled step rounding the stairwell. A woman in her late thirties, short with the wiry figure of a dancer, hangs her hat carefully in the hall.

"Down here, Mom," I call up the stairs. "Help."

"What's the matter?"

"I lost my glasses."

"Again?"

She slides off her heels and reviews the half-dozen places I've already searched. Then, hitching up her skirt, she lies down under the bed with one leg extended. With a lunge, she retrieves the errant pair. I put them on and watch the furniture rearrange itself. The table that looked like an oversized spider returns to the corner. The intricate patterning returns to the hardwood floor; the yellow glow of a streetlight slants through the sidewalk window.

From the next room, my mother calls over her shoulder. "We're going to have to get you a spare pair. Please, put them in the same place, every time, and they won't get lost."

When people resent their dependence on glasses, consciously or not, they have a hard time keeping hold of them. What we resent, we neglect. What we neglect, we misplace or abuse—even if we need him, her, or it desperately.

* * *

Today, scientists have several methods to manage the progression of myopia like mine. (What follows here shouldn't be read as the latest eye science, but as a non-specialist's take on myopia control.) Eyedrops can be used to dilate children's pupils, as is done in an eye exam. With atropine treatment, more sunlight enters the more-open pupil, increasing the crucial secretion of retinal dopamine. Unfortunately, dilated pupils also make the world uncomfortably bright and blur images at the edge of vision.

This is done to slow myopia with atropine eyedrops. The long-term effects of dripping atropine into children's eyes, however, may not be yet fully understood. (Another drug applied topically, pirenzepine, might also slow growth of the eyeball.) Though poisonous in large amounts, atropine has been clinically shown to reduce myopia in growing eyes.[35] AI is also revolutionizing diagnosis with systems like retinal imaging to assist physicians.

Scientists have also explored whether inserting a high-powered bifocal contact lens at night could slow myopic growth by reshaping the curvature of the cornea to match the eye's proper focal length.[36] In the hard-to-pronounce practice of orthokeratology, a special lens temporarily flattens the cornea by lightly compressing it overnight. (The practice has been compared to wearing braces.) Hydraulic pressure beneath the lens thins the corneal surface. Taking the lenses out the next day, many subjects see clearly without glasses until nightfall.[37] Children with already-serious myopia, though, probably won't see many benefits. Orthokeratology requires expert fitting by an ophthalmologist, but over a two-year period, the outer layer of the cornea may thin up to 45 percent.[38] This allows some children and adults to avoid wearing glasses during the day.[39]

Unfortunately, soon after stopping orthokeratology treatment, the eye may return to its original shape. Other disadvantages of orthokeratology can include its cost, thousands of dollars, risk of infection or discomfort—common problems with contacts, complicated by children's special challenges in following lens care—and possible corneal swelling or scarring.[40] Serious eye infections like the keratitis Huxley had can lead to blindness, the Center for Disease Control warns. Even among adults and adolescents, 99 percent report at least one error in contact lens care, severely affecting one out of every five hundred contact lens users annually. "And this percentage must be far higher among children just learning to wear lenses."[41]

Another possible myopia treatment is injecting the white and pupil of the eye with collagen, which slows the eyeball's growth. The result? Myopia stabilized in 80 percent of young patients a year after injection.[42] But injecting anything into nine-year-old's eyeballs is unpleasant, and cysts occurred 3 percent of the time with this treatment.[43] The most extreme approach to controlling myopia is a surgery, posterior scleral reinforcement, which must be done at an early age and also sometimes causes cysts. (Playing outside is a lot easier!)

Young, developing eyes also benefit from "myopic defocus," periodically looking off into the distance. After too much close work—peering at small screens, reading, sewing—"constant contraction may stretch the eyeball," according to a professor at Queensland University in Australia. In the absence of full light, pupils dilate so more light rays reach the edges, blurring the retinal image slightly.[44] After years of doing near work—particularly in a person who's genetically predisposed—a peripheral "stretching" of the eye globe may pull the focal point back, lengthening the eye and creating more myopia, according to scientific optician Barry Santini. Today, kids play with small screens at extremely early ages; instead of playing with blocks, they're more fascinated by phones and tablets. Cell phones as toys may not be a good idea.

So, what is the current science on whether reading in dim light promotes myopia? Myopia is multifactorial, "the result of a complex interaction between genetic predisposition and environmental exposures," according to the *European Journal of Ophthalmology*.[45] The bottom line of all this is that myopia is changing. It arrives earlier and progresses more quickly.

* * *

Seeing has a complexity beyond its physicality—a tension between sight and insight, clarity and opacity, seeing outside and seeing inside. Something half-seen at the edge of our vision resembles a half-understood phrase in a foreign language. It lingers on the porch of the imagination. Sometimes, the harder we grasp at that phrase or fleeting image—the more we concentrate on it—the less it yields. We can heighten our attention, shift focus, cup our ears—but we can't beat our senses into submission.

For adults, the suggested "permanent fix" for poor vision is often refractive laser surgery. Rather than adjusting the eye's retinal focal point, as with corrective lenses, refractive surgery reshapes the cornea, changing its refractive power to match the eye's focal length. For the farsighted, the cornea is reshaped to increase its refractive power; for myopes, surgery reduces the curvature of the cornea to push the focus backward, toward the retina.

Refractive surgery goes by several acronyms, such as laser-assisted in situ keratomileusis (LASIK), in which a thin flap of the cornea is pulled back temporarily so a laser can reshape the cornea. In advanced-surface ablation (ASA), the outer layer of the cornea is removed or folded so a computer-controlled laser can sculpt underneath—a technique used on those with thin corneas, for whom LASIK is inappropriate. Photorefractive keratectomy (PRK) uses a tiny brush to remove a micro-thin layer on the corneal surface to either flatten it (to correct myopia) or steepen it (to fix hyperopia).[46] Finally, there's conductive keratoplasty (CK) for farsightedness. In this procedure, a thin probe releases radio waves to heat the edge of the cornea. This heat causes the periphery of the cornea to shrink and tighten like a belt. Farsightedness, however, may eventually return as affected cells regenerate.[47]

For those needing high degrees of visual correction, refractive surgeries may not always be a good option. In such cases, an intraocular lens can be surgically implanted in the eye. This procedure is called a clear lensectomy. (This same procedure, done when the eye's lens is cloudy, is cataract surgery, commonly performed on older adults, nearly 4 million times per year in the United States.)[48]

Not everyone benefits from surgery. You're not a good candidate if: (a) you're satisfied with glasses or contacts; (b) you have chronic eye disease; (c) your need for visual correction is high; or (d) you're not willing to accept what the American Academy of Ophthalmology calls "the uncertainty in the outcome of refractive procedures."[49] If these surgical procedures make you queasy, well, it's better than hanging a cow's eye from your neck (and a darned sight more attractive). This might lead one to gratitude for what corrective lenses provide: consistent, clear vision without risking permanent alterations to the only set of eyeballs you're going to get.

Until researching this book, like most people, I'd never reflected on how eyeglasses work or where they came from. Now, I find glasses and contacts to be among the most important inventions in human history. The story of how humans struggled to see is compelling and mysterious. Naturally, that story has engaged the attention of authors who use eyeglasses as powerful metaphors. It also brought eyeglass fashions to the fore. Just as I was researching these topics, doubts have seeped in about whether this experiment could do all I'd hoped, amidst dreams of glasses and memories of times when their loss got me into trouble.

Tuesday

Though it wouldn't stay that way, my second day without glasses began in exhilaration. I might not have been able to see things until they were up close, but I did see possibilities. I make out familiar objects by shape, color, and location. As I approach them, they slide into clearer view, though still not in focus. My eyes were oddly relaxed from not pushing for focus every minute.

And I knew where my glasses were. I could go back to them anytime. At least they weren't lost.

* * *

This morning, I walked into the kitchen and threw my car keys into a drawer with a clang. Won't need those for a while, I figured. I'm temporarily alone, no pets or children around in a quiet home expanded from an old farmhouse at the edge of a city.

Friends remained curious. They peppered me with questions.

"Are you safe, cooking on a gas stove?"

"Yes. I guess so? Not sure."

"What are you missing most, without glasses?" Not a bad question, but come on! That's like asking what part of your life you don't really need.

"For a week, I could give up driving," one friend commented. Others suspected me of simplemindedness. "Glasses? If you don't see right, you get a new pair. What's the problem?"

I was getting used to such comments, and to the blur surrounding me. Or at least, I was fretting about it less. The bumps and grazes and band-aids kept coming; but already there were fewer. I felt a quiet pride in my adaptability.

Still, in practice, I resembled the Biggest Loser. This morning, I looked at the scale but couldn't squat deep enough to read its small numbers. So I started a No-Glasses Diet. Here's how that works: Put down your plate and walk to the other side of where you live; then maybe you won't find your food again. (This worked, except for unpleasant-smelling leftovers later.) Another trick was to say before dinner, "I'm not sure I can cook this safely," give up, and eat an apple instead.

One needs faith to change habits. Faith commands allegiance. My allegiance was to a faith that we glassers actually have more visual capacity than we realize. By forcing the issue, I thought, people like me could take a break from visual supports, still see, and thereby arrive at self-control and acceptance of our unique vision. Glasses can be an albatross around the eyes.

Others in history have experimented with sight without glasses, notably ophthalmologist William Bates (1860–1931).[1] Early in the twentieth century, Dr. Bates suggested that keeping eyes constantly in focus strains and lessens sight: "the eye possesses perfect vision only when it is absolutely at rest."[2] His muscle-toning exercises, he insisted, could remediate both near-and-far-sightedness. Bates was certain glasses do more harm than good; wearing them, he declared, was using a crutch that denied our eyes the chance to exercise their full potential. Practitioners of "The Bates System of Eye Exercises" have declared success at visual rehabilitation using eye exercises, but this takes considerable discipline and practice over months and years; one "suns" one's eyes and "palms" them to help relaxation along, among other exercises.

In the world of Hollywood émigrés before and during WWII, Aldous Huxley, Igor Stravinsky, Thomas Mann, and other European exiles practiced the Bates method with some of its leading proponents, based on his popular book *The Bates Method for Better Eyesight*. The method offered Huxley an alternative to his dependency on glasses, which he gave up wearing during the Second World War. Friends of Huxley disagreed as to whether the approach worked; some praised his progress, while one remembered him reaching for a door handle and almost falling into the street.

Bates practitioners remain active in the world today, and a related field, behavioral optometry, incorporates physical, neurological, and developmental aspects of vision—serving as inspiration for me now. "If you can relax into blur, it will help us see ourselves in a new way.... Going into blur gives you the gift of [visual] clarity," writes Dr. Samuel Berne, an optometrist who practices holistic eye care.[3] I hope he's right. Besides pursuing one's blur, Dr. Berne treats eye conditions with herbs, essential oils, carrot seeds, and light therapy. Currently short of carrot seeds, and knowing his treatment would require sessions not paid for by insurance, I'll content myself with sinking into my friendly blur. It's about all I have right now.

Ophthalmologists tend to disregard the Bates approach because it can never physically reshape the eyeball.[4] Yet with regular practice of those exercises, Huxley largely went without correction for his last two decades. (I'm learning, now, a bit of what he went through to get there.)

* * *

"All your problems are opportunities," wrote Robert Louis Stevenson. I don't see them that way today, after losing one of those yellow legal pads full of notes. Misplaced, it left a gap like the missing eighteen minutes in President Nixon's recordings of his time in the Oval Office. That pad assumed increased importance by the minute. There must be better words there than those in front of me now and if I had my glasses, I could find them. Maybe, I thought, I should just give up and try (for the fourth time) to wear contacts. I'm too nearsighted for laser surgery.

Any time one invests in an idealistic change of life, self-doubt and questions arise. Will giving up a habit really help us get the lives we think we want? Nowadays, it's trendy for people to struggle with their connection, or addiction, to technology. Many at least consider, if not actually take, vacations from social media, computers, and phones (and, perhaps in the future, smart glasses). We're collectively anxious about this technological dependence, and understandably so: A writer attending a digital detoxification camp had a woman tell him, "I am done being enslaved to a piece of technology that has robbed me and my kids of attention."[5] But she still worried, as I have this week, if she would miss out on something crucial.

One measure of our collective hunger for digital minimalism occurred when a yogurt company offered a lottery, with a prize of $10,000 and flip phones, to those willing to make a month-long withdrawal from their phones. More than 300,000 people applied. Presumably, applicants were wrestling with the pressure of being accessible to everyone and everything all the time, just as I now found myself resisting pressure from myself (and those around me) to try and see clearly every minute.

"When we give up what we think we want, we do so with a view to getting something back," wrote psychoanalyst Adam Phillips.[6] Those rehabbing their relationship with technology (in my case, the device that allows sight) expect their sacrifices to yield something better. Inevitably, a pattern emerges: wishing, hoping, bargaining with oneself. Giving up a habit rejiggers our behavior, reminding us of what we are trying to do without. According to literary theorist Jacques Lacan, this displacement of the ordinary involves something missing from its familiar, reliable place. This invokes the psychobiology of appetite, how hungers and cravings for things (including sight) unsettle us, sometimes leading to despair and even terror. To succeed in challenging ourselves to give something up, we must have faith that our action will lead us to our better selves and to the better life we intend. There are so many lifestyle cleanses—vegetarianism, committed dieting, kicking alcohol or hard drugs. Withdrawing from modern life's technological infrastructure might be nearly as hard.

In *Stolen Focus,* author Johann Hari recorded the results of his experiment in giving up his phone and the internet to learn how to focus in a distracted world. He did this in a desperate mood, feeling that by stripping away these distractions, he'd find a more balanced, sustainable way to live. He didn't intend to abandon his technology forever; we wouldn't have his book if he had done so. He took notes on an old laptop that couldn't receive the internet. I don't intend to give up my technology forever either.

One contributor to NPR conducted an exercise similar to Hari's, wanting to see how hard it would be to live without plastic for a week by avoiding buying single-use items.[7] Reducing and recycling all her plastics proved exhausting. Another reporter wrote about spending a week offline, alongside others. She relearned how to live more day-to-day. Similar to my effort, she kept the phone away from her workstation and off her night table; later, she used an hourglass to limit her social media use.[8] Though she didn't use the word "addictive," her concern centered around whether her connection to her phone could be that.[9]

Earlier, I used the term "glassaholic" to describe myself, but "addiction" is not a word to toss around lightly. Traditionally defined as a chronic brain disease, the field is reconceptualizing itself to include social environment, genetics, and context as factors in addiction. Some consider addiction a choice; others, a disease. When we apply the word addiction to TikTok or a cell phone, it raises questions: How far is an addiction from a habit? When does a habit like using social media, watching movies, or eating ice cream slide from being a preference into a compulsion and then to a dependency?

According to research cited in *The Guardian*, 25–35 percent of people worldwide have a smartphone addiction; a Stanford professor called phones "the modern-day hypodermic needle."[10] This is non-substance addiction.

For substance abuse, there are receptors and drug-metabolizing enzymes to measure. Does calling recreational shopping, or gambling, or wearing glasses or contacts all the time an "addiction" make the word flippant? If extreme video gamers arrive at the ER for dehydration because they can't stop playing to drink water are addicts, what does that say about glassers? Does demanding visual clarity at every waking moment qualify as compulsive?

Sometimes hopes for long-term change are unrealistic, more philosophical than practical. Any change in behavior is uncomfortable at first, like building new muscles. But even if that desired change doesn't or can't or shouldn't last, it gives one a destination apart from where one normally lives. And just seeing that possibility—the way life could hold unexpected benefits, the way a lack of sight can stimulate other senses. Of course for me, that benefit may ebb the minute I return to my glasses—if I haven't misplaced them as I once did on an airplane.

* * *

It's 4 a.m., eight miles above the tossing waves of the Caribbean and I'm on my way to São Paulo to teach. The flight left Chicago in the evening, and we are halfway. For once, quiet rules the airplane. No carts banging down the aisles, toilets burbling, ice clinking, or crying children worrying if they'd be safe in this skin of metal, hurtling they know not where.

In the silent darkness, the night leaves quiet thoughts. The flight attendants have vanished to their quarters. Like my fellow passengers I twist in my uncomfortable seat, until I notice an unused row to lie down. But dawn is far away. The sleeping pill has worn off. I am alone and awake. Dull movies offer no help. The darkness chases out my dreams, those unknown continents, and returns me to my native, unfocused land.

Ahead of me, fuzzy dots line the floor, telling me where to go if the plane plunges. The fuzziness reminds me to put my glasses back on. But I find they've vanished into the Pit of Lost Objects every plane carries. Somewhere in the hold is my spare pair. That's a problem with wearing glasses. You need glasses to find glasses.

In the still, humming darkness, the miles roar by. The passengers seem to be holding their collective breath, grateful for an hour undisturbed by announcements and seat-belt checks. Do I dare wake a stranger to help me find my glasses? I look around. People are out in that fretful sleep air travel offers. Is this a glasser nightmare from which I'd wake; no, I'd just put my glasses in my shirt pocket, and they've gone walkabout.

Glasses panic: What was I going to do for the next eight sightless hours? I feel in the cushions. No luck. That leaves the floor or aisle. My hands spread out in front of me as I crawl along the floor in the dark. Nothing there. The plane's interiors stretch far beyond my vision.

Groveling on the floor by my seat, I am a sight of sore eyes. Of all the lessons for glasses-wearers, one must be that lying down, glasses are unsafe in pockets. My treatment of eye shields had always been too casual. Had they now retreated, in revenge?

I've visited all the logical suspects: cushions, floor, seatback, even that annoying little gap between the seat arms and the cushion. What next? Wade up to where the rich folks fly, where someone might be in attendance? Airlines have gotten pushier about preventing invasion of business and first-class areas by putting up curtains. Then, written warnings not to enter. Pretty soon, force fields will keep the flying masses in their place.

Just then, I turn around sharply in my seat and hear a familiar thump. Released from the seat bottom's grip, my glasses drop to the carpet. I am whole again.

* * *

Remembering this, today I brought my pair out of exile. Holding them up, a flash of sharpness stirred me like a bell going off. I put them down reluctantly. What I was missing most was the *integration* of sight, far and near. I found myself constantly moving forward to find focus. Foregoing glasses may have gone a step too far. Only two days in, and thoughts of quitting arose. Well, if I was going to stop, I might as well do it now, I thought. Save the bother of the rest of the week. This is how Alcoholic Anonymous members justify a forbidden drink; it's the way quitting smokers fondle a cigarette.

Earlier, when I wrote that I felt like the Biggest Loser, I was thinking not just about weight, but about my inability to keep track of things. Once set down, objects disappeared. I was hoping not to drop-kick that cup of tea I'd put down. About all I found consistently were floaters, bouncing before my eyes. I'd thought they'd disappear without glasses. No luck. (Sudden new ones could signal a retinal tear or detachment, demanding immediate attention.)

These floaters block my vision, drifting like tiny, crazy asterisks; to read, I have to shuffle them away from my pupils again and again. They are dimming my sight.

If you've had floaters, you may know them as well as you know the neighbors. Staring at them can become obsessive. No matter where one looks, they're hanging there. I've been swinging these fellers out of the center of my eye for so long I've given them names: the Duffel Bag, which floats horizontally like a barge; the Battleship, whose sharp edges outline the horizon like a city after King Kong stomped through; the Roulette Wheel, a circle inside a circle which careens from one side of my right eye to the other. You might try another experiment: stare up at a cloudless sky or hold a blank paper in front of you. Do you see floaters? Next, if you wear glasses, pull them off and study them. Ask yourself about their color, shape, and style. What character in a movie would wear them? On someone else's face, what would you think of them?

* * *

Sidestepping my floaters, I took safe exercise—a twenty-minute walk to the end of my dusty road, step by step, head down. I had to show myself there was something I could manage. I returned refreshed. Looking around, I felt a lightness at seeing anew: My eyes seemed not merely open, but open *wider*. This, I reminded myself, was how I see organically, without plastic or glass. Right now, it didn't matter if I couldn't see precisely. Hearing clearly that faint rustle in the dead leaves compensated me for not seeing which animal was making it.

Above me, the geese were heading into the river bottom for the night, bedding down on islands where the coyotes couldn't get at them. As they descended to the water, I couldn't see their "V" twenty feet above me, but I heard crosstalk from the two ends of the formation as they gabbled by. Sitting and swimming, they're silent, but when they fly, Canada geese sound like the floor of Congress on a bad day. I heard the rhythmic slap of their wings against their gray-and-brown breasts, as they beat down the air to stay aloft.

Despite their aversion to being eaten, the geese didn't seem to notice the coyotes' first calls below them. Every night they sounded off. The younger coyotes tried to initiate the night's get-together; their high-pitched trial cry usually brought silence. Then adult coyote #1, in a deeper voice, called to order the nightly yipfest. Sounds burst out of the forest; and as at many meetings, everyone spoke at once. I closed my eyes and listened. (My ears were enjoying the attention.) After a quarter hour, the coyotes quieted and burrowed into their dens for the night.

As the second day of struggling through grievances gave way to fatigue, my exhilaration faded with it. Still, a dose of hope went with me into the night. "We walk by faith, not by sight," the Bible reminds us, and I had faith that something would come out of my visual fast. Looking back, it doesn't matter if I was always losing my glasses and being teased about them. Glasses have faced derision since their beginning. The more I understand that derision, the more I understand their place today.

3

The Glasses Stigma

There are those shy of mounting Spectacles which show their Age upon their Nose.

—DR. GEORG BEER, 1815[1]

Sometimes ghastly, absurd in retrospect, resistance to eyeglasses—on one's own face or someone else's—has nonetheless persisted. This is more than a despair-worthy footnote to humanity's long struggle to see. Discouraging people from wearing the glasses they need—for vanity or for other reasons has caused countless problems for individuals and society.

As vision aids opened horizons for those needing them, the devices also faced pushback. Three kinds of resistance ensued: for reasons of religion; for appearance and style; and, surprisingly, resistance from the very profession providing the technology. Dating from the Church's wariness of glasses in the Middle Ages, the first resistance was to wearing them at all.

Almost as soon as somebody came up with a way to hang lenses on a face, someone else denounced the idea. With few people able to read, and glasses hard to find or to afford, initially, few noticed their existence; there was no general rejoicing over an invention designed for an elite minority. As historian Richard Carson wrote: "The Church in many instances encouraged the idea that afflictions [were] sent by God and were meant to be endured in silence for the good of one's soul and that any mechanical device which counteracted them must perforce be the work of the devil."[2] Indeed, early depictions of the devil had him in spectacles. The Church's opposition to lenses in this period paralleled its opposition to music. To church authorities, the only holy instrument was the human voice. Their pagan ancestry made instrumental music dangerous, "for the pernicious influence it supposedly exerted on moral temperaments," wrote music historian Ted Goia.[3]

Other sources echo Carson's assessment: "Anything that went on in the body was the domain of God," a historian of optics suggested, "and one didn't tamper with that . . . There's also the suggestion of control: if [the Church is] in control of vision, it will control everything that's going on in society."[4] Novelty was behind the Church's rejection, suggested Dr. Neil Handley, Curator of the British Optical Association Museum: "Because glasses were unusual and rare, they were seen as having magical powers. . . . Those who wore glasses were in league with the devil—immoral."[5]

Besides immorality, Church doctrine associated wearing glasses with witchcraft: "Evil deeds, supposedly, were actuated by them, and vices stimulated—superstition continued to make them agents of sin and spiritual suffering." Even if spectacles weren't sent by the devil, wearing them in this era took courage.[6]

Enduring poor vision to serve Him better? Devil worship? Today, it's hard to imagine such a furor over spectacles. Roger Bacon, for one, fervently believed that seeing the world sharply would inspire religious awe. He wouldn't have agreed with the "no tampering with nature" argument, which in any case quickly becomes difficult to sustain: After all, the devout don't go to mass in their birthday suits, and Catholic doctors attempt to heal the sick, even if their fate was divinely given.

At the root of ecclesiastical disapproval of glasses may have been the social control codified in sumptuary laws, which discouraged extravagance and reinforced social hierarchy by limiting the enjoyment of luxury to nobility: In Bacon's time, King Edward II issued a proclamation against outrageous excess. In 1433, the Scottish parliament tried to limit the eating of pies and baked meats to the ranks of baron or higher. Wearing fur was forbidden to anyone below the rank of knight. The similar application of sumptuary laws to eyeglasses was to be expected, as in China where at court, commoners were expected to remove their glasses when someone entered the room with a larger pair. It's not a far leap from these laws to later fashion dictates for glasses, such as this satire from Aldous Huxley's 1923 novel, *Antic Hay*: "For sport or relaxation, they tell you, as though it was a social axiom, you must wear spectacles of pure tortoiseshell . . . For semi-evening dress, shell rims with gold earpieces and a good nose-bridge. And for full dress, gold-mounted rimless pince-nez is refinement itself," wrote Huxley. "And since there are few who would not rather be taken in adultery than provincialism, they rush out to buy four new pairs of spectacles.[7] A fair question is, when and how did this religious objection to visual correction fade?

Perhaps ecclesiastical resistance diminished alongside the church's visehold on piety after Luther's rebellion against corruption and single-minded orthodoxy in its ranks. Did the shift to acceptance occur as clerics realized they, too, needed spectacles? Surely the myopic among them had tired of the charade of hiding their spectacles when visited by a religious superior.

Did commerce lessen anti-glasses prejudice? No records exist, but it seems logical: There was money to be made. Before the glasses peddler, only statesmen and high-ranking clerics could afford pairs other than the do-it-yourself models circulating. As glasses began to be manufactured, and prices dropped, the wealthy instead distinguished theirs with jewels and frames of silver and gold. One's wealth and status could be judged by frames. The lawyer reading a brief, the banker counting money, the bishop preparing a sermon—these cared little about violating dogma.

My notions about alternate ways of seeing, and spending my time without visual correction wouldn't have impressed the artisans struggling to grind lenses, or the manuscript copyists having to hide their visual aids away because of the Church's opposition. Around 1400, at a convent outside of Hannover, Germany, one resident hid spectacles where she hoped they wouldn't be discovered. Hundreds of years later, what might be the oldest surviving pair of glasses was discovered under the floorboards of the choir room, according to the *Online Encyclopedia of Antique Spectacles*. Its lenses had a visual correction of 3.5 diopters, useful for a myopic woman who needed them to read but who also feared exposing her spectacles habit. Typical of the time's clerical anti-glasses sentiments is this line: "the newly invented Optik glasses are immoral since they prevent natural sight and make things appear in an unnatural and false light.[8]

The second category of opposition to glasses concerned revealing physical imperfections. This led to the idea that wearing glasses showed personal weakness or a public display of aging. This sentiment goes way back. Shakespeare, in his famous "Ages of Man" speech, likewise associated spectacles and old age: "The Sixth Age shifts into the lean and skippered pantaloons [trousers] with spectacles on the nose." Poet Emily Dickinson acknowledged this same association: "[A lock of hair] will serve to make you remember me when locks are grey, and the quiet cap and the spectacles," she wrote.[9]

Men also sought to avoid this stigma, recorded as far back as 1793. As one observation put it: "Mister Du Quesne is far advanced in years but will not own it. He is by no means fit to drive a single Horse Chaise. He cannot see the ruts distinctly. He will not however wear spectacles at all. He cannot bear to appear old but must be as young in anything as the youngest person."[10] Sometimes, this avoidance could prove fatal. There's the case of a likely vain man, Admiral Collingwood, second in command at England's Battle of Trafalgar (1805). Without his specs, he leaned too far over navigational charts to scrutinize them, causing a stomach blockage that killed him. Hitler was only mildly farsighted, but in the 1930s, the Reich suppressed pictures of the Führer in glasses as a potential barrier to Germans "making a close and personal connection to its adored leader."[11] Eventually, spectacles and those nose-pinching pince-nez gained respect—but only for men.

* * *

Lucy (her last name lost to history) loved to play the piano. One New England spring day in 1835, Lucy's fingers were animatedly striking the keys when she heard a door open. In walked her suitor. Unfortunately, there she sat, bespectacled, for she could not play the Mozart and Rossini she loved without spectacles.

This was *not* how Lucy chose to be seen. According to her cousin, "her spectacles were kept as great a mystery as a murder or a ghost."[12] But now she was caught *in flagrante*.

That was the end of the relationship, but not for the reasons one might think, according to the account in *Godey's Lady's Book* of April 1836. For as soon as the suitor discovered Lucy's terrible secret, she discovered his. Seeing him clearly for the first time, she suddenly realized he was extremely unattractive—not someone she'd want to curl up with (a good thing to learn before the wedding!).

Like Lucy, many women were phobic about being seen in glasses. Not long after Lucy was caught at the piano, Elizabeth Payson Prentiss, daughter of a prominent New England minister, complained to a friend about eyeglasses. The future novelist, twenty-two, didn't need spectacles and didn't like them. They embarrassed her. "Mr. —— talked to me as if he imagined me a blue-stocking. Just because my sister wears spectacles, folks take it for granted that I also am literary." "Blue-stocking" was no compliment; it referred to dangerously literary females wearing glasses in public. Prentiss's sister risked being seen bespectacled, and by doing so she marked herself—and her family—as "transgressing traditional gender boundaries," as a scholar put it.[13]

Besides revealing one's age by wearing spectacles, young women who showed a physical deficiency might be deemed less desirable as mates, lest their weak eyes be passed on to their children. Historically, women with weak eyes have been caught between appearing imperfect and seeing well. To avoid revealing aging and infirmity, elderly women could carry easy-to-hide monocles on strings, the so-called quizzers. But these too were assailed, and their wearers were considered "grotesque, leering, and licentious, failed attempts to appear fashionably younger than they actually were," a journalist suggested. Is it coincidental that the first paintings of females in glasses appear only in the 1620s, while men are portrayed in glasses centuries earlier?[14]

For a few women, spectacles added gravitas: authors or teachers could get away with wearing them in public, as Ms. Prentiss did. Such bravery still sometimes brought disdain: In 1844, a spectacles-wearing five-year-old girl and her sister, both so talented they could recite the Greek alphabet, were considered "pallid, meager little creatures with dull, sunken eyes."[15] Women were caught between looking glamorous and fulfilling domestic duties that required close work: sewing, letter-writing, teaching, and drawing. They generally wore their vision aids in private. Even at the dawn of the twentieth century, the *Optical Journal* admitted: "Glasses are very disfiguring to women and girls. If glasses are alright, [sic] they will seldom or never have to be worn in public."[16]

In 1929, Dorothy Parker wrote the most famous demurral on eyeglasses in her short poem "News Item": "Men seldom make passes at girls who wear glasses."[17] People have been both repeating and challenging this line ever since. Two young women from Wisconsin didn't buy it: "The statement is entirely erroneous . . . a survey made among repairing opticians would show that Monday is a very busy day for straightening girls' glasses."[18] The French have a proverb which reverses this assertion: "*Bonjour lunettes; adieu fillettes*," ("Hello, glasses; goodbye girls").

In our time, it's harder to take this notion seriously; but glass-shaming over time has evinced many blame-the-victim tropes, like body-shaming. Typical is this remark, from the *Saturday Evening Post* in 1938: "As for glasses, the average smart woman would almost rather shave her head or wear high-laced boots to a dance than put on spectacles for permanent wear in public as well as in private."[19] "It was a bit like brandishing your wooden leg in public," wrote one writer.[20]

Actress Peggy Wood's mother never hid her distress at her daughter having to wear glasses. "Well she knew the toll of the world, especially the female world, would take for so visible an infirmity, and well she knew that 'Four Eyes' would dog me to my grave."

This sounds ominous; but Peggy was simply absorbing what to her was an important rule: "In frivolous contacts with the male which is to say, the stern business of life, it was poor policy to try to look either like one of the school mistresses or as if you might know as much or more than the superior sex. They are touchy about that."[21] At a concert or play, as soon as the lights dimmed, she noticed how glasses mysteriously appeared on many women's faces, and then as quickly disappeared when the lights came back up. "Bespectacled maidens have suffered from all allusions to their allure," as the *New York Times* put it.

Another woman looked back on her youth in a 1950 issue of the *Atlantic Monthly*: "I joined the ranks of these doomed creatures [with glasses] at the age of 8 and never would I hear the sweet music of long, low whistle." (Of course, modern women might argue this was doing her a favor.) Despite getting a rimless pair, "practically invisible . . . my rimless horrors went through high school in my purse." Finally, her worst fear arrived: a boy she had a crush on called her "Four-Eyes."[22] Or, as Len Snowden, the writer of a 1990 *Mademoiselle* essay entitled "Specs and the Single Girl" remembers about wearing glasses in sixth grade: "I knew perfectly well I looked like the pathetic four-eyed geek, as kids reminded me daily. It was a fact of life that if you wore glasses, you were just the queerest, no matter what you did."[23]

"When you really need glasses like I do," Len Snowden continued, "people spontaneously bring up issues like hiring the handicapped, the career of Roy Orbison, and why it is so hard to find Coca-Cola in bottles. This is why my friends never see me wearing glasses."[24]

Even more dramatic reactions occurred: "I really ought to wear my glasses," complained one woman. "So my mother kept telling when I brought these monsters to dinner. The thing is if I wear my glasses, I wouldn't go to the cocktail parties at all . . . I'd feel terrible when wearing glasses. I'd want to hide . . . I'd kill myself."[25]

Resistance to wearing glasses was and is by no means limited to ladies. Despite needing spectacles, some literary gents shared the earlier rejection of Jonathan Swift. Charles Darwin considered glasses to be "something vicious." Goethe hated them with a passion: "How fatal glasses are. As soon as a stranger enters with his spectacles, I think at once: he has not read your latest poems; or he has read them, he knows your own peculiarities and goes beyond them and that's even worse."[26] Because of their near work, writers were particularly susceptible to eyestrain headaches and dyspepsia, which glasses might help. A 1938 study suggested that eyestrain harmed the health of many great scientists and authors, including Kepler, Balzac, Carlyle, Darwin, and Huxley.[27]

"I never move without a plentiful supply of optical glass," wrote Aldous Huxley in 1925 in "Spectacles," a penetrating essay on living with lenses. After his blinding at Eton and having to put in atropine eyedrops at Oxford to see around his damaged cornea, Huxley depended on a typewriter with large type and on glasses. His array of lenses was simultaneously his salvation and his nemesis. For travel, Huxley's optical armory included three pairs of prescription sunglasses: two green (light and dark) and one black; reading glasses; and a monocle—all he really needed, with sight in one eye. "To break all these," he said, "it would need an earthquake or a railway accident."

> A pair of spectacles must inevitably break or lose itself, just when you can least afford to do without and are least able to replace it. But inanimate matter, so called, is no fool; and when a pair of spectacles realizes that you carry two or three other pairs in your pockets and suit-cases, it will

understand that the game is hopeless and, so far from deliberately smashing or losing itself, will take pains to remain intact.[28]

Assuming his glasses survived, they made the landscape "more nobly dramatic and romantic." (Another large job for glasses—and a comment that went unnoticed when Huxley publicly declared he was giving his pairs up.)[29]

To counter widespread appearance anxiety about glasses, the twentieth-century optical industry desperately tried to promote eyeglasses as fashionable and sexy. First came the "Bespectacled Beauty Pageant" (1938), with a bevy of models sporting eyeglasses, followed by Miss Specs Appeal (1953) and the Miss Beauty in Glasses pageant (1954–62). (Were the male judges allowed to wear glasses?) It was an uphill battle: glasses made makeup more complicated, or reminded people of the stereotypically unattractive "Plain Jane." In 1942, one American restaurant is recorded as refusing to hire bespectacled women.[30]

Change would come in time.

"No longer need parents shudder lest their four-eyed daughters be left 'out of things' socially or be deprived of friends and admirers. It's actually getting to the point where some put on 'cheaters' to make themselves look smarter," Peggy Wood concluded in 1932.[31]

Many women still demurred. Up to the 1960s, "if a doctor recommended glasses to a girl, it approached a minor tragedy. It seemed like no matter how well one saw afterwards, one paid for it in lessened attractiveness."[32] This led to the widespread practice of fooling oneself in the vain belief that somehow, if one refused to wear glasses, one would cease to need them (a fallacy paralleling my current undertaking).

* * *

A third category of resistance to glasses—and perhaps the most surprising one—came from, of all people, optometrists. Besides that 1583 quote from Dr. Georg Bartisch, that "a person sees better when he has nothing in front of his eyes," even into the twentieth century, a few optometrists hesitated to recommend visual correction. In 1921, Dr. George Gould issued "A Warning Against [Pince-nez]": "The ribbon or chain attached causes them to drop on one side and thus change the correction . . . if patients will not wear spectacles [eyeglasses] . . . we cannot in the future prescribe."[33] One optometrist W. C. Wallace opposed patients wearing glasses at all.[34] Another eye specialist, Dr. John M. Wheeler, urged his colleagues to prescribe as few as possible.[35] Myopia was overdiagnosed, he declared; it was not for the patient to decide whether he needed glasses. [36](The reply of opticians was probably unprintable in the *New York Times*.)

In 1929, the Executive Committee of New York City Optometrists declared that for almost 50 percent of patients, eye exercises might be better than glasses. "We have been simply correcting the eye as an optical instrument, like a cornea. Hereafter, we will deal with it as an organization of muscle. . . most of the eye defects can be corrected so that the defect itself will disappear."[37]

Even driving in glasses was considered suspect. In the early 1930s, the *British Medical Journal* wrote about accidents caused by spectacles: "The driver wearing horn-rimmed spectacles is blinded by the heavy rims and hinges at the side . . . half of the vision is occluded on both sides at eye level." All this ink reflected a continuing prejudice against those needing visual correction. Contrary to the contemporary stereotype of glasses-wearers as "nerds," in New York City's public schools in the 1920s, students with poor eyesight were associated with "backwardness, stupidity, apparent laziness, and truancy." Many were classified as "backward, mentally deficient, stupid, or habitually left back" in schools.[38] Is it any wonder taunts followed on the playground?

* * *

Another way of avoiding glasses, of course, is by using contact lenses. Even the earliest tinkerers with lenses sought a better way: Why not put the lens right *on* the eye, rather than suspending it on frames or laying a magnifier on the page? In 1508, Leonardo da Vinci imagined how contact lenses might work. To demonstrate the principle, he mentioned sticking one's head in a bowl of water to see. (Not the most useful approach.)

René Descartes designed, but didn't build, a contact lens in 1636. Two centuries later, a French lens maker tried slicing off the ends of test tubes. That didn't work either. There the idea sat until 1887, when a maker of artificial eyes in Switzerland developed a protective lens for a man whose eyelids did not fully close.[39] Because these first contacts were large—covering the whole eye, not just the pupil—they couldn't be used for long; they were wearable but unbearable. In addition, the heavy lens tended to slide to the bottom of the eye. When that happened, one had to grab a cheek and pull down to see through the fallen contacts.

What made contacts so tricky to develop is that the cornea itself, the outer layer of the eye, has no direct supply of blood: It relies on tears (and the air) to supply needed nutrients and oxygen. Tears lubricate the eye and wash away cellular waste. Thus, anything blocking the eye from the air or from tears can be uncomfortable and cause corneal ulcers.

Contacts, like glasses, went through many steps to become what's worn today. Their ancestry dates to 500 BC, when Romans began to make artificial eyes from painted clay. These were worn outside the socket for damaged eyes. Once refined, this technology eventually led to what people wear today.[40] Among the first commercial devices were those *Scientific American* called "glass discs" for the eye in 1931, "simple little eyeball caps of optical glass, thimbles instead of frames." They didn't catch on. In 1935, Zeiss, the German optical manufacturer, ground only 450 pairs for Americans, mostly for unusual optical problems. As might be expected, bias against glasses likewise extended initially to contacts; in 1936, *Fortune* magazine suggested they're for "over-sensitive young souls who might get inferiority complexes if they wore glasses . . . 50% of sales are made to women who are, justifiably enough, vain of their looks and realize that they are more beautiful without spectacles than with."[41] In 1957, 79 percent of women who bought them credited "vanity" as their motive.[42]

The invention of Lucite (clear plexiglass) allowed for "hard" contact lenses to be stronger, thinner, and lighter than anything made before. In 1948, people began wearing contact lenses covering just the iris and pupil, which is the current method.[43] Over time, contacts had developed from blown glass, ground glass, and molded glass to gas-permeable lenses and finally to a plastic compound infused with salt water (saline), which takes the place of tears, for a "soft" contact lens, what 90 percent of contact lens wearers choose today.[44] The future belonged to plastic (lenses), as actor Dustin Hoffman was told in *The Graduate*.

Today, plastic rather than glass is used for most optical lenses. Plastic gained traction in the early "1970s, when fashion favored larger frames, making glasses significantly heavier (though the invention of 'low index' lenses reduced thickness and weight)." In the 1990s, lens processing technology advanced. "A higher grade of poly became available that was clearer and free of imperfections that impeded good vision," wrote glasses technologist Andrew Karp. "Plus, tinting improved, and hard coating protected the relatively soft material from scratching."[45]

Still, resistance to glasses continued. Opticians knew the hide-the-glasses phenomenon sold contacts, which were explicitly marketed to those avoiding the "nuisance value" of glasses. As many as 90 percent of wearers chose contact lenses for psychological reasons. "I never felt the least bit glamorous while wearing glasses," commented a new contact lens wearer. Today, options available in contacts include bifocal and progressive lenses, and ones that darken outside, and soon, perhaps, with cameras fitted.[46]

Resistance to glasses, and to those wearing them, has been dogged through the centuries. Wearers have been disregarded, dismissed, and all-around dissed. Later in this book, I investigate the extent to which negative attitudes have changed— both by those judging wearers and by wearers' attitudes themselves. I resolve not to dwell on the nasty things people have said about glasses or how people look in them. But I couldn't stop myself reliving my personal experiences of that judgment, inside and outside my own head.

Wednesday

No bird soars too high if he soars with his own wings.

—WILLIAM BLAKE

Today's hump day, halfway there—but halfway to what? Unfocused, the day stretched before me on a conveyor belt to nowhere; and the belt was stopped. I couldn't push it forward. That loss of control remained as I found myself stripped of even simple pleasures and productivity. My day was a tree without leaves.

On the levee behind the house, a coyote slunk by in a whir of gray and dusty brown. Who else was out and about? Was that a lizard running up the wall? In the bosque (woods) by the river, I don't often find rattlers, but they're out there. Today, the hot air squatted on the land with the stickiness that foretold a storm. Even the mountains at the edge of town frowned at the heat. Along our muddy Rio Grande—a quarter mile wide and three feet deep—only the current moved. Even the insects napped. The weather's stuck, just like me.

Compiling the resistance to glasses as unholy and disfiguring has taken a toll. What had people thought of the bargain-basement pairs I wore growing up, white rims circling thick lenses like visual handcuffs? In the mirror, I saw stubble, a glassy-eyed look, and reddish eyes from lack of sleep.

* * *

In last night's dream, I was at the state fair, New Mexico's biggest event of the year. I was a child, arriving early and standing in line by myself. I visited the pie café, the sheep-shearing competition, and the dancing seals. At the optical exhibit, I stared at the cool gear. Just as I was wondering if another eye test would help me, a boy came up. He said his name was Henry, and he wanted to trade glasses. I said okay. He said he wanted to see if my glasses would help him see better. I said I hoped the same thing.

Now, I've never been big on glasses trading. Too often in childhood, letting someone see through my glasses ran like this: "Four Eyes can't see without his glasses! Hey, I got 'em," the bully would cry, playing Keep Away with my link to the world. It's considered cowardly to make fun of the blind, but the semi-sighted are fair game. It's like that glasser kids' game, "Who Sees Worse":

"Wow, you really have a thick pair!" says one.

"Bet mine are worse than yours!" comes the reply. Glasses are pulled off and traded. I regularly heard: "God, you really *are* blind."

Meanwhile in my dream, I saw around me the way I do now: blankly, wondering where everything went. I put on Henry's pair and saw even worse, all blurry. I handed them back.

The next day in my dream, everything repeated: the pie café smelling of warm cinnamon and the frames on display. Henry showed up. We traded glasses again, and this time, it worked! I could see so clearly I flew up in the air and looked down at the clouds. I saw the whole fairgrounds with the Ferris wheel turning, the animals in the petting zoo, the parents leading kids by the hand. Everything was amazingly sharp. Cotton candy—I could see every strand. I even saw Henry down below, waving at me, and I remembered these were his glasses, so I went back down and returned them and asked the smiling, grandfatherly optometrist if I could have glasses like Henry's someday.

* * *

Afterwards, I spent the day hunched over a desk, my head a few inches above the yellow pad. My back ached, my neck ached, and my eyes, well, they wished they had their glasses back. Close up, my trusty old eyes worked as well as ever. I was enjoying Dickens-length novels in whose depths I forgot to worry, and I'd found books about kids' glasses. (How come fiction isn't written about other useful devices, like scissors or flashlights?) I'm also reading about our life before glasses. Twenty-eight hundred years ago, the Assyrians in modern-day Iraq and Iran told of a king who would take a magnifying glass and hold it to the sun to light fuel on an altar.

Before glasses, the mildly nearsighted were integrated into society in appropriate roles, though prejudice remained. One Roman stood up for glassers: "One who is by nature nearsighted is as sound as one who runs more slowly than others." As illustrators and scribes, the heavily myopes were prized for their unique ability; one report suggests they were inbred to preserve this.[1] The tiny lettering on Babylonian manuscripts had to have been done by someone with what today might be called a disability. (This reminds me of the eugenicist beliefs of one Dr. Rice, a state health officer I'll discuss later who suggested the weak-sighted be bred out of the population.)

* * *

Outside my window, I heard a storm forming. The wind groaned. Leaves trembled like a child. A few drops fell.

In New Mexico, storm-watching is a spectator sport. Above, platinum clouds parted reluctantly, like lovers at a train station, before a hard rain fell. The winds stirred the cottonwoods, and a sweet scent blew in the window. A few drops more, and the storm retreated, leaving the land thirsty. The air smelled of sage, and then the wind quieted, the thunder faded, and the drops disappeared.

By the storm's end, the temperature had dropped ten degrees. I had the urge to make a fire. I built it hesitantly, in the log-cabin style I learned in Boy Scout camp. I checked if the flue was open. I lit a rolled newspaper and then dropped it into the center of paper and wood. I positioned the fire shield and sat back. The day was gray, and I was gray too, needing a friend. Sometimes fire is the next best thing. The indistinct flames floated like cream in coffee before it's stirred. The room smelled greenly of pine bristles I'd tossed on top. As it crackled, flames rose and fell like waves before my eyes. I sat up near, as close as I would to a friend on a couch and closed my eyes. Behind my eyelids, in a yellow-orange glow, I saw as I used to. Just me by the fire, propped up on my elbows, while the windy breath of fall poured down from the high Rockies. The wind sounded like a distant call from my past.

* * *

"Four-Eyes! Hey, Four-Eyes!" The phrase ricocheted like a stone across the asphalt playground of my new elementary school in Pleasantville, New York—a middle-class suburb hoping to graduate into the pricey company of its Westchester neighbors Scarsdale or Tarrytown. "Come here!"

I looked around. Three kids in the corner were kicking a big red rubber ball around behind me.

"Four-Eyes! You, with the glasses!" Ronnie Kazorzak yelled at me. The Slavic planes of his cheeks resembled white cardboard pasted together in flat triangles. He was the school sports hero, a tall twelve to my skinny nine.

I looked around again, like he couldn't be talking about me. Then, reluctantly, I headed over to see what he wanted. My brain was slowly registering that name. Four-Eyes? Who has four eyes?

Kazorzak towered over me by a foot. He was buff, in the dawning era of physical fitness. His bristly black hair matched the long black coat he half-wore, half-dragged; he looked like a ghost from *The Addams Family*. Up to now, I'd never been on his radar. Mostly, I stayed in the school library. I'd just met Tom Sawyer, and he and Huck were doing cool things like exploring caves. There was a wildness there that would be in me too if I was their friend and cut my thumb and pressed it together with theirs in a blood oath. I hadn't ever paid attention to Kazorzak, whose face now hung over me like the prow of a ship.

"I'll see you after school, Four-Eyes." Then he turned and returned to his hangers-on.

I don't remember the day stretching on like it does in the movies. I could be wrong, but I don't think I thought about him much, except to wonder what he was talking about. Instead, I sat guessing who Becky Thatcher liked. In class, I was seated in the back row with the book splayed open in my lap, trying not to look down too often.

After school, I walked out the school doors and turned right down Bedford Way toward our little apartment under the stairs. Kazorak stood down the street waiting. My hands were tight around my *Adventures of Tom Sawyer*. The autumn clouds hadn't lifted, but my chill wasn't from the breeze.

"You going to read on your way home, Four Eyes?" (By now I'd figured out what he meant.)

"What do you want?" My voice quavered, though I tried not to let it.

"I want to do this," he said, punching me in the arm and snatching the glasses off my face. He kept punching my upper arm, not hard enough to bruise, but hard enough to hurt.

"Quit it," I said, but he didn't, until we reached my driveway and I'd grabbed back my glasses.

"What's wrong with you?" I asked angrily.

"What's wrong with me? What's wrong with you, and those goggle eyes you're wearing?"

From that day on, my walk home from school became a racecourse. After the bell, if I took off quickly, I outpaced Kazorzak halfway. Halfway, he got in half as many lumps. Sometimes, he just gave it up; scaring me was enough punishment for my thick lenses. He trafficked in fear. When he did show up, though, his snorting face was beet red and hard for no reason I could see.

We all have sudden realizations of life's unfairness. This was mine.

Yet another afternoon walk with Ronnie Kazorzak: His hair stood up from where he'd run sweaty palms over it, like a patch of weeds after a rain. Do little bullies grow up to be big bullies? I wondered.

"Go away, you oversized tick!" I yelled.

"That's it—now you've made me mad!" Thunk, thunk against my arm—which by now was both calloused and well upholstered; Mom never understood why I wore so many layers.

"Listen, Four-Eyes." But that day he had time for only one insult because we were drawing up to my driveway, where my mother had previously threatened to swat him with a broom.

"You know what your problem is?" His voice rattled like a pinball hitting the sides of the game. "Your problem is you read too much." He accented his words with three sharp jabs to my triceps. "It's messed up your eyes." He snorted in triumph. "My mother says that reading does that." Then he turned back to his house across from the school. (Ironically, my mother would be his reading teacher at the junior high he'd attend.)

That must have been the day when she finally called his mother and talked tough. Afterwards, Ronnie would eye me from across the playground: the hunter and the one who got away. Today, if Kazorzak is still around, I bet he wears glasses and doesn't remember any of this.

* * *

Just as I'd finished the house's easy-to-access food, my spouse returned and announced we were going shopping. "I'll drive there; you drive back," I said. She smiled and took the keys.

That drive was unnerving. Streets I've been down a thousand times looked eerie at night. Streetlights floated above like ghost lights in a swamp. At traffic lights, I saw their colored circles a hundred smaller ones. Streetlights floated above like ghost lights in a swamp. Inside the supermarket, I couldn't read the signs.

With glasses, I realized, I could be spinning my cart through the aisles, tossing items in. I kept my distance from the bulk-food bins; the bakery, on the other hand, was just fine for my No-Glasses Diet. On my right, a guy was standing and talking. To me? To someone else?

Out in the parking lot, I stopped cold. Whoah! There was no way to find the car. I just stood there. At home, N. unpacked the food and then repacked for a meditation retreat. In the morning, I was alone again, wondering if I'd make it to the end of the week.

In twilight's moody shadows, some sigh and think of other places they might be. I had no such desire; I was home. Soon, the world around me would sleep; the night needs no glasses. Hopes were parked safely for the day. Yet, despite the cozy fire, mine were restless and precarious, as I relived a younger self's challenges. I was feeling pulled into a current I couldn't steer, without a paddle. While others might be at home, trying on frames they hoped would look fashionable, I was waiting impatiently for the day to end.

4

Fashions in Glasses

Men don't seem to worry about their tortoise-shell badges, but with us women, well . . . There are still some who take a chance on seeing in order that they may feel fully confident that they are seen well.

—ACTRESS PEGGY WOOD, 1932

Fashion in glasses began the first time someone picked up two pairs and decided one looked better than the other. That decision reflected our need to define ourselves. We fashion ourselves daily as we choose clothes or one pair over another. In choosing frames, many select glasses that let us live large: a bolder us. Yet sometimes the jazzy frames we liked in the store or online aren't the best for clear sight. And so unfolds a schism separating fashion trends and vision care. This tension between stylishness and visual necessity is rooted in how we see best and how we'd best like to be seen, a need to fit in, versus a need to construct a unique identity.

When it comes to style vs. necessity, there's also the matter of where one buys them. Today, many people order glasses online, but though frames bought online may be cheaper and the selection wider, they don't come with expert fitting and adjustments from your friendly local optician. "You are either committed to optical excellence or only out for the best-looking cosmetics," writes columnist Barry Santini in *20/20*, the optical magazine. "So instead of thinking of optics as in continuous war with cosmetics, try approaching it with a touch of Zen."[1]

Zen is not a bad word to describe the distance sometimes needed from craving-induced fashion choices. It's grand to be recognizably distinct in your glasses, yet many modern glassers have a nagging anxiety that everyone but them is making better selections, with better results. Some like to be in with the in-crowd; others want to avoid fashion faux pas, akin to showing up in shorts to a formal lunch. They may hope that a better, nattier self awaits behind more up-to-date frames. (Probably in a trendy store they've never heard of.)

Extreme styles of glasses sometimes cross the line of functionality—it's remarkably hard to see behind pairs of glasses in the shape of piano keyboards. Advertising, meanwhile, comes down on the side of glasses as self-expression: Be different, be really you—but don't go too far; you can't go wrong in frames with designer labels.

* * *

It wasn't always this way. The first glassers weren't contemplating style; they had no more interest in fashionable frames than in fashionable dentures. Their aging eyes simply needed to see better in the days and nights before electric light. I'm not the best guide to eyewear fashions. Others have done better.[2] (I grew up clothed at factory-second stores and thrift shops; for me, like those earliest glassers, fashion never came up, only durability.)

The story of fashions in glasses might be said to begin with their mass production. Europe's elite wanted something fancier to stand out from the hoi polloi wearing mass-produced pairs. Here someone added a jewel; there, a carved ornamentation on a frame. At the other extreme of glasses fashion were plain, nonprescription lenses worn just for show, against which the author of *Pilgrim's Progress*, John Bunyan, sternly warned in 1686:

Spectacles are for Sight and not for Shew:
Necessity doth Spectacles commend;

Was't not for need, there is but very few
That would for wearing Spectacles contend[3]

The concept of spectacles for Shew and not for sight echoes this persistent quest for balance between looking good and seeing well. Eyeglasses serve many ends: as a handy tool, as a fashion statement, or as "instruments of modern bourgeois reasonableness," as an Italian critic suggested, "as though sight were only a mechanical action."[4] Of course, fancied-up frames can still hold excellent lenses. Yet some critics of eyeglass fashion have suspected that as glasses developed from a medical device into a color-coded accessory, they may have been "taken hostage by, and subjected to, the caprices of the fashion world."[5] Which raises the question: Can one ever be fully fashioned in eyewear?

More practical than scissors glasses, lenses held on a pair of short handles, were lorgnettes, glasses on a stick used mainly by women: two lenses embedded in a handle and often bejeweled as an accessory. Many well-to-do glassers of the eighteenth century might also carry prospect or spy glasses, with a sideways mirror so wearers looked ahead but saw alongside. (Such lenses were also embedded in fans; Marie Antoinette used one.) Theater-goers made use of small telescopes, opera glasses.

As new technology for attaching glasses to faces superseded previous ones, fashion followed along. By the end of the nineteenth century, the pince-nez—nose-held glasses—had become so fashionable that Conan Doyle included one in a Sherlock Holmes mystery. But wearers of these spring-mounted "fingerpinchers" had to exercise care. Fashion dictated how they were worn: with the ribbon behind one's ear and hanging down loose, they lent a distinguished air. When the wind blew, however, the ribbon could get in one's mouth, interfering with conversation or eating. ("Care must be used when smoking a cigar," a doctor pointed out.)[6] University students were also expected to remove their pince-nez in the presence of professors, denying visual clarity in classrooms.

Meanwhile, glasses prejudice persisted alongside innovations. This time, though, opposition to spectacles wasn't a result of the Church's take-what-eyes-you-have nonsense but against those showing off fancy pairs. Decorative frames were ridiculed mercilessly in drawings; wags sent up the avaricious in spectacles and operagoers ogling young ladies. The rich used eyeglasses the way they used the rest of their vestiture, a tendency that reached its apogee in a 1950s platinum frame decorated with diamonds called the Crown Jewels from American Optical.[7] Today, for those not needing vision correction, sunglasses can serve much the same purpose.

* * *

The earliest sunglasses were inspired not by the sun but by snow. Millenia ago, the Inuit and other indigenous groups made snowglasses (slit-goggles) out of whalebone ivory to dim reflections off ice and sea. Sunglasses' most important use was eye protection, not style nor inscrutability; these came later. In Chinese courts, judges wore them to conceal their expressions from those being investigated. Additional protective uses developed in travel and industry: Railroad passengers in open carriages avoiding cinders and early motorists dodging grit from dirt roads. Out of these two concepts—protection and concealment—modern sunglasses were born. Today, sunglasses are less about protection and more about looking sharp.

To devise sunglasses protective against UV rays, among the first scientists to study colored lenses seriously was English chemist William Crookes. In 1913, his experiments with different minerals and tints produced Crookes Lenses. The new sunglasses were not universally welcomed: Optical researcher William Kitchener insisted "green or colored glasses veil objects with gloomy obscurity and can never be recommended . . . all colored glasses increase the labor of the eyes and soon bring them into an irritability state."[8] (Tell that to the 70 percent of Americans and Brits citizens who own pairs.) As time wore on, the use of sunglasses for protection gave them an air of adventure; pilots in open-cockpit airplanes had them. Soon, fashion ads began to suggest one might wear them down here on earth. Ads for "sun glasses" appeared in magazines aimed at tourists and holidayers.

While today associated with various varieties of "cool"—ironic given that ordinarily, one wears them in the heat of the day—when sunglasses first became stylish, they too were derided. As in the days of John Bunyan, people faced criticism for wearing them only to make an impression, "for shew," because most sunglasses sold had only plano (noncorrective) lenses. Initially, critics associated them with loose morals and hedonism.[9] Even before the advent of mirrored lenses, sunglasses had become inherently voyeuristic, placing early adopters in a stance disengaged from the world: Wearers saw out, but the world couldn't see in, a trend some of the unglassed resented.

Until the 1930s, fashion designers didn't engage thoroughly with sunglasses. In that decade, sunglasses came to be newly trendy on film stars like Greta Garbo, who wore them in public to be unrecognized. That this effort was unsuccessful did not discourage other stars from trying to hide behind their shades, their dark lenses saying, in effect, "I deny you the right to see me offstage." Movie stars also used them to avoid blinding from early flash bulbs fired at close range by photographers eager to snap a picture. Ironically, this privacy-seeking effort was soon turned around by commoners, who hoped that by wearing sunglasses they too might be mistaken for celebrities.

By the postwar era, everyone, it seemed, suddenly had sunglasses. *Popular Science Monthly* wrote that sales in this period jumped from tens of thousands of pairs per annum to millions.[10] Smokey and amber-colored glasses were all the rage at beach outings, sometimes with playful shell and starfish decorations on frames of wood and bamboo. There were other reasons for the use of sunglasses, too, such as jazz musicians hiding eyes reddened from marijuana use. Impassive, barricaded from sight, cinematic heroes and heroines of the late 1940s wielded sunglasses as weapon, to make themselves inaccessible, or played with the erotic potential of hiding their charms from viewers.

By the 1950s, styles in sunglasses became increasingly ornate. Upswept and cat-eye shapes were accessorized with rhinestones or jewels, styles that continue to the present. Women in this era wore teardrop "aviators," cat-eyes, or Lolita heart-shaped sunglasses. In the 1970s, Yves St. Laurent, Givenchy, Pierre Cardin, and other fashion brands licensed their names to sunglass manufacturers. This mania for branded sunglasses (which, it must be said, apparently work no better than plain ones) still dominates the industry today.[11] Today, companies like Pangaia and Twelve even make sunglasses from captured carbon.

* * *

For untinted glasses with corrective lenses, the journey from necessity to fashionability has taken much longer. About a hundred forty years ago, in 1883, the *New York Times* reflected on the already persistent tension between optics and eyewear fashion—most glassers prioritized looks over clarity. "99 in every 100 who consult either oculist or optician are advised to wear spectacles," the newspaper wrote then. "As a rule, 4/5th of them refuse to accept the advice because pince-nez look more stylish."[12]

The first book on eyewear fashion, published in 1911, described glasses as "a necessary evil, something to be slightly embarrassed, slightly apologetic about wearing."[13] As a prominent optometrist concluded, "Women who were interested in looks didn't want glasses to begin with."[14]

To promote glasses in place of pince-nez, optometrists even suggested banning pince-nez like that worn by President Teddy Roosevelt. "The prescription or sale of such tools should be adjudged as malpractice and subject to heavy penalties."[15] In the continuing struggle between appearance and refraction, over time this diabolical choice—seeing clearly while avoiding the display of weak eyes—fueled an industry dedicated to persuading us that we look better in highly styled frames.

By the early twentieth century, lorgnettes, pince-nez, and monocles gave way to the glasses of today, frames with temples. The efforts by optometrists to promote healthy eyewear had found success; spectacles came out of the closet. Instead of being hidden, the *Kansas City Star* wrote, glasses had arrived at an age of glorifying an infirmity (though, the paper admitted, wearers were still being ridiculed in public). "The average human person instead of being ashamed that his eyes are on the blink, actually seems to be proud of it—wearing [glasses], he looks as wise as a tree full of owls and as conspicuous as a red-headed man at an Italian picnic."[16]

In the 1920s, after an actor, Harold Lloyd, started a glasses trend, youths of the "tortoise-shell-spectacle generation" displayed pairs like his without shame. Wearing glasses no longer seemed a sin, though it did invite styling. "Glasses and Appearance," a 1925 radio lecture, suggested that making glasses beautiful "may strike some of you as a little faddish, a bit extreme," but listeners should select frames with "attention to design, material, harmony of color, and, most importantly of all, becomingness."[17]

The burgeoning commercial success of eyewear led to a battle over who could sell it. Trade associations of optometrists attempted to block sales in stores. In 1928, these groups succeeded in limiting access by sponsoring a law in New York State requiring a licensed professional to be in attendance when dispensing glasses. It would be cynical to point out that as eyewear was medicalized, its price rose significantly.[18] This cost was sometimes unwittingly passed along to other consumers: "When I put these spectacles on," a lawyer told his optician, "it will cost five dollars more to talk to me."[19]

In 1930, English humorist P. G. Wodehouse advised novelists on how to write about glasses properly. "Spectacles may be worn by good uncles, clergymen, good lawyers, blackmailers, and moneylenders. Pince-nez are reserved for good college professors, bank presidents, and musicians; monocles for good dukes and all Englishmen. (Wodehouse should know: The year before, in *Summer Lightning*, he passed pince-nez to a squire, a monocle to a suitor, and "menacing spectacles" to an offensive job-seeker): "It's futile to argue that glasses are unromantic, they are not. I know because I wear them myself and I am a singularly romantic figure."[20]

* * *

The Second World War brought spectacles worn under a gas mask and tied around the ear. In the post-war years, fashionable eyewear took off as many women gave up factory work for entertaining at home.[21] Seeing a trend, in 1949 American Optical hired a designer to design pairs for ladies. The Harlequin frame appeared frequently, modeled after a masked character in Italian commedia dell'arte. Stylish sunglasses, untethered to the optical profession, surged in popularity after Bausch & Lomb introduced their Ray Ban style in 1936.

The 1950s offered classic styles, including the black, trapezoidal Wayfarers worn by actor James Dean in 1955's *Rebel Without a Cause* (and later by the stars of *The Blues Brothers*). Women could choose among frames with names like "Sweet Delight" and "Coquette." For men fewer choices existed, mostly browline frames that masked the eyebrows. On campuses or in big cities, one found heavy "intellectual" or "library" frames—wide, thick, and black, projecting masculinity: these appeared in films. Michael Caine, in *The Ipcress File* (1965), and Marcello Mastroianni, in *8 ½* (1963), made these dark glasses sexy.

In yet another effort to hype eyeglass fashion, spectacle beauty competitions, first attempted in the late 1930s, restarted. The winner of 1953's "Miss Specs Appeal"[22] commented, "Of course men make passes at girls who wear glasses. It simply depends on the frame."[23] *Vogue* ran a headline that urged, "BE GLAD YOU WEAR GLASSES." Or, as *Harper's Bazaar* declared, "Today glasses are out on the town." A turning point for fashion frames had arrived.

By the 1960s, wire rims appeared grandfatherly and browlines stuffy. Resisting a buttoned-down era, musicians like Thelonious Monk and rocker Buddy Holly adopted new, signature styles. Out popped op-art glasses frames in black-and-white geometric patterns, and hexagonal or triangular lenses in hues from yellow to lilac to turquoise. Women could now order custom frames covered with lizard skin or snakeskin to match a handbag. Anything went: glasses with windshield wipers, glasses in the shape of whiskey glasses, pairs with a built-in clock. (Unfortunately, only those facing the wearer could tell the time.) Buyers looked on with amazement but mostly didn't buy. "Eyeglasses may be a nuisance to plenty of us who need to use them," wrote *Woman's Wear Daily*, "but now there's no stigma attached. Quite the reverse. We make a feature of them." This transition from "invariably disfiguring" to "a feature" suggested fashionistas, at least, could be satisfied by their pairs.[24] In 1965, *Vogue* insisted glasses for men had to be recognized as fashion: "They're no longer glass crutches."[25]

The increasing use of makeup posed a unique obstacle for women. For farsighted glassers, applying makeup could be challenging because of their inability to see the mirror close up. For glasses wearers of all stripes, the kind of makeup applied behind them is important: volumizing rather than lengthening mascara; applying brighter, bolder eyeshadow; and using eyeliner to set off the eyes behind lenses.

Not everyone was impressed by the new styles. It took years for highly myopic John Lennon to admit to wearing glasses; he routinely pulled off his specs when performing. "Mustn't spoil the image," he told a devoted fan, even after 200 female fans petitioned him to wear them at a concert with a note backstage.[26] (And if a Beatle couldn't reveal himself as a glasser, who could?) Eventually, he gave in. His plain, wire-rimmed ones from the National Health Service, "tea shades," became central to his image. To Nina Mouskouri, one of Greece's best-known singers, glasses were essential: Competing in the Eurovision show in 1963, Mouskouri fought organizers for the right to wear hers. (According to Travis Elborough's excellent *Through the Looking Glasses*, she had actually been fired from a night club in Athens as "inelegant" for refusing to take her pair off.)[27]

In the 1970s, maxi fashion arrived with "disco frames" and oversized sunglasses like those worn by Jacqueline Onassis or Audrey Hepburn. With

Elvis Presley's glitzy, seventeen-carat-gold sunglass frames, and singer Elton John sporting glasses with ostrich feathers, eyeglass fashion took an over-the-top turn away from function. The size of these new fashions was made wearable by acetate and new, lighter plastics as polycarbonate and CR-39 lenses (made from a resin used in the Second World War bombers) replacing glass. Molded frames allowed precise adjustments by opticians, but the new, oversized frames made prescriptions more challenging to fill with the best optics. The new plastics also made soft contacts easier to wear, and prices again dropped; one pundit announced that with the popularity of contacts growing so fast, eyeglasses would soon disappear altogether. [28]

In reaction to fashion excess, the end of the 1970s brought ripped skinny jeans and punk styling to glasses. The Ramones and London punk band X-Ray Spex thrust their eccentric glasses style at audiences. The 1980s, in turn, went retro, returning to classic styles of the 1950s; rocker Elvis Costello wore Buddy Holly's Ray-Ban Wayfarers. After Tom Cruise wore them in *Top Gun* (1986), 360,000 pairs of Aviators sold in five months. At this point, novelty frames that once alarmed buyers in the 1960s seemed well, normal. Artists conceptualized glasses as art, designing pairs never meant to be worn, like scissor glasses made from actual scissors (not great for jogging) or frames in the shape of two whiskey glasses. (Drink to me only with thine eyes!)[29]

By the end of the 1980s, frame-making was a business worth billions of dollars annually.[30] "It is time to enjoy wearing glasses," read an ad for the Silhouette line. Glasses had come a long way, from being a source of shame for wearers to being a lucrative source of revenue for major fashion labels. "You can say a lot with eyewear without saying anything," wrote Patricia Marx in the *New Yorker* in 2010. Though the Food and Drug Administration still classifies glasses as medical devices, "in the world of fashion, your eyeglasses may have more personality than you do [but] Really, now, should a piece of plastic and a couple of breakable hinges cost more than the laptop I'm typing on?" Marx complained.[31]

The culprit for Marx's unhappiness (and that of many consumers) was branding. By the 1990s, most designer names on eyewear were largely licensed to or owned by the same company, Luxottica. As they aged, baby boomers showed a willingness to pay for those fancy frames, particularly when logos rode the outside. Slap a trademark on a pair of frames, and instead of paying extra to talk to the lawyer, you paid $200 extra to the optician. (The price of eyeglasses frames was originally based on the pricing model for jewelry—a markup of 300 percent—which might have made sense back in the 1800s, when jewelers made them of silver.)

* * *

The twenty-first century has brought spectacle connoisseurship. Every year, glasses couture slides along the catwalk in shiny new materials and colors. Redwood, bamboo, and frames made of titanium (flexible and nearly weightless) mean glasses can be super-light and polished to a futuristic look, like those in the *Matrix Reloaded* (2003). Haute-couture styles from brands like Armani or Oliver Peoples attracted inexpensive Chinese knockoffs, allowing wearers to try out snazzy frames. Perhaps consumers crave them because glasses are a relatively inexpensive fashion badge; fashion frames are a lot cheaper than gowns of the same brand. The mass production of acetate brought frame prices still lower, and individual craftsmen designed their own pairs, even as Warby Parker challenged the survival of small opticians by sending out batches of inexpensive frames on inspection.

Today in China, Europe, and the United States, conspicuous consumption of brand-name eyewear is nothing people are ashamed of. The prices of designer sunglasses jumped 30 percent in one year as the sunglass industry topped sales of 3 billion dollars annually.[32] Fashion frames meant anyone with plenty of disposable income or a purse stuffed with credit cards could join the fashion brigade. Still, the jousting between optical excellence and fashion preference continued. "Retailers concentrated on fashion and forgot the utility aspect," Marx added in the *New Yorker*.[33]

These days, however, if people prefer fashionable glasses, they don't admit it. A 2019 survey by the Vision Council asked wearers if they preferred the best style or the best vision; 73 percent said they chose the latter. Two-thirds claimed designer names were unimportant. Yet people keep buying these frames by the billions to stand out.[34]

* * *

My glasses stood out, all right. The pairs which in middle school had attracted bullies like ants at a picnic remained in my wardrobe. At the turn of the twenty-first century, I was still wearing those old browline frames, hoping in my economical way they'd someday return to fashion. (I'm saving them. You never know.)

Though my glass lenses could not break, they chipped. Playing basketball in high school, mine were knocked around like a bumper car. After one baseball practice, I was grounded for coming home with a pair that looked like they'd been hit with the bat rather than the ball. I can't blame my parents. Glasses were the most expensive thing I owned.

They once protected me from a line drive I couldn't quite see. It smacked my glasses so hard that it bent the frame. Fortunately, the lenses didn't break. While others were considering frame tints to match their hair, I was oblivious, underwhelmed by fashion. Later in life, my attitude softened. I began to wonder if nicer frames might help my looks. I had no income that was disposable. Some finally arrived from a fluke, century-old investment from my granddad. This coincided with yet another drop in my vision. In graduate school I finally paid for high-index (thin) lenses and less-than-cheapest frames.

I visited an optometrist in the Sunset district of San Francisco, near a campus where I was teaching. Of the thirty frames displayed, a smoky red pair caught my eye, ordered for a client who never picked them up. Red matched my color, as well as the local politics. After a lifetime of brown and black, I wondered if I could wear these. Would people laugh? I ignored the question and put down my card. I was going to signify.

In doing so, I was joining the consumers who've been collateral damage in the skirmishes over frame prices. Does that $25 frame from China fit any worse than the $1600 one advertised in the *New Yorker*? In the struggle between "spectacles for Sight and not for Shew," today "Shew" seems firmly ahead. "Every day, in almost any optical office around the country, someone is making decisions that prioritize an eyeglass's cosmetic appearance rather than good optics," writes optician Barry Santini.[35]

"Where is the line between individual identity and group identity, and which side takes precedence?" asked the fashion editor of the *New York Times*. "Do you want to fit in or stand out? Play the game or change the game? Have the courage of your own convictions?"[36] These days, to find the courage of a true fashion statement, a buyer would go beyond the choices at the local optician to, say, a pair with miniature tires surrounding the lenses. (Would they bounce if dropped?) "I was always anti-fashion," actor Woody Harrelson reflects. "Because it always seemed to me there were more important things to care about—like melting ice caps, the Amazon burning and the pollution of our water, air, and food."[37] Preoccupied with appearance, buyers may forget that eyeglasses exist for sight.

It's ironic how long seeing clearly and being fashionable have been at odds. In the end, fashions in eyewear are either a critical match to one's "lifestyle" or expensive padding for a device millions critically need. Behind whatever frames we choose remain our poor eyes, straining to connect our brain with the world outside. Yet to this day, when choosing effective glasses, we inevitably wonder how others view them, a concern born out of popular culture and its stereotypes.

Of course, when one's not wearing glasses and can barely see in the mirror, as I am right now, it matters not how they look. As the week without glasses continued, I would soon be violently reminded of the irrelevance of vanity to the larger conversation about the purpose of glasses.

Thursday

In my unconscious, glasses are working overtime. Again I dreamt about them—not about my pair but about one that's rectangular, thick, and black, the pair a judge wore on the lawyer show *Perry Mason*. After I put them on in my dream, I saw worse; though it was morning, a gray, metallic fog darkened everything. A woman waved to me indistinctly at the edge of the yard, like a zombie in a movie. Before I could say hello, she faded into the fog.

As I woke, I checked to see if my glasses had changed into the Judge's Special. No, there they were, still smug in their corner: "I knew you'd be back." I picked them up. In a flash, I saw the room's skylight in perfect focus.

I noticed a smudge on a lens and said, "Can't have that!" I washed them as I normally do and then instinctively started to slip them on before remembering. Cute trick, but I wasn't giving up—not yet, at least. For safekeeping, I moved those glowing red frames away from temptation.

Today I decided to say "yes" to driving. I needed proof I could do it. After all, another car should be big enough to spot, and roadrunners and squirrels would leap out of the way even if I didn't see them. I'd get in the car, turn the key, and back out, hoping not to run into anything or anyone.

* * *

I'm still reading about how people managed before glasses. I came across this thought from Andy Warhol: "Before eyeglasses were invented, it must have been weird because everyone was seeing in different ways. Now eyeglasses standardize everyone's vision to 20/20. Everyone becomes more alike."[1]

Actually, rates of myopia have skyrocketed in the last three centuries, despite the fact that nearsightedness may be largely a modern condition, since myopia is slowed by youthful activity outdoors, and the ancients did a lot of that. Perhaps we're noticing the problem more.

Still, those with severe myopia and astigmatism have long fared worse than their regular—or farsighted brethren. Glasses for nearsightedness appeared 175 years later than those for farsightedness and presbyopia (sight loss caused by aging); the development of astigmatic lenses with cylinder took longer still. Prior to the Gutenberg press, literacy was uncommon outside of church and government; so with only a small fraction of the population reading, nearsightedness mattered less. People also spent far more time outdoors, so fewer eyeballs elongated from lack of solar exposure. All this would change once printed volumes and broadsides began to circulate. But until the middle of the sixteenth century, literate myopes read heavy volumes the way I was now doing, bending inches from the table or rolling reading stones back and forth across the page.

The history of what happened to those with weak sight becomes haunting.

"During the dark ages, when everyone was blundering around with uncorrected vision, the myopes were rotten at finding their place in the world. Literally, they set off in the wrong path, never noticed when a wolf was waiting to pounce and were apt to lunge their sword at the wrong person. This put them at a distinct disadvantage," wrote a critic for *The Guardian*.[2]

Yet in ancient societies, people with astigmatism or minor myopia, got by. Unable to hunt, they contributed to social groups differently, particularly as their other senses rose and compensated; they relied on auditory learning and memory skills. Plus, digging or cooking didn't require eagle eyes. The farsighted served as scouts or hunters, watching for fires or enemies. Shorter life expectancy meant fewer experienced presbyopia or age-related visual problems like cataracts or glaucoma. "People ended up in jobs that suited their abilities; rather than finding technical innovations that made everyone equal," according to Neil Handley, optical historian.[3] Later, myopes were considered blessed with a talent for illustration; medieval illustrated manuscripts and Ireland's magnificent Book of Kells required artists who could write words not much bigger than a grain of rice. Finely wrought gold pendants and ivory scrimshaw likewise demanded short-sighted artisans.

Earlier, however, those with very weak eyes would have been in trouble. Unless they possessed connections or a particular talent, they'd have had to depend on kin for food, shelter, and survival. Their inability to hunt cost nomadic tribes traveling to find food and shelter. Put plainly, they were a liability. Those with severe myopia wouldn't have survived without staying productive. In the worst case, the short-sighted may have been left behind. Those unable to defend themselves might even, one historian suggested, have been encouraged to kill themselves so as not to burden their community.[4]

Hey, thanks a lot! Leave me behind when the crowd moves on to warmer pastures, just because my parents' genes left me myopic? What if somebody particularly disliked my cooking—would they have left me tied up while the horses were loading? I'm taking this too personally, I know: but how would *you* like to be abandoned after all the berries in a clearing were picked out?

* * *

Today it finally happened, and I have the bloodstains and scar to prove it. The predator was a humble coffee table, one my son sat at to glue paper together for school—just a simple affair of wood rising a foot off the ground. I'd been writing the rant above about the fate of the physically challenged in early times. The more I wrote, the tenser I became. Finally, I stood up angrily and stormed toward the kitchen when I slammed my leg against the sharp edge of the coffee table. I yelled and stepped back in disbelief as blood ran down my jeans and across the brick floor.

I tied a dishtowel around my leg and limped to the bathroom for antiseptic. The blood from a two-inch gash was filling my shoes. Though my hands were shaking, I staunched the cut, put on antibiotics, and wrapped gauze around the egg-shaped bump on my shin. Damn table! Damn eyes! Damn glasses! I took three aspirin and sat with my leg elevated and fumed and tried to read.

I had dreaded this happening, and not only for the pain and mess it had caused. This was what everybody had warned me against—and I hadn't wanted them to be right. I'd wanted to manage on my own without lenses, and now this.

After a while, I felt calmer. Dried blood, it turned out, came up easily from the brick floor. I wore baggy pants.

I decided not to tell anyone about what happened except Katherine, my new editorial assistant. She'd begun stopping by twice a week to keep an eye on me, transcribe letters, and do research. She was puzzled by what I was doing and why. Surely others had an easier time giving up glasses, she offered. I smiled vaguely. "Sometimes you move so far," the Swedish author Jan Myrdal writes, "that all the perspectives you once saw have been twisted out of proportion and lost all connection with the new reality surrounding you."[5]

I quit calling myself names and began asking hard questions. If I'd known as a child the cost to my eyes of reading into the night in my basement room, would I have kept turning the pages? Why had I persisted, this week, in an exercise that brought me so many troubles? But I'd acted in desperation. My declining sight had raised the possibility that a day could come when glasses might be of little use to me.

Enough, I said to myself. Going cold turkey had turned calamitous. This was no stubbed toe. I glared angrily at my glasses, headless in a corner, ostracized when I needed them. Maybe I should just give it up already before I slipped and gave myself a concussion. Upset after my injury, I'd tipped soup all over the stove, and the boiling liquid ran down already battered legs. On the stairs, I couldn't see the bottom step. Or rather I saw it, but not how far away it was. My world was unsafe. "To see what is in front of one's nose needs a constant struggle," George Orwell once wrote.[6] How right he was.

I had aligned myself with those who fast, or go through a "dry" January, or on silent yoga retreats. My fast had turned dispiriting, like Huxley's poem "Cicadas" about what he felt after losing his sight: "My own spirit's dark discouragement, deprived of inward as outward sight who seeking . . . a lamp to beckon through my tangled fate, found only darkness and, disconsolate, mourned the lost purposes and the vanished good."[7]

My goods had vanished too. I couldn't pry anything loose in the packed freezer or find the broom.

What a day. It could hardly have gone worse. Three more to go, assuming I stayed the course to the end of the week. An aching leg and painful memories made it challenging to sleep. Behind closed eyes, I saw children bullied and straining to make out the blackboard.

Fortunately, my eyes haven't failed me. Reading is still clear though I am tiring of holding the book up, and of the dismal messages books on glasses send.

5

Glasses Turn Literary

The greatest magnifying glasses in the world are a man's own eyes when they look upon his own person.

—ALEXANDER POPE, 1778

In "Spectacles," a story by Edgar Allan Poe, Napoleon Bonaparte, twenty-two, is a man about town with a problem. His eyes are "weak, to a very inconvenient degree," but he doesn't want anyone to know he needs glasses. "Being useful and good-looking, I naturally dislike them and have resolutely refused to employ them. I know nothing, indeed, which so disfigures the countenance of a young person." They reek, Bonaparte declares, of "sanctimoniousness and of age."[1] Daring to disregard glasses? He'd soon receive his comeuppance.

Glasses have long fascinated authors, perhaps as a holdover from the days when spectacles were either a miracle or a sign of the devil. When first eyewear began to appear, a whiff of sulphur or an aura of mystery hung over it; if glasses helped people see, what other powers might they possess? Besides sharpening vision, writers have imagined glasses revealing secrets, allowing 3D vision, performing magic, and avoiding mistakes like those of Poe's hero—in love at first sight, "riveted by a glance" but too vain to check matters out with his glasses.[2]

One night at the opera, Bonaparte notices a woman across the hall, "the most exquisite I had ever beheld." Surprisingly, he finds his impertinent stare is returned, and the next day, he pours out his soul to her in a love letter, including his secret: "the disagreeable and inconvenient, but hereto carefully concealed, weakness of my eyes."[3] He visits and, completely smitten, on the spot Bonaparte asks the woman to marry

The lady stares at Bonaparte in dismay. Then she smiles and accepts, with one puzzling requirement: She wishes her new fiancé, "to wear spectacles."

After a lightning courtship and marriage, Bonaparte at last puts on glasses, and finally he sees his new bride clearly: "Those wrinkles! and what had become of her teeth?" He throws the spectacles violently to the ground and confronts his bride, "speechless with terror and with rage. . . . 'Y-y-you villainess old hag!'" he foams.

"I mean, I not very old after all. Not a single day over 80," the woman stumbles in broken English.

From there, the story wraps up all too neatly. Implausibly, Bonaparte's love turns out to be his great-grandmother. And they weren't really married, she tells him—the ceremony was just a sham, to teach him a lesson. "I am done forever with *billets doux* [love letters]," he laments, "and I hope never to be met without SPECTACLES."[4] Bonaparte has discovered the cost of visual vanity and of hiding his ocular weakness, a well-worn tenet of glasses fiction.

* * *

In stories about glasses, protagonists shy from them for many reasons: they might be uncomfortable, ungainly, unflattering, or just don't represent well who people think they are. A better, less trammelled you lurks without lenses, goes the logic. Tuck them away lest anyone notice. Well, if hiding or resisting glasses has so persisted in tales of the past, will things look better in more recent work, once bias against them has ebbed?

No doubt part of the benefit glasses brought to literature is their visibility. Using the face for characterization has always been irresistible to authors. Describing lips, chins, mustaches, beards, and particularly the eyes serves writers well in revealing personalities and emotions. The inherent externality of glasses—the *New York Times* once called glasses more public than underwear, because we wear them outside—is more readily described than thoughts. As novelist Sinclair Lewis pointed out, "there is character in spectacles—the pretentious tortoise-shell, the meek pince-nez of the school teacher, the twisted silver-fashioned glasses of the old villager."[5] Or as humorist P. G. Wodehouse once counseled authors: "Have you ever considered the latent possibilities for dramatic situations of short sight?"[6]

In addition to their presence on the face, that most prominent of human features, glasses are a deeply personal article—so personal that their association with a particular wearer is definitive. In Arthur Conan Doyle's "The Adventure of the Golden Pince-nez" (1904), a detective protégé of Sherlock Holmes rushes in with news of the murder of the assistant to a Professor Corum. The sole clue? A pince-nez with a broken silk cord, snatched from the face of the murderer. That clue is sufficient for Holmes: "It would be difficult to name any article which afford a finer field for inference than a pair of glasses." From the outset the case hinges on the murderer's corrective lenses.

To prove this, he scribbles his immediate conclusion. "Wanted: A woman of good address, attired like a lady. She is remarkably thick-nosed, with eyes which are set close upon either side of it. She has a puckered forehead, a peering expression, and probably rounded shoulders." And because "her glasses are of a remarkable strength, she should be easy to find."[7] Then, to the customary amazement of his listeners, Holmes explains his deductions: the killer's gender, from the glasses' delicacy; her wealth from the golden frame; her nose's shape from the size of the pince-nez's clip; her age "from the physical characteristics of such vision, which were seen in the forehead, the eyelids, and the shoulders."[8]

* * *

In fiction, glasses often possess magical powers. They do far more than let people see: They pierce hypocrisy. They allow wearers to read people's thoughts, predict tragedy, and show the future. They can be contradictory: avoid them at one's peril, like Poe's protagonist Bonaparte, yet be mindful that wearing them can prove dangerous, even fatal. Before exhuming any bodies, however, we might review how writers used eyeglasses to make their other points, authors assorted. All the way back at the end of the fourteenth century—about a century after their invention—eyeglasses caught the attention of Geoffrey Chaucer, the poet of pilgrimage. In the Wife of Bath's tale, he wrote that poverty is the eyeglass through which one can verify his true friends:

Poverte a spectakel is, as thynkith me,
Thrugh which he may his verray frendes see.

Seventy-five years later, French poet François Villon willed that at his death, his glasses should go to the short-sighted, so that at cemeteries they'd know "if they were singing at the grave of a sinner or pious soul." (You'd need more than specs for that, surely, but it's a generous thought.)

Once spectacles became more common during the Renaissance, they appeared more regularly in literature. In sixteenth-century German folklore, the character Till Eulenspiegel was a glasses peddler and trickster. In 1555, the fabulist Rabelais promised his readers to "saddle my nose with spectacles" in order to do his job well.[9] Glasses were also a central concern of Samuel Pepys, the great seventeenth-century diarist who blamed his loss of sight on long nights of writing by candlelight. By thirty-five, he had trouble reading his pages. His attempted solutions were "Being bled, changing his brewer, using green glasses, using 'young glasses' as opposed to 'old spectacles,' wearing 'tube' spectacles, a vizard (type of visor) with lenses, and the use of a water globe [as Romans tried]." Despite all these attempts, Pepys ultimately quit his diary, unable to manage it any longer: "[I] undo my eyes every time I take pen in hand."[10]

Reading glasses appear frequently in Shakespeare: In *Henry IV, Part II,* the king thunders, "Wilt thou ... seek sorrow with thy spectacles?" In *King Lear,* it's politicians' turn to receive glasses-scorn:

> Get thee glass eyes
> And, like a scurvy politician, seem
> To see the things thou dost not.

Poets particularly imagined magical pairs: "[By] the benefit of certain spectacles, I know not of what making.... I saw all the channels in the bowels of the Earth," John Donne wrote in 1612.[11]

The first time someone got excited enough about spectacles to sing about them seems to be the Heidelberg Ballad (1670):

> If old age has made our sight weak
> So we cannot anymore see noble writings
> Then we take a light, clear lens,
> Which illuminates the writing
> And make it visible as we see through it
> (Well, it scans better in the original German.)

Over a century later, Jonathan Swift assigned glasses as shields to defend against the Lilliputians in *Gulliver's Travels*. Surrounded by the tiny men, Gulliver brushed off their arrows harmlessly in all but one place: his eyes. "I kept, among other little Necessities, a Pair of spectacles.... These I took out and fastened as strongly as I could upon my Nose; and thus armed went on boldly with my Work in spite of the Enemy's Arrows; many of which struck against the Glass of my Spectacles."[12] Later in *Candide*, Voltaire's Dr. Pangloss declared that noses were made for spectacles rather than the other way around. Flaubert characterized Emma Bovary as pretentious by attaching a gold handle to her quizzing glass.

In Goethe's *Wilhelm Meister's Apprentice*, the hero sees with glasses "more that I ought to see;" Goethe believed one should accept one's vision as is. Vehement on the subject, he couldn't "speak a sensible word to someone through a glass." They annoyed him so much that he sometimes turned away visitors if they wore lenses.

Other authors accepted eye correction as helpful. To Jane Austin in *Emma*, they represented a treasured device worth mending. When Emma's mother breaks her glasses, the rivet holding them together must be refastened quickly. "And by the by," Austen digressed, "everybody ought to have two pairs of spectacles. They should indeed."[13]

Dickens used spectacles as props on lawyer Keage in *Bleak House*, teacher Binber in *Dombey and Son*, and most prominently at the MUDFOG ASSOCIATION FOR THE ADVANCEMENT OF EVERYTHING:

> Mr. Tickle displayed his newly invented spectacles, which enabled the wearer to discern, in very bright colours, objects at a great distance and rendered him wholly blind to those immediately before him.... [He] could see, with the naked eye, most marvelous horrors in West India plantations; while they could discern nothing whatever in the interior of Manchester cotton mills.[14]

* * *

As acceptance of corrective lenses increased, authors took a different tack, warning what could happen if needed lenses went unused. Ignorance of one's surroundings from not wearing needed glasses meant one could be dangerously out of touch (as I have been). In the nineteenth century, the world was spinning ever faster as people dashed around in trains and automobiles. Hundreds of inventions poured in daily to patent offices, including the electric light, cylinders that recorded sound, and telephones that sent that sound across continents. To approach such a changing world without visual clarity was a forbidding prospect.

In Henry James's gripping 1896 story "Glasses," hiding from them has tragic results. The fate of Poe's Bonaparte was now to be visited on a twenty-year-old ingenue.[15]

Flora Saunt (from the French "*florissant*," meaning flowering or glowing) has a face so distractingly beautiful it stops passers-by and causes men to follow her into railway carriages. At the opera, glasses pivot in her direction. On holiday by the sea, she meets a portrait painter—the story's narrator whom she stuns with "the most agreeable eyes I had ever seen." Unfortunately, though, he decides that she is also "abjectly, divinely conceited."[16] A female Narcissus, she is in love with her reflection which hides a terrible secret: that Helen-of-Troy face conceals a degenerative eye disease. Corrective lenses would help, but Flora refuses to have her face "glazed in and cross-barred."[17]

In this and in other stories of the era, spectacles are called "a defect," "hideous strength" or, as James suggested, "monstrous gear" artificial aids to be worn only in private. After such tripe, who could blame Flora for rejecting glasses, no matter how badly needed?

Anyways, Flora won't have it. She coasts blurrily through the world, a Magoo in pearls. Finally, the game's up. She's caught in the act of wearing: "This exquisite creature, blushing, glaring, [was] exposed, with a pair of big black-rimmed eye-glasses defacing her. Her beauty was all there was of her," the painter laments, "wholly sacrificed to this huge apparatus of sight."[18] He is disgusted, "as if a great rare sapphire had split in my hand."[19]

Flora, in turn, is embittered. "Would you like to paint me now?" she taunts the painter. "My face is all I have! And such! A face! I knew from the first I could do anything with it."[20] After the lord courting Flora sees her in glasses, he deserts their published engagement. In frustration, she turns to glasses as the penitent returns to church. The painter loses track of Flora until one night, again at the opera, when he spies her looking more beautiful than ever. "That 'great vitreous badge' was no longer needed"—for Flora had gone completely blind. But she found a man to marry her, who says, "I would take her with leather blindness, like a shying mare." The man, as one might expect by now, is himself rather unattractive—but then again, Flora will never know.

The modern reader may be puzzled why people avoided what helped them see; the immediate cause—fear of revealing visual weakness and lessened attractiveness because of that—may today seem ludicrous and improbable.

Yet in the time of James and Poe, this fear was all too common. Glasses were Flora's punishment for her delusion of perfection, a tax on her vanity. Hatred of glasses was her tragic flaw. It's beauty and the beastly glasses all over again, according to one critic, pondering that continuing duel of sight vs. appearance. "Flora lives the tragic conclusion of her choice of form over function, nature over technology, beauty over ugly."[21] Yet, who could blame her for shunning a device from which people shy "as from a leper?"[22]

* * *

In other stories, the narrative power of glasses turns from avoiding them to the danger of putting on the wrong pair. In his fifties in 1879, English novelist Wilkie Collins needed glasses badly. Yet he hated his small, wired together ovals of glass. In vengeance, he invented a pair that lets its wearers see altogether too well, "The Devil's Spectacles."[23]

On an expedition to the Arctic north, an old sailor is lost without food or drink. In his failing moment, the Devil appears and transports him back home safely. He also gives the sailor a pair of magic spectacles: "They'll help you see more than you bargained for. Look through them at your fellow mortals, and you'll see the innermost thoughts of their hearts plain as I do."[24]

The sailor, wisely, is not sure about this gift—it sounds fishy. "Suppose I don't want to look? May I throw the spectacles away?"

"They'll come back to you,' says he."

"May I smash them up?"

"They'll put themselves together again."

"What am *I* to do with them?"

"Give them to another man."

After the old sailor's death, the glasses pass to the local squire, whose mother and fiancée complain about the pair's "hideous ugliness." He blames his oculist but puts them on anyway. Why wouldn't he want a pair that shows what people really think?

Being super-sighted, however, is like a sudden inheritance: gratefully received but often foolishly spent. In the harsh glare of sour truth, the glasses function like Cassandra's unheeded prophecies, always true, but always bad news.

The squire first tests the spectacles on his butler, discovering the family retainer takes kickbacks from merchants. He's fired. Next, an old friend asks to borrow money. Through his glasses, the squire learns he's been thought of as a cash cow; he refuses a loan and loses a valued friend. By now, he's realized these are "contaminating spectacles," which "failed to show the higher and nobler motives, instead revealing the little superficial irritabilities and distrusts."[25] Fortunately, the people he loves pass the test. In the end, he gives the rankling pair to a man secretly trying to court his fiancée.

Actually, who among us would welcome, or even be able to withstand, such scrutiny? As a species, we are too uncharitable. What the Devil's glasses showed the wearer was that brute truth can be a knowledgeable pain; for even when we see clearly, we sometimes don't want to. The problem was that the Devil doesn't give the sailor a choice. Beneath Collins's dramatic premise lies the idea that putting on spectacles transports one to a new world—and what we do there shows our character.

* * *

At the turn of the twentieth century, authors still struggled with the place of glasses in society. Though no one knows exactly where the term originated, the first published mention "four eyes" dates from this era in *The Iron Pirate* (1892), a novel by Sir Max Pemberton. The tale is a fantasy of a gas-driven, iron-clad pirate ship terrorizing Atlantic shipping, and "Four Eyes" is its mate, "a brawny, thick-set Irishman with gray-blue eyes "keen-looking and large."[26] What inspired Pemberton to call his pirate "Four-Eyes," no one knows. Oddly, the first character called "Four Eyes" didn't wear spectacles at all.

Occasionally, authors saw the good in spectacles. In 1911, Australian journalist and editor Arthur Adams wrote A *Touch of Fantasy, or Romance for Those Lucky Enough to Wear Glasses*. The novel's hero, Hugh Robjohn, a government clerk by day and author by night, discovers he needs glasses. He asks the usual questions: "I must wear spectacles? My eyes will be all right after?" His personality and worldview are suddenly transformed by bifocals from Jena, Germany, where the renowned optical company Zeiss was founded in 1846.

Robjohn considers his optician in Sydney a magician, somebody who "gave new sight to lucky mortals."[27] His spectacles, though, have sides both good and bad. Their exactness shows him the abstract book on economics he's writing in a new light, revealing "The truth that his blurred vision had never before been able to discover. To think that all these years he had lived in blindness."[28]

Eventually, the spectacles' insightful magic wears off, and "the bloke with window-panes" returns to the doctor who prescribed them. Checking Hugh's pair, he finds them inappropriately rosy. The *new* glasses Hugh gets are the glasses of fact, showing him "the brilliant crudeness of unblinking reality."[29] In the end, Hugh decides he's willing to take life "as it was, without a blur, even though the blur was beautiful." "Yet," the book closes, "it would be a poor world, this of ours, if there was not for each of us, for a moment or a year, the chance of wearing the spectacles of illusion."[30]

Aldous Huxley was more indifferent toward lenses than Adams. In 1926, he wrote a short story about the embarrassment of wearing lenses, "The Monocle." His protagonist was an awkward fellow with a tight preacher's face and weak eyes, Gregory C.[31]

"Why *do* you wear a monocle?" a friend teases him at a dinner party.

"Well, if you really want to know," he answers stiffly, "for the simple reason that I happen to be shortsighted and astigmatic in the left and not in the right."

"Shortsighted and astigmatic? God forgive me—and I thought it was because you wanted to look like a duke on the musical comedy stage."[32] (Chalk up another glasses put-down!)

"His eye-glass," Huxley wrote, perhaps from experience, "had done nothing to increase his self-confidence. He was never at ease when he wore it." Most of the time his monocle dangled at the end of its string, dropping into soup or tea, marmalade and butter. Fashion fear had prompted him to make, "the occultist's diagnosis an excuse for trying to look smarter, more insolent, and impressible. In vain."[33]

For Huxley's character, eyeglasses got in the way of his sight. It could have been worse. In the next yarn, visual correction nearly costs someone their life. For what if wearing glasses made you an outcast hunted in the streets? Impossible, right? Yet, before Arthur Miller wrote *The Crucible* and married Marilyn Monroe, he wrote a strange little novel, *Focus*. Set in New York City during the Second World War, Miller metaphorically imagined antisemitism being triggered by glasses. On the book's cover, light rays splinter as they pass through a lens.

* * *

Larry Newman is an ordinary guy with an ordinary job and an ordinary life. He returns from work to an ordinary house where his mother listens to the radio as Catholic priests like Father Coughlin rail against Jewish conspiracies, an antisemitism her son shares.

His job is in a glass-walled front office, where he hires women as clerks. One day a young woman applies; but her voice is too loud, her accent too Brooklyn. Newman guesses she's Jewish. "The company doesn't hire . . . we prefer people who . . . I'm sorry," he says, shaking his head. Then the boss calls him into his office and hands him a newspaper. Newman can't make out the words.

"You can't read it, can you? Why in the world don't you get yourself a pair of glasses? Good god man! . . . You can't *see*, Newman."[34] Newman's new glasses have thick lenses. He's glad to see better. Given his strong prescription, the optometrist had offered contacts, but they're expensive. Why bother?

The next morning, he finds out why. In the mirror, his now farsighted lenses bulge, making his nose prominent. Oh, no, he thinks: It's like Kafka's

Metamorphosis where a man wakes up to discover that he's turned into a bug. In Newman's case "A Jew, in effect, had gotten into his bathroom."[35] Maybe no one will notice. No such luck. At work a corporate vice president happens to visit, and Newman's troubles begin. He's again called in to talk to the boss, who tells him he's being moved to a back office.

"Why? Haven't I done a good job? I've got my glasses."

"We don't feel you'll make a good impression on people who might come into the outer office for the first time."[36] It didn't matter that his Episcopalian family had come over from England in 1861. Glasses had morphed Newman. His neighbor in the pro-Nazi Christian Front confirms the transformation: "Well I'll tell you . . . since you got glasses, you got to admit you look a little Hebey." The result of all this is terrifying. First, somebody dumps garbage on Newman's tiny but neat lawn. Then anti-Semites attack him, tear his jacket, and throw him into the street. At the police station where he reports the crime, the clerk also assumes he's Jewish. Wearily, setting down a weight "he'd been carrying and carrying," he finally accepts the cross his glasses have brought."[37]

* * *

The year after *Focus*, glasses continue to define characters to readers in Raymond Chandler's *The Little Sister*—and not in a positive light.

Orfamay Quest arrives at Phillip Marlowe's office seemingly a Ms. Innocent—little-girlish voice, no lipstick or jewelry—who's hunting for her brother. Marlowe immediately notices Ms. Quest's "prissy-looking" rimless glasses—but he sees right through them to her larcenous, treacherous soul. "Get yourself a pair of those slinky glasses with colored rims," he advises. Or, "if you're going to wear those rimless glasses, you might try to live up to them."[38] The characterization of Orfamay Quest is a case study in how an author applies eyewear: In rimless frames, she conjures up an artless Kansan. In slinky ones, she's a cosmopolitan blackmailer, one who with melting eyes whispers, "Take my glasses off, Phillip," after, dabbing perfume behind her ears, parting her lips. Glasses are a protective gate she raises when needed.

Tellingly, by the novel's end, she's reverted to her old model—right back where she started, despite selling out her brother for a chunk of cash to a gangster who wants to kill him. She reaches up and touches the rimless glasses: "These feel wrong now. I liked the others, but they couldn't play well in Manhattan, Kansas."[39]

Attitudes towards glasses at midcentury improve only when they are necessary for survival. Not only are eyeglasses literarily duplicitous and perilous, in William Golding's *Lord of the Flies*, wearing them brings down a leading character.

Lord of the Flies tells the story of two dozen boys marooned on a deserted island after their plane crashed. To survive, they re-enact the development of society. The thick glasses of a little boy nicknamed Piggy play a leading role. Someone figures out that his lenses could start a fire for cooking and offer a way to signal ships; and so Piggy becomes Prometheus, the Greek god who gives fire to humanity. His spectacles transform him from the weakest member of the group to one of its most powerful. His lenses turn from a symbol of weakness to a device to save lives, for lenses have reverted from their long-perfected evolution to their original function: a burning lens.

Power does not reside with Piggy himself, he discovers; it passes with his glasses. As the boys devolve from rule-following to savagery, his pair is snatched off, and his complaint classic: "Giv'm back. I can hardly see," he howls. Just as Zeus chained Prometheus to a rock for stealing fire and giving it to humanity, so Piggy sits "expressionless behind the luminous wall of his myopia."[40] At the end of the novel, a boy accidentally starts a forest fire with the glasses. That alerts a ship, which rescues the survivors—but Piggy is not among them.

* * *

Perhaps the relentless stigmatization of glasses in literature is the reason at least forty books attempt to convince kids, in a sometimes-sanctimonious manner, that wearing glasses is not the end of the world. Many children's books follow the same pattern as those for adults, with glasses provoking unnatural visions of ghosts, faeries, fearsome portents, and the future, casting spells or opening portals to new worlds. (Famed writers in this category include Ann Beattie, in whose *Spectacles* special glasses show the protagonist her great-grandmother as a girl, and Astrid Lindgren's *I Don't Want to Go to Bed*, where glasses let a boy see through the floor beneath to mice curled up asleep.) There are glasses books that let kids take command by reading minds, granting wishes, even settling scores. Ghostly glasses cast spells, force the principal to be a kid, make people do whatever the wearer wants—and these are the good pairs. Otherwise, they bring chaos, revenge, and manipulation.

Just as in Poe or James, resisting spectacles is the main theme. Authors see their mission as encouraging kids to accept visual correction: "Don't feel bad about wearing glasses," they seem to say. Only ignorant kids make fun. Books of this ilk address kids whose first pair of glasses proves traumatic—an invisible scar rarely discussed. Teasing about glasses can be one of the hundred little cuts of childhood, leaving kids ashamed for wearing them, uncertain, and shy.

Two Strikes, Four Eyes is typical of the "just wear them anyway" genre: Toby the mouse loves to play baseball, though he can't see beyond the end of his whiskers. Not wanting to be the first on his team to wear glasses, he hides them. Without glasses, when the ball comes at him, "he leaped when he should've twisted and twisted when he should've leapt."

"He's the pits!" teammates complain.

"He's two left feet!"

But Toby can't take the idea of being called a "sissy" or "four eyes." So he leaves his glasses in his pocket. The big game arrives: Rats versus Fowls. The rodents are ahead 4–3, and the fowls are at bat, with one bird on base and two outs, when Toby misses a pop fly, and the manager sacks him.

"Well," he thinks, "as long as I'm off the team, I might as well watch the game." He puts on his glasses. But suddenly, Toby has a chance to bat. With glasses, he can see the pitch for the first time: THWACK. The crowd roars; girls swoon.

"Why didn't you ever wear your glasses before?" his teammates ask.[41] Moral: Mice who wear glasses do well with the lasses.

Boris the Hedgehog also dislikes his glasses. He doesn't know he needs them until a TV repairman checks his set and tells him it works fine. Receiving glasses, he remarks, "I had no idea there was so much to look at." But then he notices the mess in his room. Boris takes off his glasses. Everything is nice and fuzzy again like he's used to. He decides to wear glasses only when he picks up turnip sandwiches at the hedgehog bakery, so he can eye the pretty baker's assistant.[42] Moral: Hedgehogs without glasses can still make passes.

The sting of others' judgment is a potent fear for children, and despite all the happy endings, it's this fear that often rings truest in children's books about glasses. "I am going to be the class nerd," protagonist Alex thinks darkly in Marilyn Levinson's *The Fourth-Grade Four*. "The biggest jerk. The only boy in his fourth-grade class who had to wear dumb glasses."[43] Similarly, Wagner the mouse in Kate McMullan's *Pearl and Wagner: Four Eyes* says: "I hate my glasses. They pinch my nose. They poke the backs of my ears. They make me look like a guppy." Eventually Wagner, too, sees the light and wears his pair.[44]

In *Franky Four-Eyes*, the hero half-screams when given spectacles: "He was not looking forward to another day of 'Four Eyes' and 'bug face' and names of that nature."

"If he's the teacher's pet," a student snarls from the back of the classroom, "then he must be a seeing-eye dog. But I've never seen a dog with glasses!"[45]

Recently, accepting glasses has become a winning strategy. Take one of America's most famous cartoon characters: Charlie Brown and Peanuts. In *Linus gets Glasses (2016)*, when Charlie and his buddy Linus are walking home from school, Linus shouts "a snake!" (Turns out it's a stick.) Then he walks into a tree: "Ouch! Where did that mailbox come from?" Charlie tells him he'd better see an eye doctor. Linus takes his glasses home. Newly surveying his family, he cagily tells his older sister Lucy: "now that I have glasses, I can see . . . how smart and pretty my big sister is." It works. Instead of being angry about a stolen apple, Lucy admires his pair. Snoopy the dog wants to look spiffy too. The book ends as the dog snatches the glasses. Everybody is happy except the dog, who like me can't see straight.

With time some prejudice improves. The most famous children's books where glasses figure are the Harry Potter series. Harry's thin, fragile wire rims are held together with magic and tape because of all the times he's been punched on the nose. In Harry Potter's world, charms (*oculus reparo*) fix broken spectacles. Though in films, Harry's glasses are less prominent, in books, they're essential to professors like the wise Dumbledore with his wire-rimmed half-moons or the dubiously clairvoyant Sybil Trelawney, in *Harry Potter and The Prisoner of Azkaban*. There, Professor Trelawney's wide, farsighted lenses bulge and her enormous, gleaming eyes moved from face to nervous face.[46]

Harry's glasses characterize him as both intelligent (evidenced by his love of reading) and vulnerable (due to poor eyesight and those delicate frames). J. K. Rowling, the series author, insisted Harry's glasses were symbolic. The reason she gave Harry glasses was because she'd worn them as a child and wished for heroes and heroines in glasses—so she created one.[47]

Well, have contemporary attitudes to glasses changed? Somewhat. Sixty years after *Lord of the Flies*, cautionary tales about hiding from glasses persist. In Camille Bordas's 2018 story "The State of Nature," an ophthalmologist's home is burgled. The investigating officer looks at her glasses suspiciously, "as if an ophthalmologist were required to have perfect vision! I wear contacts when I work, because patients tend to feel the same way." At her office, a patient asks to avoid wearing glasses: "I don't want to depend on [glasses] anymore. They make you look weak, and I don't want to look weak. I want to be ready and have perfect vision when the world collapses."[48] (This comment echoes a famous episode of *Twilight Zone*, "Time Enough!" wherein Burgess Meredith's character longs for time to read. Surviving an apocalypse, the first time he reaches for a book, he breaks his glasses.)

The ophthalmologist hunts for her stolen property at a flea market. She sees her glasses-avoiding patient but steps away: "I was wearing my glasses and didn't want the secret of my bad eyesight revealed."[49] At the market, she subsequently learns that her patient had shied away from *her*, because he wasn't wearing his pair. All this sounds like Shakespearean farce, with characters dashing offstage to hide their glasses, including both ophthalmologist and patient.

The myopic heroine of Randa Abdel-Fatteh's *Ten Things I Hate About Me* (2009) masks her ethnicity and visual shortcomings behind blue-tinted contacts and a blonde wig. In Stephanie Laurens's *The Reason for Marriage* (2017), a homely girl hides behind a glasses, only to have a handsome man look beyond her appearance to her spirit. In Cynthia Williams's "Full Court Seduction" (2017), a straitlaced scientist hides from his past behind spectacles he packs away. These characters still hide from their glasses, just like Napoleon Bonaparte and Flora Saunt more than a century ago.

Why, in the 2020s, does glasses-shame persist? These days, nearly everyone wears vision aids if they live long enough. That thin layer between us and the world can be as light as a breath on a cheek, in contacts, or as weighty as the comically oversized pairs on celebrities like Elton John. Rowling's heroes in glasses fix their pairs with magic; can't our culture undergo a similarly positive shift?

"It takes a great deal of history to produce a little literature," Henry James wrote. Hopefully it won't take a great deal more literature to produce a more positive image of glasses and glassers. The closeting of glasses remains in books and films.

Voluntary for many, a necessity for some, the messages and images of glasses in books are likely less influential than those from films, which we'll take up next after seeing what new disaster happens to this bumbling, maladroit, ill-sighted author.

Sketch of medieval spectacles. © iStock / Getty Images Plus / Alhontess.

Roger Bacon Optical scientist. Courtesy of the author.

North American Native Inuit eyeglasses. Courtesy of the author.

Reading stone. Courtesy of the author.

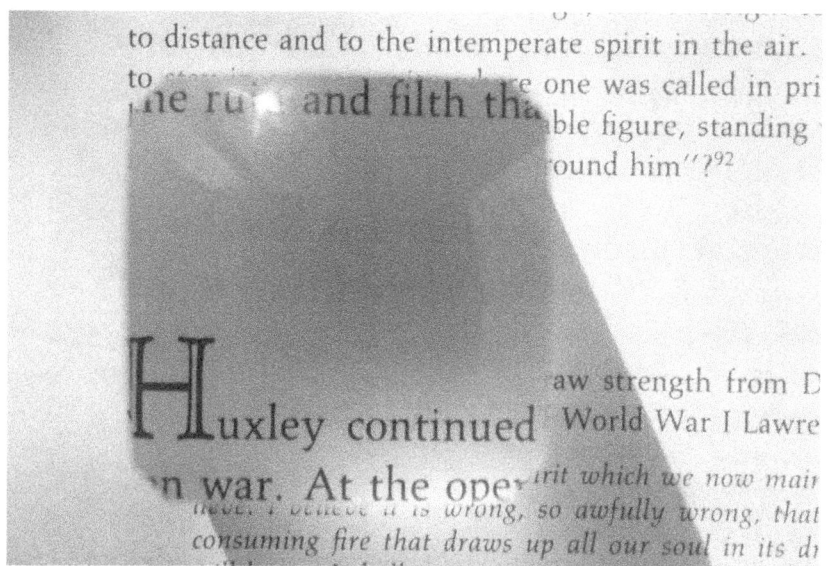

Reading stone on page from Huxley in Hollywood. Courtesy of the author.

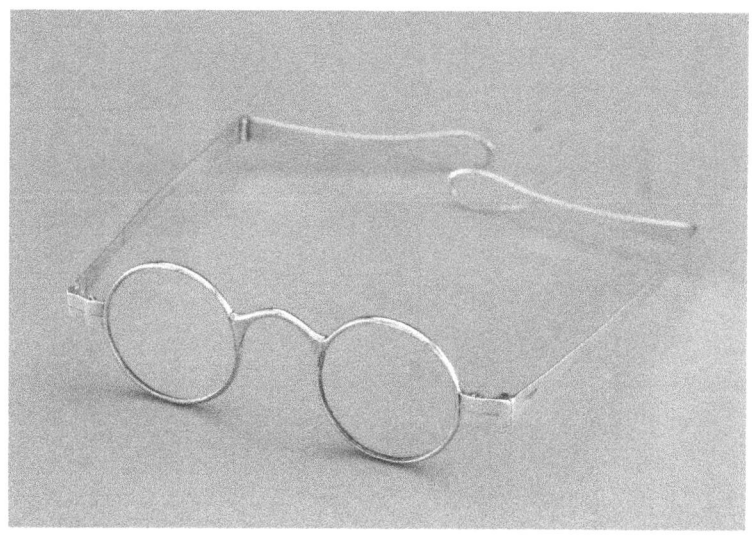

18th century glasses with folding side arms. Courtesy of the author.

Tools for grinding lenses. Courtesy of the author.

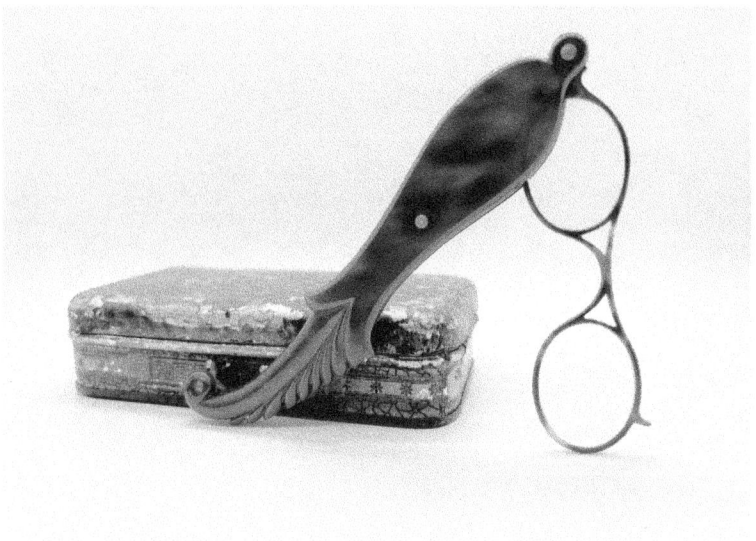

Lorgnette with folding handle. Courtesy of Fabulous Fanny.

Theodore Roosevelt in pince nez glasses; their case saved his life by stopping a bullet. Courtesy of the Library of Congress.

Actor Danny Kaye in monocle. Courtesy of the Library of Congress.

Pince-nez eyeglasses. Courtesy of Fabulous Fanny.

Quizzing glass. © iStock / Getty Images Plus / Alhontess.

Benjamin Franklin's eyeglasses. Courtesy of the Library of Congress.

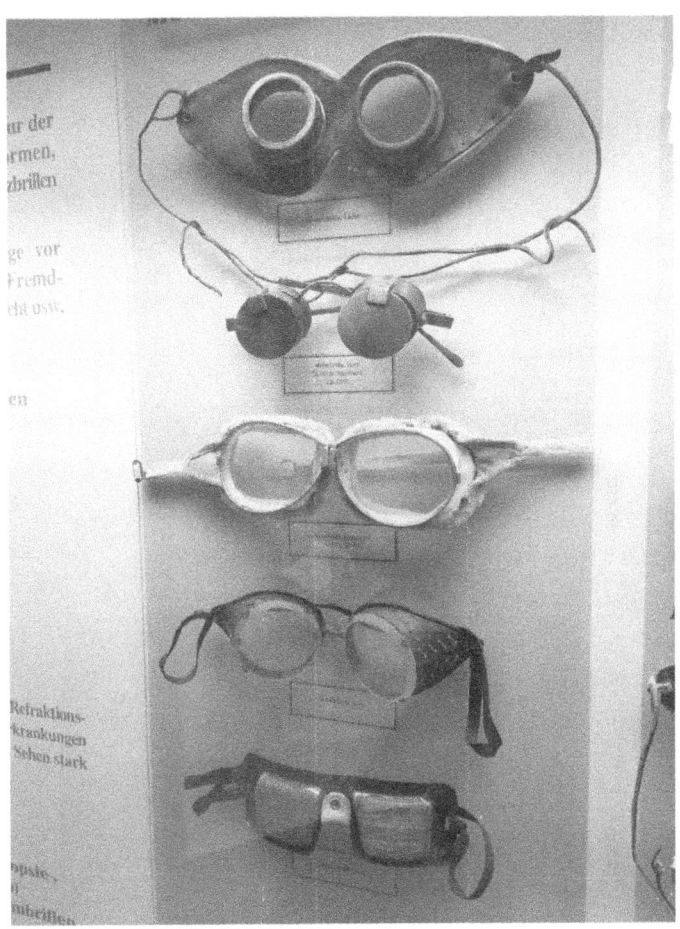

Early Railroad passenger glasses. Courtesy of the author.

Travelers' glassers. © *iStock / Getty Images Plus / JerryPDX.*

Aldous Huxley, c.1930. Courtesy of the Aldous Huxley Centre Zürich, Switzerland.

Aldous Huxley, c.1960, after giving up glasses. Courtesy of the Aldous Huxley Centre Zürich, Switzerland.

Aldous Huxley: Learning to see without glasses. Courtesy of the author.

Library frames. © iStock / Getty Images Plus / Marina Khromova.

Cateye glasses. © Ablestock.com / Getty Images Plus / Ablestock.com.

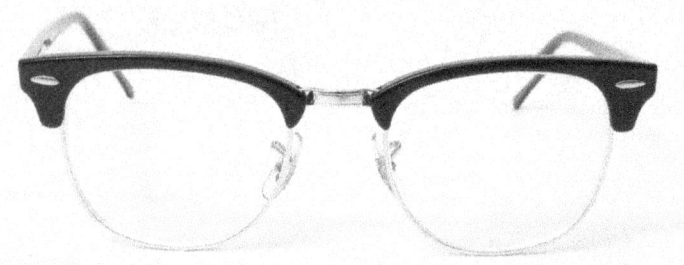

Browline glasses. © Moment / Getty Images Plus / Witthaya Prasongsin.

VR glasses are fun and growing popular. © iStock / Getty Images Plus / ArLawKa AungTun.

Author's glasses over the years. Courtesy of the author.

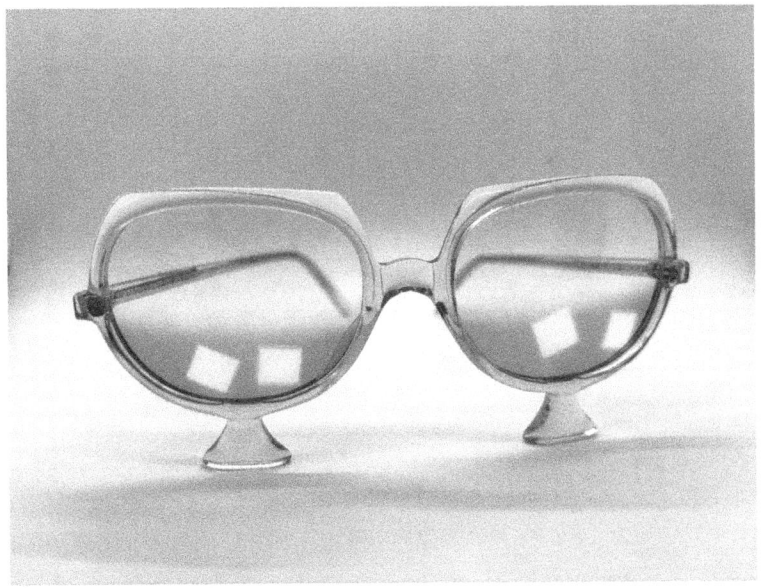

Whiskey glasses. Courtesy of Fabulous Fanny.

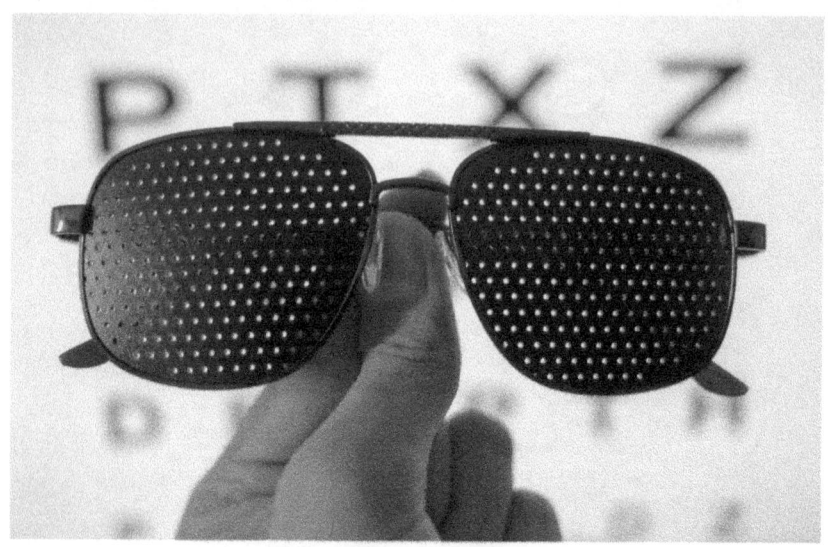

Novel (pinhole) spectacles, used by Huxley. © iStock / Getty Images Plus / Ployker.

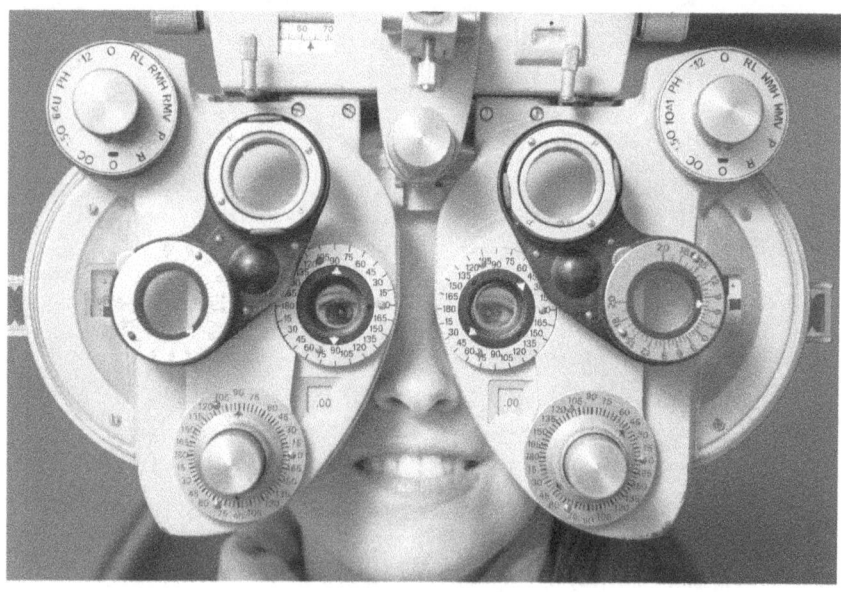

What the optometrist sees. © DesignPics / Getty Images Plus / Ben Welsh.

Friday

The egg on my leg is turning an ugly purple. It affects how I move: gingerly, half expecting another disaster. Tiptoeing around, I move the table and extra chairs to the edges of rooms. My old VW, with its manual shifting, would hurt too much to drive.

My current answer to the often-asked question, "What are you getting out of this?" is unprintable.

A few doomsayer friends all along expected to visit me in the hospital. A philosopher friend called my effort a "phenomenological inquiry." On my knees cleaning up spills, I call it a wet mess.

Last night I sat out back with an old friend, as darkness rose around us. The cicadas had started up, and the stars glinted like silver pins in the purple-black sky. Ordinarily, our time together has a peaceful, easy feel, but last night she was worked up.

"What do you think you're doing?" Claire asked pointedly. I shrugged, tired of the question. Her tone demanded an answer. I could have kept asserting I saw fine but differently; but that notion was aging quickly.

"I don't know. I just had to do this. It's different, wearing and not wearing."

"That's all, just a difference?" she asked. Actually, it's more than a difference. A part of me has departed—but that's hard to explain. Something dark lingered in her questions, the way that twilight brings anonymous confessions. Worry cascaded down her face.

"Let me tell you *my* story," she began. "As a child I was −9 diopters in one eye, −11 in another—worse than you, terribly near-sighted. I got glasses, but I wouldn't wear them. Up to that time I'd been the blonde princess everybody liked. I was popular. I put on my glasses, and people made fun of me. So I put away my glasses pretty quick. I faked it. I could guess what the teacher was writing on the board. I could guess what friends were holding up. At home, I'd bring out my glasses. In public, I kept them in my pocket. Nobody—only an intimate partner—has seen me in glasses.

"Taking off glasses to see up close and putting them on to see farther creates a visual duality. When I was forty, I grew tired of this dual life. I had the operation. I could see without glasses. But that habit of being private, then public: it kept on. I didn't talk about my eyes with guys I was dating.

"So, did glasses make me a more private person? Or was it the other way around: did I need to be private, and glasses were my way of separating myself? I'll never know."

Like in those nineteenth-century novels, not just Claire but the world seemed set on reminding me of the pitfalls of avoiding glasses. Last night sitting a foot from the TV, my leg elevated, I watched a commercial for contacts. The man was about to brush his teeth in the morning before he put his glasses on. He reached down for a tube of toothpaste. He couldn't see that it read "hemorrhoid cream." Ugh. Don't hide from glasses, the ad insisted; or else.

* * *

Learning how people managed before glasses had me imagining myself in that era: chipping stones into axes, or throwing pots. A millennium ago, I wouldn't have had a choice of occupation.

Until yesterday, I'd thought that if I stayed close to home and paid attention, this experiment would work out. I'm reconsidering this after pouring a glass of water 150 percent full; the surplus spread across the slippery floor. I made lunch but left a sixth of it on the counter. Then I nicked a finger cutting cheese. And instead of a dash of hot sauce in my soup, I'd accidentally tripled that, and the only dash was me running for water. After all that, I tried to mix a margarita. Its proportions were so far off, it was undrinkable. I can't live like this.

I could identify with what happened to the nearly blind author James Thurber: "'Do you raise them?' I said to a lady on the bus.

'Raise what?' she asked.

'Those chickens, like the one on your lap?' She pulled the emergency cord and brought the bus to a halt . . . what she had in her lap was a white handbag. I may be put away any day now." Another time, he had to give up wearing glasses after an operation. "I am getting crosser and snappier and sadder every minute straining and struggling to type and read and draw," he wrote. "At first I bumped into horses by day and houses by night, but now I only hit the smaller objects, such as hassocks and sewer lids that are slightly ajar."[1] I get it.

The other day I complained about losing control. Today, my problem is with distances. They're too great. Before glasses, I had to hover around new people and objects to see. Glasses changed that. They allowed me to step back from the world. Every culture has a notion of a comfortable personal space—how close you can approach someone if you don't intend to nuzzle them. Now, I'm back to interacting with everything from less than a foot away, which makes some activities awkward and others unmentionable.

How much easier this week would have been if I were farsighted. Instead of bringing things close, I'd have tromboned my arms. I would have been able to drive a car easily; I'd ask people to step back so I could see them. Unlike nearsightedness, farsightedness is a metaphor for prophecy in literature. My Scottish ancestors talked of "second sight"—the way the blind could foretell the future, as Tiresias did to Oedipus's father.

How are the farsighted people viewed differently by their peers? I was about to dive into the research on how people stereotyped glassers. I didn't expect it to be pretty. I never had a choice. Glasses were my antennae, my feelers reaching into the world. Without them, I grasped at the wind. Avoiding one's glasses resembles turning off a hearing aid, which some might call an anti-social act. It's giving up responsibility, being unaccountable. It's an imposition. Choosing to be indefinite. I hoped friends would forgive me.

At the close of this fifth night, I lay in bed rubbing my leg and listening to the coyotes bay. I turned out the light and pulled the cover tight. If I could injure myself in my living room, what would happen when driving or going out in a crowd? About the only thing I looked forward to was the prospect of watching films about glasses on a borrowed tablet, brought up close. I had no idea how I'd manage tomorrow, going to the Albuquerque Press Club Golden Anniversary gala.

6

Glasses Go Hollywood

Fortune is like glass—the brighter the glitter, the more easily broken.

—*PUBLILIUS SYRUS, C.BCE 24*

On sick days when I stayed home from school, my mother would leave tomato soup and a sandwich by the stove. Sometimes she'd turn on a movie. Watching films in the afternoon, I hoped to grow up like the classic stars with big shoulders, Robert Mitchum or Humphrey Bogart. These guys had everything—except glasses. No steamed-out vision for them on a rainy night when they swaggered into a bar to thrash the bad guys.

Staring up at the screen, I noticed few characters onscreen with glasses like mine, "Coke-bottle" lenses—the kind so heavy they seemed to tip the wearer forward like a flower outgrowing its stem. Hollywood's male leads were muscular, striding decisively in tailor-made clothes. They cracked wise; they had happy endings. There was plenty of food in their cupboard, and they towed along stylish companions. Why, I wondered, didn't they ever look like me?

In *Play It Again, Sam* (1972), a Bogart character offers dating lessons to Woody Allen, urging him to be more daring with women:

Allen: "But what if you're slapped?"
Bogart: "I've been slapped before."
Allen: "Yes, but your glasses don't fly across the floor."

Anyone exploring glasses stereotypes has to watch them in movies, where we see nerds, geeks, professors, mad scientists, Nazis bent on mayhem, and severe librarians aching to peel off their glasses. As with glasses' literary portrayals, films warn against hiding our pairs away. At least, in the darkness, no one notices what glassers have in front of their eyes.

Science fiction author Isaac Asimov captured the absurd way movies characterize bespectacled women:

> A superbly beautiful actress, whom we shall call Laura Lovely, is ugly, provided she is wearing glasses . . . A kindly female friend of Laura, who knows the facts of life, removes her glasses. It turns out, suddenly, that she can see perfectly well without them, and our hero falls passionately in love with the now-beautiful Laura and there is a perfectly glorious finale.
>
> Is there a person alive so obtuse as not to see that (a) the presence of glasses in no way ruined Laura's looks and that our hero must be completely aware of that, and (b) that if Laura were wearing glasses for any sensible reason, removing them would cause her to kiss the wrong male?[1]

That about nails it. Glasses in films have historically indicated a character's disability or inadequacy. Yet, this message can be contradictory: Both Nazis and Santa Claus wear wire-rims. Librarians in lenses are kind, but also naughty and sexy. In close-ups on the big screen, glasses are considered unsexy, even on Marilyn Monroe in a strapless evening gown. They make men either vulnerable, as in Steve Martin's *The Jerk* (1979), or creepy, like Pierce Brosnan as James Bond in *The World Is Not Enough* (2002), who slips on X-ray glasses to identify hidden weapons but can't help peeking at women's lingerie.

Understanding eyeglasses as a cultural touchstone in film requires researching how they're tagged. Dozens of websites track the presence of glasses in films through articles like "30 Bespectacled Characters on Film" or "We Need to Kill the 'Ugly Girl in Glasses' Trope."[2] It's surprising by how opinionated we are about stars' glasses. And watching films for weeks on end to tease out categories wasn't as much fun as I'd thought. Seeing women repeatedly treated like dogs until they shed their eyewear—the classic geek-to-chic makeover—grew old quickly. Below, I've prioritized those films where glasses figure prominently. (TV shows and video games, I leave for someone else to track.)

* * *

Eyeglasses do occasionally become the hero of films. They solve crimes, spot hidden weapons, and add color to the world. Take, for example, *They Live* (1988), where a drifter looking for work in a strange city hears a street preacher haranguing a crowd. The world is run by aliens masquerading as humans, the man insists, but nobody notices. "Awake!" he shouts. "We're living in a condition half-asleep, the world lulled into a trance. We're focused only on ourselves and entertainment."

The hero, "Nada" (Spanish for "nothing") stumbles across a box of odd sunglasses in an alley. He puts a pair on and, to his horror, discovers that the preacher was right. Seen through the special glasses, the surrounding aliens are an ugly bunch, with metallic heads and screw-bolts for eyes. When Nada turns on a television in his room, a hacker breaks in and repeats the preacher's message. It turns out aliens have walked unnoticed for decades. They installed a massive transmitter with a signal sent through televisions, even when off, that prevents people from seeing them clearly. Nada has accidentally stumbled on the world's biggest secret, and he couldn't have done it without glasses.

Nada marvels at the aliens using those super-sunglasses,. Dressed in human clothes, the aliens blend in while sucking up the world's wealth; our hero finds soup kitchens and factories closing while well-dressed screw-heads dawdle over lunch. He joins other sunglass-wearing folks, the Glasses Resistance, whose motto is:

"They Live. We Sleep."

After bumping into an alien dressed in mink, he can't help himself. "You look like your head fell in the cheese dip back in 1957, formaldehyde face," he sneers. The alien uses a wrist phone to call Alien Central: "I've got one that can see!" Fortunately, the Glasses Resistance finally blows up the jamming transmitter and aliens are revealed as TV anchors and politicians (some suspected this all along).[3]

"I began watching TV again," the film's director John Carpenter reflected. "I quickly saw that everything we see is designed to sell us something: the film's about "unrestrained capitalism."[4] In *They Live*, it takes glasses to see society clearly.

* * *

There's no character in film shown behind lenses as often as the Nerd and his cousin, the Geek. The first author to coin the word "nerd" was apparently Dr. Seuss (in 1950's *If I Ran the Zoo*), whose nerd is a whiskery, monkey-like figure.[5] The first movie character regularly shown in glasses was silent film actor Harold Lloyd's "The Boy." (Lloyd is the guy hanging from the hands of a giant clock in *Safety Last* [1923].)

Lloyd developed his glasses-wearing persona after a conversation with his producer, who insisted that without a disguise, Lloyd's face might be too handsome for comic roles. So, Lloyd agreed to wear glasses—albeit lensless ones, to avoid reflections under the lights.[6] To find his prop, Lloyd tried on two frames: the first pair too heavy, the second too large. Finally, in a little optical shop in Los Angeles, he hit upon the perfect pair of horn-rims, costing him seventy-five cents. They lasted a year and a half. When the frame broke, Lloyd, like Harry Potter, went on patching it with everything from paste to spirit gum.

To optometrists of the 1920s, Lloyd was a saint, "the man who popularized the use of glasses, especially horn-rims, to a population who resisted the use of spectacles."[7] Lloyd's soft, nerdish character normalized eyeglasses for the general public. College students adored him, buying thousands of pairs of round, horn-rimmed glasses like his.

How the nerd-in-glasses stereotype became negative is a mystery. Originally, the nerd was someone accessible and friendly: like Lloyd's character. "When I adopted the glasses," Lloyd told newscaster Harry Reasoner, "I became a human being, not a mannequin."[8] His character acknowledged a physical defect but moved on, offering glassers new pride. Ironically, Lloyd didn't need visual correction at all.[9]

So why in glasses do nerds (obsessives lacking social skills and focused on studying) get a bad rap? Or rather, why do eyeglasses get such a bad rap because nerds wear them?

The classic Nerd, 1950s style, is Terry "The Toad" in *American Graffiti* (1973), with his brow-line frames, pocket protector, frightful hair, and dirty and scratched lenses. They're sexually immature or wimpy. A decade later, their image improved. At the finale of *Revenge of the Nerds* (1984), they stand up for themselves: "All our lives we've been laughed at and made to feel inferior. Why? Because we're smart? Because we look different? . . . Nobody's going to be free until we stop Nerd persecution." (Glassers of the world, unite; you have nothing to lose but the chains on your pairs.)

Invariably a loser at the beginning of a film, the Nerd often shows potential. Though picked last for teams and popular only as a homework-checker, the Nerd can instantly turn into a hunk or hottie—if he stows the glasses, the way Clark Kent does while transforming into *Superman* (1951, 1978). "Let's face it, John Wayne, Clint Eastwood, Charles Bronson, Chuck Norris, etc. would not wear glasses in their movie roles," a blogger wrote on *Neatorama*.[10] Yet, in the end the Nerd often triumphs, winning a bigger salary (and better frames).

* * *

In glasses, the Nerd's alter-ego, the Geek, often appears as an absent-minded professor. Henry Fonda wears professorial specs in *The Male Animal* (1942), an innocent bystander caught up in a free-speech struggle at his university. After doing hard time in the library, historian Nicholas Cage in *National Treasure* (2004) uses his pair to reveal a vast treasure, which he turns in, because his glasses serve Truth and Light. In *The Nutty Professor* (1963), Jerry Lewis joins the faculty in half-glasses, but he's forgetful to the point of blowing up his laboratory. The bespectacled professor can also be melancholy, like Colin Firth in *A Single Man* (2009), confronting students bored at discussing that week's author, Aldous Huxley. The most hapless faculty member in glasses, though, must be Professor Wagstaff (the comedian Groucho Marx) in *Horse Feathers* (1932). At Huxley College, he wisecracks as he teaches geography: "The Lord alps those that Alps themselves."

In their tortoise-shells, the geeky profs appear distracted. In *Bringing Up Baby* (1932), Cary Grant plays Professor David Huxley, a paleontologist who stares through narrow brown ovals at a brontosaurus skeleton he's assembling for a museum. Katherine Hepburn decides to marry him with only one reservation: his specs. In a turn of the (optical) screw, the man is told, "You really are handsome without them!" Millions of viewers got the message.

In *The Jerk* (1979), another geek, Steve Martin, works as a gas station attendant. He meets a fussy little businessman whose glasses keep falling off. Martin fixes them by soldering a handle onto the frames, an "Opti-Grab." Years pass. The invention's a success, and the man tracks Martin down, handing him a check for "250 big ones." Excited, Martin runs to the bank, thinking his patron means $250—as a jerk he's strictly low-rent. But then he's sued. Comedian Carl Reiner appears in court cross-eyed, insisting the Opti-Grab is responsible. The camera pans to the similarly cross-eyed judge. Martin loses his fancy house and girlfriend and ends up living on the street. If only he had visited an optometrist for glasses to help him see into the future.

* * *

Optometrists or ophthalmologists occasionally show up as leads in films.[11] One of the most detailed treatments is found in *Four Eyes and Six Guns* (1993), whose story indulges fantasies of the Old West where one finds an optometrist who knows how to shoot. Villains cower at his sharp-sighted sharp-shooting.

Ernest Albright (Judge Reinhold) has always dreamt of one day living in the West. He saves up and finally rides a train to Tombstone, Arizona. But this is the Old West, so of course train robbers pop out of nowhere and steal his leather case of test lenses, which they pour out on the ground and stomp on. Then, Ernest arrives in town only to discover that the "optical store" he bought, sight unseen, is a dusty shack. Like the glasses peddlers of yore, he's forced to wander the countryside on foot selling pairs. Finally, a break: he discovers that the town's marshal, Wyatt Earp, is so nearsighted he can't catch outlaws but still refuses to wear "sissy glasses." Ernest takes over as marshal and hunts down the bad guys, wearing his golden wire-rims. After his success, the town's mayor promises Ernest that every man, woman, and child in town will have an annual exam at his shop.

When *Four Eyes and Six Guns* premiered, the *Los Angeles Times* called it the best Western of the year. Maybe so. This might be the most favorable portrayal of opticians since *The Spectacle Maker* (1934), a short about a lens grinder in the Middle Ages who makes two kinds of lenses. The first makes everyone look good and beautiful. The second shows people truthfully, which is so dangerous that the lensmaker is accused of heresy. He's released only after the first kind of lens shows his hidden goodness.

Badness in glasses, however, is easy to spot: the cool octagonals on the villain of *For Your Eyes Only* (1981), the ominous wire-rims on assassins in *Mirage* (1965), or sunglasses in *Léon* (1994). What is it about wire-rims that oozes madness and criminality? To see glasses personified as evil, turn to film portrayals of Nazis and Neo-Nazis, for whom wire-rims are requisite.[12] If a movie turns scary, mad scientists crawl out from the woodwork in metal frames, as in *Dr. Terror's House of Horrors* (1965) or *Dr. Caligari* (1920).[13]

Some celluloid glassers go mad without notice, like the off-center Brad Pitt in *Fight Club* (1999). But the largest group of bespectacled crazies is thoroughly criminal, like the canny but debonair murderer in Hitchcock's *Strangers on a Train* (1951).[14] One of Hitchcock's best-known films, written by Raymond Chandler based on Patricia Highsmith's novel, the plot of *Strangers on a Train* revolves around glasses. Fast-talking Bruno wants his father dead in order to claim his inheritance. To avoid getting caught, he strikes up a conversation on a train with Guy, a tennis star he's been stalking. He boldly proposes they swap murders—Guy will murder his father, in exchange for Bruno getting rid of Guy's blowsy ex-wife, Miriam, so Guy can remarry. She's a party girl with eyebrows tweezed into little slashes—the sort who, confronted about borrowing a purse and not returning it, only smiles. Her thick lenses are bright circles around conscienceless eyes. Those glasses will be the only witness to her death.

In one of Hitchcock's most famous visual sequences, Bruno strangles Miriam at a carnival. During the struggle, her glasses fall to the ground, and her murder is reflected off them. (The director created this shot by placing a reflector on the floor with an oversized lens on one side and the actress on the other. She seems to float backward, a scene Hitchcock ingeniously double-printed.)[15] Miriam's glasses are the evidence Bruno shows Guy to persuade him to kill Bruno's father, but Guy refuses and, as the film ends, the camera zooms in on Bruno fixating on his next victim, a teenager wearing transparent frames (Hitch's daughter Patricia).

* * *

Pre-1970s, the range of roles for bespectacled women in film is narrow. Despite the occasional outlier—like magazine editor Miranda Priestly (Meryl Streep) in *The Devil Wears Prada* (2006), who gnaws at a stylish, two-tone pair of glasses before scolding her staff—female glassers onscreen tend to be meek and bookish. Pretty much any woman associated with books—book sellers, librarians—arrives in glasses, ready for that common cinematic transformation—rehabilitation by pushing their frames off to one side. (The problem with many ugly-duckling transformations is that the heroine wears glasses which are exaggeratedly ugly.)

Bookstore owner Dorothy Malone, in *The Big Sleep* (1946), flirts with Humphrey Bogart's Philip Marlowe. She cares about him; he cares about not much. But he has a flask of rye in his pocket, and soon the "Closed" sign hangs on the door. As they get to know each other, he points at her glasses and says: "Do you have to . . . ?" She turns away, takes them off, and shakes out her hair—a classic part of the ditch-the-glasses maneuver. "Well!" Marlowe leers, eyeing Dorothy anew.

Onscreen, librarians range from the wholesome—Donna Reed in *It's a Wonderful Life* (1946) and Goldie Hawn in *Foul Play* (1978)—to that persistent Jezebel, the Naughty Librarian.[16] Few depictions of gals in glasses are as spicy: There are even sexy librarian coloring books for adults. Young or spinster, mousy or flirtatious, they start out shushing the room like Georgia Backus in *Citizen Kane* (1941) or Rachel Weisz in *The Mummy* (1999); but once liberated from glasses they heat up fast as a brushfire.[17] When they drop that glasses chain, a second identity surfaces. (This happens with a vengeance in *Personals* (1990), wherein a librarian quiet by day becomes a slasher by night.) Occasionally, glassy librarians simply pop their cork, like the one in *Major League* (1989) who hollers, "I have a better body than Miss Fuel Injection of Detroit!"

No portrait of bespectacled librarians could overlook the sexiest of them all, Marilyn Monroe in *How to Marry a Millionaire* (1953). Monroe plays nearsighted Pola Debevoise, one of three young women trying to bag rich husbands in "the greatest plot against Mankind since Helen of Troy, Marie Antoinette, and Venus de Milo," as the film's trailer touted.[18] In her opening scene, Monroe gets off the elevator without her glasses and walks straight into a closet. "It's all right, put them on. No men here yet," fellow gold-digger Lauren Bacall hollers. Later, midway through a dinner date, Monroe joins the gals in the powder room and learns the man buying her supper is sketchy and wears an eyepatch.

"Honestly, Pola, why can't you keep those cheaters on long enough to see who you're with, anyway?" Bacall asks sarcastically. "No, I'm not gonna take a chance like that. You know what they say about girls who wear glasses." Monroe scrunches up her nose and squints.

On a plane, the man next to her changes his sunglasses for a heavy brown pair. Monroe pretends to read. The man stares at her.

"Don't you wear glasses?"

"Oh, no! Whatever gives you that idea?" says Monroe.

"You're reading upside-down. Is it astigmatism?"

"No, just blind as a bat," she admits.

"Me too."

"Really? Then why aren't you wearing glasses?" she asks.

"I *am* wearing glasses . . . I used to bump into fire plugs and shake hands with lampposts. All because I didn't want to be called 'Four Eyes.'"

"But it's different with girls . . . Men don't attend [sic] to girls who wear glasses."

When a woman known the world over for glamour shows up in glasses, it's a cinematic moment. If Marilyn Monroe could get away with it, who could call female glassers unattractive? Anyone watching Monroe's freedom-for-women-to-see moment may remember her sparkly black cat-eye frames. "It was Marilyn who first sexualized glasses because she got the man without taking her glasses off."[19] For bespectacled women, this was liberation. "Why don't you put [your glasses] on and find out?" the man asks. "If you're worried about me, I already think you're quite a strudel."

Monroe gingerly lifts her cat's eyeglasses out of her purse as if they're iron and slides them on.

"You don't think they make me look like an old maid?" she worries.

"I've never seen anybody in my life that reminded me less of an old maid!"

Many agreed. But decades later, even the value of a cinematic moment like this one would be called into question. "Are all women who wear glasses [in movies] just waiting for a dashing prince to rescue her from her spectacles-induced black hole of unpopularity?" asked a blogger in *Fandom*.[20] "So we shouldn't accept these horrible and harmful tropes in our pop culture."[21] If women in film eventually gain the freedom to be beautiful with or without glasses, they may still lack the freedom *not* to be beautiful—to wear frames as they need without regard to what men might think. This glasses-as-shield avoids what a feminist might call the male gaze. In the years predating feminism, though, Monroe's glasses bit was so popular producers brought it back in *Some Like It Hot* (1959). While flirting with Tony Curtis (thick black frames and an English accent), Monroe confesses her attraction to Guys with Glasses: "They're gentle and helpless and myopic from reading all those tiny little columns in *The Wall Street Journal*."

Actors have always valued a good pair of frames for the opportunity to turn them into a prop like the cigarette, which offered endless opportunities: pulling the cigs out, tapping them against a table, lighting them with a meaningful glance. On film, glasses can be pulled out of cases and purses, unfolded, straightened, tapped on a table, breathily cleaned, looked over with a grin or frown, gnawed, pulled and pushed off and, of course, lost. Meryl Streep's fiddling with her frames reaches fine art; half of her acting is "glasses business." She dramatically removes them, nibbles and fondles them, and snatches them off her face.[22]

* * *

No glasses-wearing character in film is more controversial than Mr. Magoo, patron fall-guy of spectacle-wearers. His Academy Award–winning career in cartoons spanned forty years and reached audiences worldwide. In ads, he appeared in oversized black glasses, which framed his face like a death notice. His problem was that he rarely wore them, instead walking around in a perpetual squint. In an olive overcoat, umbrella, and brown porkpie hat, Magoo was a walking disaster movie: power lines fell as he cut down a tree; buildings tumbled: manholes gaped; lampposts loomed. His was the dominant characterization of the short-sighted in 1950s popular culture. (In that era, a list of those similarly marginalized would be a long one, with minorities, the physically challenged, and gays heading the list.) Magoo cartoons and films delivered a moral to pre-teens of the 1950s and 1960s: glassers are dangerous. If you saw someone with thick lenses, better watch out.

Magoo—his name suggesting someone caught in goo—is short and stubby. Like most trickster characters, he takes it for all of us: "Oh Magoo! You've done it again," the voice of Jim Backus proclaims. And then the safe falls a little to the left and the bullet goes through his hat as he marches through life like one of those ancient gods of destruction. But since he's innocent—he just can't see—the world can't blame him. And Magoo never seemed to mind his fate, even when suffering multiple-personality disorder: Freshman Magoo, Rich Uncle Magoo, Misguided Magoo (in orbit), even Beatnik Magoo—with jive, beards, bongos, and poems Kerouac wouldn't have dug. There was, it seemed, just no end to comic uses for a half-sighted character.

One day, a producer at NBC got the bright idea of Magoo taking on classical stories like *Robinson Crusoe* and *The Three Musketeers*. 1957 brought *Don Quixote*'s turn. Oddly enough, purblind Aldous Huxley was hired to write the script.[23] "Huxley showed up bright and early the first morning, all smiles and eager to start, and in very short order we became painfully aware that he was on the verge of total blindness," wrote a journalist under the name Dun Roman. "He was bubbling over with enthusiasm about what fun we would have rewriting *Don Quixote* 'for little Mr. What's-his-name, McGrew? McGoogle?' Everyone working on the Magoo project agreed not to embarrass themselves and Huxley by telling him that Magoo was as ill-sighted as he was."[24]

Today, Mr. Magoo is so entrenched in popular culture that singing sensation Rihanna once paraded around New York City in oversized Magoo-style glasses.

And "Mr. Magoo" was the name Trump called his slighted attorney general Jeff Sessions—hardly a compliment. *TV Guide* rated Magoo twenty-ninth in its list of "Top 50 Greatest Cartoon Characters." Was there ever a character more laughed at for lacking sight?

Most everyone very nearsighted was called "Mr. Magoo". My thick lenses inspired the usual lame jokes: "Where's your cane?" "Hey Four Eyes!" Or a personal favorite: "You reading that book or smelling it?" I'm hardly the only one. "I am legally blind," wrote Rob Wishart, an editor in *The Los Angeles Times*, "and have been called 'Mr. Magoo' by taunting jerks with great frequency since childhood."[25]

There must be scientific surveys on just how and how much viewers incorporate cinematic images into their personalities. In some way, we must. Enough pictures of skinny waifs in bikinis, and a girl might starve herself. Enough bespectacled nerds in films, and a boy knows that in glasses, he's bumbling and unmanly. "I was bullied for my braces, my glasses," wrote a commenter on YouTube. "I'm 39 and I still have social anxiety, and it's hard for me to talk to people." [26]

Just when Hollywood producers and writers could have turned the page on glasses-shaming, they began a new chapter: a feature-length remake, *Mr. Magoo* (1997), starring Leslie Nielsen. Objection to Disney's decision to make the film was immediate, vehement, and public. "Now, millions of young viewers can laugh at some slob walking into walls and mistaking mailboxes and fireplugs for people—and then go yell 'Mr. Magoo! Mr. Magoo!' at classmates, neighbors, and strangers with poor eyesight," Rob Wishart concluded in *The Los Angeles Times*.[27] Yet, like the character himself, the film charged past a boycott from the National Foundation of the Blind, and into production. Unlike Mr. Magoo himself, though, Disney Productions soon discovered how badly they'd stumbled.

The film had drowned twice in development before Disney picked it up. (Sony passed it up in favor of a Godzilla movie, a fair trade.) The film's firestorm began with a letter in the *Tulsa World*. "The Disney people . . . hope that Americans will think it's funny to watch an ill-tempered and incompetent blind man stumble into things," a writer observed, comparing the character to Little Black Sambo.[28] Bringing back Magoo was as hateful as returning *Amos 'n' Andy* to the air for African Americans. Not everyone found Magoo as hilarious as the film's producers. "We do not mistake a bear for a person dressed up in a fur coat, as Magoo does," wrote the president of the National Federation of the Blind. "We do not mistake a fire hydrant for a small child, as Magoo does. And we do not mistake long-play records for dinner plates."[29]

Critical response to the movie was universally poor. Many agreed with bespectacled critic Roger Ebert, who awarded it ½ star of 4: "It soars above ordinary badness as the eagle outreaches the fly." On Rotten Tomatoes, a popular film-review website, someone posted, "audiences will feel like they've stepped on a rake." Not entirely blind to its effect, the film closed with a disclaimer: "All people with disabilities deserve a fair chance to live and work without being impeded by prejudice." But tell that to Kathi Wolfe, writing in the *Washington Post*: "Kids pick up myths from the characters. The visually impaired [are presented] without grace or competence; it is fun to laugh at blind people." Wolfe quotes the author of *Cinema of Isolation: A History of Physical Disability in The Movies*: "The movie industry has perpetuated . . . stereotypes so durable and perverse that they have become mainstream society's perceptions of blind people."[30] Viewers claimed the film may have scarred them for life and suggested that all its prints be destroyed.

After a few weeks, Disney pulled *Mr. Magoo* from theaters, losing $20 million. The film did win awards, though: "Worst Resurrection of a TV Show," and "Most Painfully Unfunny Comedy."

* * *

Why care about negative images of glasses? In 2005, investigators from Bristol, England interviewed thousands of children with glasses aged 7½ to 8½ and found that 35 percent endured everything from name-calling and body anxiety to physical assault.[31] Wearing glasses makes preadolescents one-third more likely to be bullied, according to *Investigative Ophthalmology Visual Science*.[32] The CDC states that this kind of bullying increases risks of depression, anxiety, sleep disorders, low self-esteem, and a hesitancy to go to school. In extreme cases, some consider ending their life.[33]

Anyone wondering about the seriousness of anti-glasses bullying might consider a family whose child committed suicide after the Magoo remake. In 1997, a bright-eyed African American woman was concerned about her stepson, Musa. Unbeknownst to her, the boy had faced taunts and beatings at school for wearing glasses; but at fourteen, he thought he should handle his own problems. Tragically, the teachers and staff at his school never told his mother what was happening: "The first we knew the full extent of Musa's agony was when we discovered his body."[34]

"These children are very fragile," she said. "I have no words to convey my anxiety when I think about what will happen when the children in our area see the movie about Mr. Magoo. Perhaps the name-calling and laughter and tricks will be only a little worse because of the movie, but how much worse do they have to be before one of our younger children decides to follow Musa's example?"

A lot worse. It would be comforting to think glasses prejudice belongs only to past generations. Yet, as recently as November 2021, in New Orleans, eighth-grader Tierra lived in constant torment at school. "It's her glasses," her mother insisted. "Muffin," as the thirteen-year-old was called, found a gun at home while her mother was out grocery shopping. Her mother returned to find her with a bullet in her head.[35]

In May 2024, Sammy, a fourth grader in Greenfield, Indiana, was watching his big brother's soccer match on a Saturday night. The phone kept ringing with threats from bullies. This had been going on for some time; his parents say they'd complained twenty times to school authorities, without results. Sammy loved his glasses; he'd picked out nice frames. But when he returned from school the day after wearing them for the first time, he said, "I'm never wearing those things again. Today was horrible."[36] "He was beat up on the school bus and the kids broke his glasses," his mother told the *New York Post*.

On that fateful Saturday, the phone rang again with a call from their neighborhood bully: "Monday I'm going to get you!" Monday morning, instead of Sammy getting up for school, his father found him laid out in his bedroom. His father has held on to the frames that his son wore. "I have his broken glasses sitting over there in a memorial shrine the kids made." [37]

It's one thing to trace glasses-shaming back to the Middle Ages, and another to view YouTube interviews with parents whose children were bullied to death for wearing glasses. I meet people who tell me, "That bullying thing was a long time ago; now, glasses are cool," but stuffing this behavior into the closet of the past doesn't make it go away. Hassling kids for glasses or intense bullying for disability cannot be dismissed as child's play from olden days.

* * *

Today, better images of glassers are far easier to come by. The Harry Potter movies, for example, sent kids to optometrist looking for glasses like his, according to optometrist Stephen Oppenheimer. "Fifty years ago, parents were saying, 'I don't want my kids to wear glasses' . . . . That's disappearing, more or less, from education and from seeing more and more people in glasses on television or in movies. Directors want to make a statement. They want a kid smart, so he's got glasses. Self-perception is influenced by what the kids around you, your friends, and family say. Parents and friends are now more accepting."[38] Far more female characters today wear lenses proudly. In *Predestination* (2014), when a schoolmate calls a girl "a four-eyed little bitch," the girl hits back with a solid punch.

Partly, this change in the ways lenses wearers are portrayed onscreen is due to the courageous advocacy of filmgoers like Lowri Moore. Growing up in Nottinghamshire, England, Moore always felt unattractive because of the glasses she'd worn since she was a baby. In 2019, at the age of only nine, Moore began a campaign for change, writing to a film producer.

"I've grown up watching Disney princesses and always admired them and thought they were beautiful. Unfortunately, none of the princesses wore glasses, and that made me feel like I wasn't beautiful enough."

"So I hope that you understand. And please may you make a Disney princess who has glasses. There's lots of little girls who wear glasses and I don't want them to feel like I did. Sadly, most of the characters who wear glasses are called geeks and nerds and I don't think that's fair. It would help people to know that they are beautiful no matter what."[39]

News of Moore's effort was reported as far away as New Delhi. Her request hit home with Jared Bush, the director of Disney's *Encanto* (2022). He decided that Mirabel, the films' heroine, should indeed have specs. One of Moore's admirers later wrote, "Every girl in glasses thanks you (even those of us who are slightly older!)." On Twitter, Colette Smith wrote, "Hard to believe in the 21st century that people still tease those who wear glasses."[40] Lowri later ended up writing a children's book, *Princess Rose and the Golden Glasses*, about a glasser who thinks she's not pretty enough. Now, Moore lobbies to have some emojis wear glasses.

* * *

Lowri Moore asked for her glasses not to be marginalized, and no doubt as girls and women (and men too) stop hiding their eyeglasses, a new, less judgmental world opens. Yet, has Lowri Moore's princess in glasses truly defeated the ghost of Mr. Magoo?[41]

In a time when 16 million Americans wear glasses with no-correction clear lenses, focusing on older portrayals might not seem to make sense. Eventually, glassers will no longer be defined by what they wear to see. Good roles exist for glasses and contacts in films; they're not always being cast. Glasses could be presented as protective, the way they were when glasses deflected a bullet in Eisenstein's *Potemkin* (1925) and saved a Russian woman's life. Scriptwriters could scrub dark associations with criminals and mad scientists. Culture shifts more slowly than a movie script, however, and stereotypes persist long after they have molted into something more positive. All this leads to reconsidering how glasses-shaming in films, books, and other cultural products has deflated self-esteem in children. One way to analyze this is to understand the reactions to glasses which researchers have measured over time. The studies I've been reading about how people evaluate glassers, often from a moment's glance, is quite disturbing. Today's destination is my public debut, unspectacled. I don't know how I'll fare in a room full of people I know but can't identify.

Saturday

Yours truly finally realized how far he'd isolated himself from society simply by being visually unconnected. I thought about what I'd missed, "the direct and intuitive way you grasp the personality of another through gestures, the way the eyes move, the pattern of movement," as Myrdal wrote in the book I'd just finished.

On this, the next-to-last day, I listed what I had gotten used to, and what I hadn't. Losing slippers, watch, or whatever I put down aggravated me. The challenges of communicating and moving around riled me, as did friends demurring from stopping by, unsure what they'd find. After the list became a whine, I stopped writing it. Then yesterday, a contract for a consulting job came in the mail. Signing and scanning it was no problem. But the letter insisted I had to submit the original at their offices, in person and urgently. Here was an excuse to try driving.

* * *

I walked to the kitchen and rummaged for the keys. I strapped myself into my car and turned the key, a familiar sound; yet nothing was like it was before. Was that ring of logs protecting the cottonwood still there? Not sure. Swipe it and I'd break an axle.

I put the car in gear and inched forward. The tree wasn't clear until a foot away. (Crunch.) Backing up, I pulled around the tree. Gravel flew. I kept to the center of the road; no one seemed to be coming at me. Once I got going, driving was fun, like one of those carnival rides where you don't know which way you'll be thrown next. I wanted to drive all day. But, moving forward turned out to be easier than stopping. I couldn't gauge the right distance for braking and swerved. The long lane wobbled in front of me. I heard traffic ahead.

I braked, and the car slid on the gravel into the roadway. I stopped, backed up, and drove back home. The papers were dispatched back by courier. "Curses," I could almost hear my glasses mutter. "Foiled again."

* * *

That night my assistant Katherine drove me to the Press Club for my out-of-focus debut. For me, the evening was a masked ball—people familiar but to me unrecognizable. We arrived at dusk. Perched on a hill overlooking downtown Albuquerque, the building is a century-old, three-story log cabin modeled on the famous El Tovar Lodge at the Grand Canyon. During the First World War, back when Albuquerque was little more than a train depot and trading post, El Tovar's architect built himself this large cabin. Back in newspapers' glory days, reporters and editors leaned on the polished wooden bar after work. Today, the horse-drawn wool wagons are long gone, the urban Indian population is growing, and Amtrak still stops here.

A dusty wind blew from the mesa outside town, and the sun delivered a blazing western sunset. I walked up the steps with Katherine holding my arm protectively. After she pushed open the front door, I suddenly realized I'd never been in a crowd without glasses. Across the room, faces moved but offered no clue as to what they were saying.

Instinctively, I held my breath, as if inhaling would bring the out-of-focus world inside. I sat down on an armrest that rocked the chair. In the dimly lit room, I had arrived at an emotional cliff. I felt like a nervous breakdown was getting ready to happen. I wanted out of there. Just then, from across the room someone waved at me. (At least I thought they were waving at me.) I smiled weakly and waved back. Here I was, out of control again. The bartender called out, "Who's next?" (Like I'm supposed to know?) People climbed past me from the billiard room to the wooden porch overhanging the city.

Food was laid out on a long table. I kept dipping my knife into the mayo jar for a sandwich; it kept coming up empty. I felt incompetent and wizened; taking off my glasses seemed to have accelerated my aging.

After a few drinks, though, I viewed my personal, portable blur more gently. I minded it less. I fantasized about Sightless Vacations, where people sharing just one trait—visual weakness—got together for a vacation from focus, a Club-Med-type place with signs in very large type. Partygoers wouldn't bother with makeup or grooming; nobody could see them anyway. Instead of a hat-check, there'd be a check-your-glasses desk.

Someone came up to me.

"Steve! Good to see you."

"Eh—er, I'm not Steve." Did I become a Steve when I took off my glasses? Like Jekyll and Hyde?

"Oh! You look just like Steve!" the woman said to me. Close up, her face was flushed by drink.

"What's your name?" I asked. She told me; but of course I'd never recognize her later.

I moved in the direction of a table, faking a confident step, and promptly put my elbow in an ashtray. We fake a lot, I mused this week. As a guest, we might fake taste for an uncomfortable meal, or our opinion of a friend's favorite film. We may fake income for taxes. So much faking goes on—online, offline—that a search for a private truth becomes a moral journey.

I faked my way out of the door of the Press Club, faked my way down the steps and driveway and into the car. Safely inside, I found mayonnaise on my lap.

* * *

After washing up, I decided not to return to the club for a few weeks. Other than injuring myself, that panic at the club was the worst thing that happened this week. I got through it, though.

It was finally lifting, that sadness that had descended these last few days like a thick San Francisco fog. In my eagerness to try out this idea, I'd overlooked what I needed to remember—how much I needed to connect. Being unrecognizable without glasses proved uncomfortable; so why cry over spilled mayo? The point had been to function as best I could.

Still, like anyone, I couldn't ignore how I'd appeared to others as I stumbled about. I calmed myself with hopes that learning how people react to glasses—separating fact from casual impressions—would help me better understand how I and my fellow glassers were viewed.

7

What People Think of Those Wearing Glasses

[With their glasses], I serve strangers as an object for strict examination; as if with their armed glances they would penetrate my most secret thoughts and spy out every wrinkle of my old face.

—JOHANN GOETHE, c. 1830

In 1930, just as nations reoriented themselves to the jobless Depression and fascism rose in Europe, a tall, thin medical school professor in Indianapolis, Indiana, wrote "If I Were Mussolini." It told how he'd choose who should be allowed to live with physical defects.[1] An enthusiastic eugenicist, author of the book *Racial Hygiene*, his work echoed efforts then underway by Italian fascists and Nazis to create a master race. Dr. Thurman Rice suggested the elimination of weak-eyed folks like me.

Rice appears in a cameo in T. C. Boyle's book about Dr. Alfred Kinsey, *The Inner Circle*. There, his hygiene course is a running joke, "an exercise in innuendo, misinformation, and Victorian nice-nellyism."[2] Rice believed visual defects molded personalities. Readers in glasses or contacts should consider what he expected life had in store for them.

By any standard, Dr. Rice was Indiana's medical heavyweight. Not only a senior professor at Indiana's medical school and acting health commissioner for the state, he edited the *State Board of Health Bulletin*. In 1930, as he was writing "Physical Defects and Character," a dark characterization of children with near and farsightedness, he was promoting sterilization of visual "defectives."

"My friends ask me how I would decide who should be sterilized," he wrote. "I shouldn't think it would be hard here in Indiana." Rice's generalizations are essentialist. To him, a farsighted personality is active, even aggressive, "a jolly good fellow" who scoffs at wearing specs: "I don't want those darned old glasses," Rice imagines him saying. "They look sissy, and they're in the way."[3] A farsighted girl, according to Rice, is likely to be a tomboy, more comfortable in the park than in the classroom. Teachers call the farsighted boy names: lazy, a mischief-maker, dumb, inattentive. As he ages, he's likely to get sullen and resentful, "old and poor and unkempt. He presents a pathetic picture."

To characterize the nearsighted and the astigmatic, Rice takes readers to the basketball court, where the hoop's a blur; and unless those bookworms wear their glasses, there's no point in their going to the theater or to movies. Playing golf, other players stood by "in disgust and told him the particular kind of worm that he was," the sort who, deciding they need more sunlight, buys a sunlamp. Dr. Rice's "myopic personality" has a dark side: the more myopic, the less people fit in. "She gets the reputation of being a know-it-all, popular only on the days before a final examination," he wrote in the popular health journal *Hygeia*.[4] "Ballgames, hunting, and fishing are a waste of time," he imagines myopic kids thinking: "What's it matter I can't do these things?" A person with astigmatism shares many of the myope's supposed characteristics, "a disagreeable personage." They may tilt their head slightly to see better. (Those with astigmatism experience one part of an image as sharp while another may be out of focus.)

For Rice, anyone highly myopic or astigmatic is someone the world could do without. "We [all] wish they were more likeable and adaptable. . . . Parents are often proud of their bookworm, but they should remember that such a child is a worm of quite a different sort."[5]

Some will think that Dr. Rice's profiles crazy; others might find grains of truth in this snapshot of popular attitudes ninety-five years ago. With vision exams common today in elementary school and correction offered sooner, Rice's personality profiles read improbably. Still, if you're one of the 10 percent with perfect vision, you might ask yourself how *you* might have been viewed for wearing glasses.

Does visual weakness determine personalities and destiny? Readers today won't likely accept biological determinism, but these comments help understand the negative roots of glassers' stereotypes. "When the eyes are 'wrong,'" Rice writes, a woman "may ruin her family life and make her home a place to be avoided." He recommends a law to compel cross and crabbed men to have their eyes tested. (What happens if their vision turns out fine and they're still crabby?) "Most of them need glasses–and the others need the guillotine."

In the annals of sniping at glasses, this remark represents a high point. His colleague and friend was Dr. Harry Haiselden, known as the Black Stork for his refusal to perform needed surgery on children born with birth defects. In the name of eugenics, he would allow a defective (underweight) child to die.[6] Rice's writings provide a sobering context for how those born with a need for glasses were viewed in his era.

* * *

More than seven hundred fifty years ago, the first reaction to someone wearing glasses happened when the first person brought a pair home or to work—what was said? No one was taking notes in the thirteenth century. If somebody saw better for wearing glasses, did they care if they looked odd? We'll never know.

In the twentieth century, colleges of optometry began social psychology studies to explore how people rated those wearing glasses, and then tested the accuracy of those stereotypes. Such measurements were often drawn from college students in Psych 101 classes studying photos and video of wearers; but whole elementary schools have also been polled to determine children's attitudes. The results of these studies, though unastonishing, might give you pause the next time you visit your friendly local optician or click through an online eyeglasses site.

Before serious research, doctors, optometrists, and opticians shared unscientific and anecdotal opinions about people in glasses. As early as 1910, Sigmund Freud probed the psychoanalytic implications of "visual disturbances." He concluded that effective sight, with or without glasses, is deeply connected to an individual's psychic balance. In 1943, G. R. Thornton, at Purdue University wondered if wearing glasses made job applicants more successful. To test this, Dr. Thornton had psychology students rate slides of the same people, with and without glasses. Glasses-wearers were regarded as industrious and intelligent.[7]

The association of glasses and intellectualism dates back to the fifteenth century as the Church's opposition waned. In 1455, on viewing the first printed Bible, future Pope Pius II pointed out how its clear lettering allowed priests to read it without spectacles. St. Jerome, a translator of the Old Testament, kept a pair by his desk. So did most everyone obliged to read a lot—hence spectacles' long association with intellectuals, which in surveys turns up constantly.

Not everybody thinks alike, but most everybody seems to react alike to eyeglasses. Qualities most associated with wearing glasses range from industriousness and intelligence to social awkwardness and homeliness. "Maybe glasses signal various perceptual, motor cognitive problems" and create a negative "spectacle image," one serious researcher concluded.[8] Don't judge a book by its cover, they say, but it's clear that we appraise a face from its features: Just ask, for example, defense attorneys, who have relied on what might be called a "glasses defense," encouraging those accused of a serious crime to put on glasses to increase chances of an acquittal.[9] In the eye of the beholder, glasses are transformative, like cosmetic surgery without the knife.

Researching reactions to glassers evokes feelings similar to what might happen if one wore those devilish, deprecating spectacles of Wilkie Collins, the pair that revealed people's hidden opinions. If you wear glasses, how much would you want to know about those ratings? If you're curious about what people say, just be glad you don't have to wade through reports like "Person Perception through Facial Photographs: Effects of Glasses, Hair, and Beard on Judgments of Occupation and Personal Qualities" from the *European Journal of Social Psychology*.[10]

* * *

Research on attitudes toward glassers has been intense and dogged (perhaps in part because many researchers themselves wear them). In 1952, reviewing existing research, two professors of optometry concluded that a myope was an inevitably "bad mixer," someone "introspective and more selfish . . . meticulous, dogmatic, tyrannized, and egotistical." The hyperope (farsighted), they concluded, was temperamentally opposite: outdoorsy and extroverted, just as Dr. Rice projected.[11] (These small studies, without controls, would not hold up to the scientific standards today.)

By the 1980s, larger, carefully controlled studies compared the stigma of being overweight to that of wearing glasses. The former was rated more harshly.[12] Women, of course, had known this all along—48 percent felt "a measurable decline" in their looks, when wearing glasses.[13] Then, in 1988, a study using more variables concluded that women in glasses were perceived as likely religious and conventional; and though intelligent, unimaginative.[14] One researcher found that glasses made women look stockier and men more slender. Women in glasses were rated as more timid than males, but more artistic and gentle.[15] (Stocky, timid, conventional–just the image modern womanhood seeks.)

As research became more international and cross-cultural, studies from Africa and Mexico raised an old issue, hiding from glasses. Even when kids were given glasses, researchers found that they weren't wearing them. In South Africa, only 31 percent of those with glasses had them on; in Tanzania and Mexico, only half. In one school in Oaxaca, only 13 percent wore their glasses, though a third carried them around in their pocket for emergencies. The older a student was upon receiving glasses, the less likely they were to wear them.[16]

The reasons for glasses resistance in the above-cited studies are those one might imagine: At a school in Dar-es-Salaam, Tanzania's capital, children with glasses were called "tortoise," "a cartoon" and, of course, "four eyes." "People are afraid of being ogled," one child explained.[17] Glasses reportedly made boys vain and arrogant; girls, on the other hand, said they were excited for a fashion accessory. A few African parents thought spectacles a plot of Western eye doctors, to "provide undesirable spectacles to destroy their patients' eyes."[18]

Conspiracy theories aside, the limitations of previously described studies cast doubts on their results. First, historically, glasses-wearing subjects and their evaluators have largely been students and white (a problem plaguing research in Psychology, which draws test subjects from universities). Second, rating wearers from only pictures omits interactive cues to their whole personality. Third, studies haven't distinguished between mild and extreme correction. Finally, sometimes it's not *whether* one wears glasses but *how* one wears them. Are the frames distinctly unflattering? Are they whole, askew, or chipped? (Some glasses worked well with a wearer's face; others seemed to wage war on it.)

The higher the quality of research on perceptions of glassers, the more mixed and nuanced the results. In 2010, at the University of Vienna, researchers found full-rimmed glasses made people seem "more intelligent but less attractive," but rimless pairs made people "trustworthy," perhaps because their frames were more transparent.[19] An Oxford study found the association of intelligence and glasses faded when raters observed people moving around on camera.[20] Among eighteen-year-olds in Denmark, the thicker the lenses, the higher the wearer's predicted score on intelligence tests.[21] On the other hand, a University of Melbourne study contradicted previous research, "finding [glasses bore] no association with introversion, conscientiousness, or passiveness."[22] In that study on how hairstyle, glasses, and beards interact, the researchers discovered that men with glasses and no hair had the highest rating for leadership. (No, the study was not funded by the Bald Liberation Front.) Those with both glasses and a beard were rated as the most highly educated.[23]

And what about those trial lawyers arguing the "glasses defense"—does it really work? The authors of "Is Justice Blind or Just Visually Impaired" say "Yes, but." There's more to prepping a defendant for trial than a suit, a shave, and a proper-looking frame.[24] Moreover the glasses ploy backfired in white-collar trials, where higher ratings of a defendant's intelligence led to more frequent guilty verdicts.[25]

By 2012, researchers had moved on to replication studies and meta studies (where a researcher combs through previous studies). A scientist in the Netherlands, Francine Jellesma, conducted a massive meta-study that came to an understated conclusion: Even into the twenty-first century, "wearing eyeglasses can negatively affect physical self-esteem."[26] So much research, so little change!

* * *

After reading through a foot-high pile of journal articles, the findings are getting to me. They sound like the idea that one's body type, or the way stars were aligned at birth, determines character. Did everyone I interacted with growing up write me off as unsocial, introverted, less attractive? If there is such a thing as a myopic personality, do I have one? Dr. Rice, concluded that being highly myopic has "some highly desirable points but an unnatural manner," a statement which reminded me of an exchange between hard-boiled detective Philip Marlowe and a client in Raymond Chandler's *The Lady in the Lake*:

> "I don't like your manner," said a client in a voice you could have cracked a Brazil nut on.
> "That's all right. I'm not selling it," Marlowe mutters.

Wearing glasses is a package that opens at both ends: People assume you're bright and trustworthy, but then they don't much like your looks (at least until recently). Glasses are transformative. Put on wire-rims, a white shirt and tie on a gangster, and they can resemble a banker. Put horn-rimmed glasses on a wild musician, and they look studious. Put pixie glasses on an MIT graduate student, and they might look like they're on the way to the candy store. If research shows people believe glasses make someone look smarter, does this mean they look stupider without them? Given the way attitudes arise from literature and film, adults' stereotypes turn into their kids' prejudices. So how can society end this cycle and stop people judging others—and themselves— by what's on their face?

Research suggests strategies that might help:

- Promoting children's books that praise glasses may reduce teasing.
- Providing children with glasses or contacts earlier, if needed, lessens resistance to wearing them.
- Recognizing that as more style choices appear tolerance spreads like herd immunity.

The most commonly proposed solution to glasses-shaming is to reduce negative images of glasses in media.[27] What about a Glasses Pride movement? At an Illinois elementary school, aide Lynne Speaker was upset by how few of her students were wearing their pairs. She set up the Paul Revere Glasses Club: sixty-five children showed up for its first meeting. "I gathered up all kinds of frames and let kids try them on. Children who wear glasses are often ridiculed, so we talked about why we wear glasses and what we should say if someone makes fun of us," she wrote.[28] Filmmakers could stop using glasses as the nerd-indicators, and avoid implying that "ugly people [with glasses] are just a makeover away from being a supermodel," as one blogger wrote.[29] In the last twenty years, attitudes have shifted, thanks to the Harry Potter books and films, according to Dr. Neil Handley: "Now kids in the schoolyard want to look like him."[30]

* * *

And as more people wear glasses, they're becoming more popular, so more people see glassers as like themselves. "The world has moved on, thankfully," suggests UK columnist Jenny Wilhide. "So now it's official: girls in glasses are glamorous—and you can eat your heart out, Dorothy Parker."[31]

In 2023, a twenty-two-year-old summed up her experience behind glasses:

> I really wanted glasses in second grade. It was an accessory I could wear. I even fibbed a little to get them, like saying the "E" on the eye chart was backwards. I was teased once, called "Four Eyes." I remember thinking, "That's so old. Come up with new material." Soon, half of my class had them. Yet, today, most of my girlfriends wear contacts. They only wear their glasses on lazy days when they're not going out. I remember one day in high school, I looked at myself in the mirror for a while. I decided maybe I do look better without them.[32]

Such comments suggest that though attitudes toward glasses are changing, prejudice remains internalized. To those unable to tolerate contact lenses and too farsighted, myopic, or hesitant to undergo surgery, this research may sound glum. Since when is blaming the victim acceptable? It happens all the time to people with challenges (deafness, blindness, motor impairment), and to those who appear autistic or otherwise different. Changing attitudes begins with changing behavior. Folks will go out and buy nice frames and feel good about them; but then whip them off for pictures, as if their pairs still make them feel unattractive. What I'm wondering about next is if wearing glasses still elicits so many reactions, how have those judgements affected how glassers see themselves? I'm a bit afraid to find out.

As for me, I'm not hiding from mine; very soon they'd be back on my nose.

Sunday

This last day of my week without glasses brought a quiet elation: I'm not permanently consigned to live with blurry figures, like those wandering Dante's imagination in *Paradiso*. At the end of his journey, Dante climbed that sacred staircase to heaven and, told by his lady Beatrice, looked down at Earth. At this, he is blinded and unable to see clearly.

> While I was in fear for my lost sight, there came forth [a voice] and it said: til thou recover the sight . . . be assured that thy sight is but confounded, not destroyed.[1]

Confounded, not destroyed. Thank goodness. Tomorrow I'd swim up out of this well of loneliness I had created for myself.

"On what aim is our soul set?" Dante continued. "Who dares say they have an answer?" Maybe such an answer could come only to those standing apart from the world, as I had. Yet, I saw now, this week had been a journey too far. I'd lost not only productivity but community. This reminded me of an interview with novelist Barbara Kingsolver for my radio series and book, *Writing the Southwest*. (https://www.unm.edu/~wrtgsw) She explained to me what she called "connectedness." "Everything that I write really comes down to an exploration of community. What is community? How do we fit into it? How do we hold our place and lose ourselves to something bigger in time? I think that's the only question I'm ever going to try and answer," she told me.[2]

I like that. I'd like to think that within all of us, blind or sighted, a basic humanity waits. Just as the sun pierces the clouds, empathy can shine through the cracks in our private blinds. If we see, our eyes are windows to see into our soul, those windows can shut, and the eyes and the spirit within can darken or remain out of focus. What's lost then is what makes us human—that heart-to-heart, smile-to-smile connection, the two-way radio between ourselves and others. In my case, what had started out as a vision detox had led me into what lay below the surface of my normal, refracted life.

Those highly dependent on glasses or contact lenses have split personalities: sixteen hours on, eight hours off. Every full-time glasser is out of focus sometimes. And society's persistent stereotyping further disconnects us. We can shout at the mountain, but it won't change. We can rail against injustice, and it might change. We can curse our lenses, stomp them, throw them in a lake—but that won't allow us to see better. We need a new way of understanding the world visually. In this model, using vision aids wisely might mean considering when and how to best wear them, rather than donning them automatically. Maybe there was something in that ancient, churchy insistence that people accept the eyes fate assigned us. We who are fated to walk around with glass or plastic in front of our eyes may sometimes lose sight of Kingsolver's "connectedness." Our "us" may appear vague while "them," the others, are brightly outlined. Clear sight makes it easier to connect; but crossing society's great divides takes more than glasses. What is this "little threshing floor that makes us so fierce?" Dante asked as he looked down on our divisions.

* * *

As I broke my visual fast, I had the odd sensation of approaching the surface of a lake from below. I rose toward the blue, imagining sights I would see tomorrow.

I wrote this book not only to offer the history and meanings of a device essential to billions—for some, every day of their lives. I wrote it to teach myself more respect for those whose every glance, all day and night, is hindered. For everyone who tries daily to keep ahold of their lenses correctly, and for all those whom lenses cannot help.

I couldn't decide exactly how and when I'd return to the Land of Blur. Of course I would, momentarily, as I washed or rested. But maybe now I would linger more in that purgatory between clarity and fuzziness. On this last night of limited vision, I took one more look around. I'd traded visual acuity for a chance to live differently with and within myself, and by that new view to know myself better. That it was challenging, even scary at times, hadn't negated the value of seeing on my own. By depriving myself of clarity, I've come to see myself—and the world around me—all the more clearly.

Before I end, I need to dig into what people have told me about their pairs in the emails and anecdotes they've sent me.

8

What People Say about Their Own Glasses

O wad some power the giftie gie us to see ourselves as others see us.

—ROBERT BURNS, 1786

"I was only six years old when I flunked an eye test held at the Chicago Public Schools," wrote Jane St. Clair, today a columnist and author. "A week later I was looking through a black contraption with goggles that looked like it belonged on a Russian submarine." Walking outside with her new glasses, the usual revelations struck her: the sharpness of signs, the outlines of clouds, leaves on trees. But then her parents insisted she not wear her glasses in public, to avoid visual weakness—"No matter how often I tripped over things like big dogs or walked into white doors that blended into walls, or that I could not see a volleyball much less a baseball in gym class."

"Junior prom was particularly memorable when I walked into the band pit. As my glasses got thicker and thicker, I no longer found Mr. Magoo funny." After corrective surgery, with the need for refraction gone, Jane comments, "The funny thing is, I miss them. I miss my glasses."[1]

Jane missed her glasses because, as with my own experiment, a part of her had disappeared.

* * *

Ever since I started wearing glasses—and especially when I stopped—I was curious to hear how people related to their own pairs and how they thought wearing them had affected their personalities. For years I posted invitations in magazines and online, encouraging comments. Here, I've created a catalogue of responses from the hundreds of responses sent to www.glassers.us. The stories below are organized by age of the wearers, identified by first name only. Instead of empirical studies, this chapter is anecdotal, offering the self-appraisals of glassers—the good, the bad, and the frankly ugly; these are suggestive but hardly scientific. From these accounts and interviews, I'll take a deep dive into how visual aids shape the way people see themselves from behind lenses.

As you might guess, glassers' responses to their pairs ranged widely between love and hate. Most everyone had strong feelings and at least one story: Some poetic, some funny, and a few fell into the better-have-a-hanky-ready category. For most, glasses provided a new look at life; but for others, glasses were a weight they've never been able to leave behind.

* * *

As a teenager in Southern California, Glenda made sure to pass her eye tests by memorizing the eye chart. She had no use for glasses and refused to be seen in them. The hide-the-glasses routine was well known to optometrists like Dr. Stephen Oppenheimer. "Self-perception comes from what the kids around you say." Go to the optometrist, and it's, "Oh my god, I need glasses? Something's wrong with me?" In extreme cases, Oppenheimer says, patients threatened him for prescribing glasses, like an odd client in Arizona: "You're not going to touch me. Anybody goes near my eyes, I'll kill them." Oppenheimer's threats included not just homicide but suicide: "Don't tell me I need glasses or I'll kill myself." He told me of a man in his eighties who told him he couldn't get a driver's license without correction: "The drivers' license people are crazy, I don't need them. I won't wear them."

"The reason they want you to wear glasses is not because you're going to kill yourself," the optometrist reminded him. "You're gonna kill other people."

"I'd rather do that than wear glasses."[2]

To be fair, reactions like these are extreme. Mostly it's kids and teenagers who show up at the optometrist in tears over how glasses will affect their social profile. Responses to one's glasses inevitably reflect that tension discussed earlier, between looking good vs. seeing well with glasses. Glasses ambivalence—appreciating them for what they do, yet sometimes despising their impact on others—is the most common sentiment.

Some glassers hold on to an exploratory attitude: "Wearing glasses is like alcohol. There are all different varieties all conveniently placed in an aisle, some looking pretty, some dull, some exotic—they're all there, waiting to be purchased," Chrissy wrote. "You begin to know what you want, choosing the drinks that make you feel good about yourself."

"I've been wearing glasses since I was in the second grade," she continues, "for nearly two-thirds of my life. Wearing them hasn't always been fun—sometimes I despise them—but now I can't live without my glasses. I've found the one drink for me after so many years of taste-testing."[3] Extreme attitudes toward wearing glasses often fade over time. "Glasses suit me," a longtime wearer named Mark posts. "Or they have become a part of me."

* * *

In glasses, children have the toughest time. The poorer their eyesight and the thicker their lenses, the worse kids seem to feel about themselves. Eyes, and glasses, are notable when we interact with another person: Just weeks after birth, children begin to notice eyes (and glasses) more than other regions of the face. Attitudes toward eyeglasses develop steadily: At age three, friends like each other's eyewear, but from five to six, negative comments arrive, and self-perception shifts accordingly.[4] Glasses then serve as "a living reminder of the fragility of life. [Wearers] internalize the notion that eyeglasses imply a character flaw."[5]

In 1964, a TV special aired, *Rudolf, the Red-Nosed Reindeer*. You know the story: A young reindeer is teased about his shiny nose. For some kids, the Four Eyes among us, glasses were that shiny nose.

"Back when I was in third grade, at the beginning of the school year, a girl showed up wearing glasses," Dr. Oppenheimer remembers. "People didn't want to get close to her because they said she had 'cooties' from wearing glasses; she was an untouchable." [6] This bias goes back hundreds of years: the belief that if you had something wrong with you—medically, physically, personality-wise—it was contagious, like the evil eye.

For children, the revelation of "Wow, I can see" that accompanies a first pair of glasses has historically been accompanied by, "But now I'm a target." Phil got his first pair when he was in second grade. He thought it was a miracle: He could see the blackboard! The blurry world he'd inhabited all his life dramatically came into focus. "I could actually see facial expressions." But then the problems started. "My new specs, with their light blue frames and thick lenses, didn't signal: Cool! Smart! Fun! They signaled: Hey bullies—pick on THIS kid!"[7]

That bullying or severe teasing in childhood stays with people. Whenever people differ from the norm, there'll always be a few who can't wait to take a poke at them. Perhaps this makes bullies self-important, the way a bureaucrat sits on paperwork to prove her power over others. What's important here are the feelings of the bullied, who may not take such incidents lightly or worry their glasses tell people there's something's wrong with them. "Kids needing glasses? Well, you're different," an optician told me. "Teased, it became part of your persona."[8] Children hesitating to wear their glasses often have good reason.

Occasionally, it's the opinions of those who ought to know better that cause problems. Four-year-old Lyle in Toronto also loved glasses, his mother recalled; he especially liked frames with bright colors. But the optician told him, those pairs were for girls. The optician kept pulling out frames in blue and black and other somber colors until the boy's mother grew irritated: "I tried to keep it together," Lyle's mother said, "because I didn't want to draw too much attention, but I did tell her that I thought [that] was the stupidest thing I'd ever heard."[9]

Or take Bill, who stood outside his elementary school on his very first day of school. Even before he'd stepped through the door, voices behind him called out: "Four eyes! Look like you're still sleeping!" "Four eyes! Look like you're dead!" Many kids would have stuffed their pairs away. Bill bravely pulled down his cap and walked into class. Or Paul, who had loved buying glasses; he chose a pair that made him feel like a spy. After being teased, though, he grew conflicted. His parents found his glasses hidden in various places: in the fridge, in the dog's kennel, and once in a bowl of fruit.

Parents help their children negotiate dilemmas about glasses. One choice is substituting contacts, if they've affordable. When children who need help seeing wear contact lenses early, research suggests, fewer self-esteem issues surface and they're more satisfied with their appearance.[10] (Yet, research is unclear whether that higher self-esteem resulted from avoiding glasses, or if the kids requesting contacts already had higher self-esteem.)[11] Athletic prowess may also increase.[12] Today, increasingly younger children request contacts.

Parents can also address glasses avoidance by reasoning, as Mary Ann's family did.

> I was about ten when I had to get glasses. I was shy, bookish. My two grandmothers got together and convinced my parents that if they got me contact lenses, I would feel more self-confidence, be prettier, and maybe attract some boys. Finally, my mother stood up for me. She pointed out that a lot of grown-up married women wear glasses, including some very good-looking ones like Mrs. Parker, the minister's wife and my favorite teacher. A great lesson.[13]

(Today, however, Mary Ann's grandchildren wear contacts.)

* * *

Starting to wear glasses as teenagers may be the hardest challenge. Growth spurts change teen-aged eyes, resulting in a need for glasses where that wasn't the case before. In puberty, the eyeball lengthens simultaneously to when youths develop self-consciousness. Adolescence brings young people eyeing each other newly, and gender differences emerge. Boys may see girls in glasses as sexier—though girls do not; two-thirds of women wearing glasses said that when they first wore them as teenagers, it lowered their self-image.[14] Teens can have it tough. Those who wear glasses, one study reported, "are subject to social criticism, ridicule, and perhaps rejection." One study reported teens saying glasses "disfigure" them.[15]

"I'd been wearing glasses about three years," Richard wrote. "This was way before designers thought there was any money to be made crafting frames for the nearsighted. Pretty much everyone who wore glasses back in 1967 looked like a dork. If you already looked like a dork without glasses, then you were really in trouble."

> So, one day I'm at Bob's house, and he's rummaging in his older brother's forbidden music. He pulls out a Lovin' Spoonful's album. The next to last song was "4 Eyes." Bob turned up the volume loud and sang along with the record. *How many fingers . . . hahaha* he taunted as he danced around the room. That was about when our fortunes diverged, Bob heading upward into borderline popularity, and me joining the sixth-grade band.[16]

Brad wrote, "I'm not myself anymore. I'm myself *with glasses*. And I don't believe in augmenting myself to compensate for physical flaws because that only ends in, you know, cyborgs."

"Why don't you just get contacts?" a commenter on his webpage asked.

"I can't get contacts because my eyes are fragile, sensitive newborn kittens, and any poking/prodding causes acute pain and uncontrollable crying," ran Brad's response.

Another teenager continued the thread: "Every time someone asks how many fingers they're holding up, I respond by flipping them off and asking the same question. The stupid questions stop pretty quickly after that."[17]

What's positive about wearing glasses for teens is how they provide sorely needed gravitas while seeking a driver's license or a job.[18] "They make me look more trustworthy and less threatening, especially me being a young, muscular black man," commented someone identified as Ulinvisiber.[19] Additionally, for teens, choosing their own glasses becomes a self-assertion.

Some just like the look of a face with frames and choose to wear clear (plano) lenses.

> Wearing glasses for fashion is actually a little crazy, which is why I didn't want to admit to it the first time," one woman wrote. "It's really no different than someone wearing a knee brace as an accessory. People would ask if I had a knee injury, and because I'm doing this honesty thing now, I would say no, I'm just into knee braces. That's odd, we all agree. But glasses are more acceptable because of the way they change your whole look.[20]

In changing that look, social media advises teenagers to go all in. "Wear them all the time. This will give everyone the chance to get used to the 'new you.'"[21] One young woman, who thought she'd finally found the right guy: "Finally, he asked for a date!" the nearsighted collegian gloated. "We went to the library—a safe place to get to know each other, sat at a heavy oak table, chairs close together, then opened our books as if to study," Nancy remembered. "He began staring, leaning too close and looking through my coke-bottle glasses and said, 'Don't ever marry anyone who is nearsighted.'"[22]

Avoiding comments like this one is one reason teens seek contact lenses if their family can afford them. My family could not. Raised by a single mom, as a teen-ager I had to fend off the contacts spiel every time I picked up new glasses: "They'll let everyone see your eyes!" (I thought they could see them already.) "They'll make a New You!" (I was ok with the old one.) "You'll see much better, and they don't cost that much." (Back then they cost three times as much as glasses.)

As a regular winner of only one game on the playground—"Whose glasses are stronger?"—I tried to rise above slights and self-doubts about how glasses made me appear. The snubs galled me. At times I've resented this tether, like an addict perplexed at how they have to drink, shoot, or smoke just to feel normal.

* * *

As presbyopia sets in for adults, they may reconsider previously negative attitudes. "I always looked at [people who wear glasses] as being, umm, nerdish, slightly eccentric, or super intelligent people who were just almost-not-misfits, but different," said Julie.[23] Then, wanting to be taken seriously in the business environment at her office, she purposefully changed from contacts to mock tortoise-shell frames. Why not roll with the stereotypes?

At another office, a woman identifying as "my own bad self" took a different tack:

> I work with a younger woman who used to give me grief because of my deteriorating eyesight (early-onset cataracts). After both eyes were operated on and I was cleared, I went back to work. This little snot soon slithered around and said, in her usually condescending voice, that I looked far better without those stupid, stupid, Coke bottles on my face. I replied that it was amazing how clear everything was now, and that I could see all sorts of details I could never see before, such as the lines around her eyes and the wrinkles on her forehead. "It's like you've aged 10 years,"[24] this glasser told her bully.

Adults give freer rein to feelings about lenses than the young, perhaps because by this point many have long worn them, or because of their surprise at needing a too-public sign of aging. For millennials, the perception of glasses differs from Baby Boomers. "I wouldn't say I hate my glasses. I have a lot of affection for them, actually, even though I leave them abandoned all day," wrote Helen Jung in *Cosmopolitan*,[25] about a woman who, ironically likes her glasses only when kept in a drawer.

Some adults still picture themselves with the perfect 20/20 vision of their youth, even though their eyes have objectively changed. At a family wedding, for example they'll take their glasses off because glasses don't fit their self-perception. Even the elderly may deny they need glasses, though without them they'd never try to drive. Leslie wrote me a memory: A group of five women "of a certain age," strangers to one another, were invited to a mutual friend's honorary dinner in Massachusetts. All wore both high heels and glasses. Leslie wondered "if they're as concerned about how they look in their eyewear as I am," she wrote, "as anxious about the stairs as I am."

Finally, one woman turned to the rest. "I'm having a terrible time determining where to put my foot down. And with these heels, it's even scarier. I never realized bifocals could not only be unattractive but create such a depth-perception problem." Another exclaimed, "Whew, I thought I was just me who's having anxiety about bifocals, heels, and stairs!"[26]

The arrival of age-related farsightedness can be discombobulating. "Well it really pisses me off when [people] say to me 'Oh you look so pretty without your glasses on . . . you look five years younger,'" a woman wrote. Ageist discrimination can push responses to wearing glasses to the extreme. "I'm not ready for a cane. I'm not ready for a hearing aid. So why am I ready for glasses?" asked another.[27] "The day it dawned on me that I needed glasses was not a happy one," wrote Phil. "I would never wear contacts—the idea of sticking things in my eyes makes me feel ill. The idea of people firing lasers into my eye has a similar effect. So, I stick with my spectacles. If you have gone through your first 30 or 40 years of life and you haven't had to wear glasses and suddenly you do—that's the sign of aging."[28]

So many reasons lead people to contacts or surgery. Steve Hoffman, former CEO of Reddit, is a glasses survivalist with myopia; he had a different reason for avoiding glasses. He underwent eye surgery not for convenience or appearance, he told the *New Yorker*, but "for a reason he doesn't usually talk much about: he hopes it will improve his odds of surviving a disaster, whether natural or manmade. 'If the world ends—and not even if the world ends but if we have trouble [when optometrists become unavailable]—getting contacts or glasses is going to be a huge pain in the ass.'"[29] (It's hard to run from zombies if you can't see them.)

Responses to glasses among today's adults fall into consistent categories. There are the *glasses-ambivalent*, such as Betty, who grew up intimidated by Hollywood's starlets without glasses. Contacts opened new possibilities: "In losing my glasses, I had passage to the enchanting, and frequently confusing, world of parties, bad boys, and blue eyeliner." To her surprise, though, she discovered her female pals also needed glasses.

> It took me months to find out—because they wore contact lenses in public. Sometimes I feel badass, smart, and fearless behind my tiny plastic windshields—a kind of Lois Lane who doesn't have to rely on sappy old Superman to get stuff done. Other times I just feel frumpy. It doesn't help that the women society upholds as beautiful and brilliant on a daily basis don't have glasses on.[30]

In general, females are three times as likely as males to say wearing glasses affects their self-perception.[31]

Then there's the *never-glasses* contingent. These may own pairs but refuse to put them on. Or all their life they may have refused to have a vision exam. They may feel glasses offer them little or nothing. One writer, David, compared needing glasses to finding a large, dead insect on the floor.

> I hate glasses with a passion. You're always aware of the rim, beyond which the periphery of the world is a blur; they always get grimy, no matter how scratch-free they remain. . . if it's raining they're covered in droplets. If it's

cold, the world is consumed by fog when you come inside; they invariably slip in some way, shape, or form; you're aware of the thing sitting on your nose like some malevolent skin eruption.[32]

The *pro-glasses* contingent identify so completely with their pairs they can't imagine themselves without them. "As someone who's been using specs for the past 21 years, I've never understood how it defines me in any way. It's just a part of my face! I'll not have a sudden personality transformation if I take off my glasses and start wearing contact [lenses]. I'll still be me," wrote July.[33] Glasses have become who they are: "Honestly without them I feel a little naked."[34]

The *glasses-forever* adherents love them so much they experience anxiety after laser surgery. They may keep their glasses on a shelf as artifacts. Rose wore glasses all her life but, in middle age, contemplated surgery as she wrote to me. "Will I be able to throw out my glasses?" she wondered.

> Shed my life-long identity as a four-eyed girl and live non-myopically ever after? I guess I'll just have to see. My glasses are so much a part of me that once, when my son was a baby and I removed them for a second, he gave me a look of pure horror and then burst into sobs. To him, it was as if I'd suddenly taken off part of my face.

Then, too, as eyeglasses become more fashionable, some adult wearers want them in multiple styles and colors matching their wardrobe—the can't-wait-to-have-glasses crowd. "You can switch out your clothes all you want, but you can't really replicate the way glasses can completely transform you. It's like presenting an alternate version of yourself. When I wear my glasses, people often don't recognize me; they say I look completely different. What other accessory can do that?"[35]

* * *

It would be optimistic to consign negative self-images on the part of glassers to the distant past. Studies in 2013, 2016, and 2017 in countries as diverse as India, New Zealand, and Ghana suggest that glassers still struggle. In India, those in their early twenties were asked about glasses. They resented an unwelcome dependence and didn't like their looks wearing them.[36] In New Zealand, bespectacled females with higher social acceptance and athletic competence wanted contacts. Given the chance, in Ghana, more than twice as many females opted for contacts over glasses for cosmetic reasons.[37] Similarly, a study suggests that when American women accustomed to contacts put on glasses, their anxiety surges.[38] Understanding these reactions takes us into the field of "psycho-optometry" and other behavioral fields that study the mind-eyes relation and how anxiety affects vision.[39]

Comparing previous ratings of glassers to the self-reflections here, differences emerge. Assessments of glassers—smart, trustworthy; but unsocial, less athletic, nerds—are more consistent than wearers' self-appraisals. Glassers quickly learn how they're seen by others; whether they accept that perception or turn away from it is more individual. But whatever people feel about their glasses, visual aids invariably evoke a torrent of feelings.

Monday

"My eyes have returned from a foreign country," wrote French poet Paul Eluard in 1926. I know what he means.

I woke up, grabbed my glasses, and whoa! immediately sat down hard on the edge of my bed. Everything was dippy. I looked down, and the floor rose up. Once I'd adjusted, I walked out to my backyard. There was the neighborhood cottontail hopping about. I watched New Mexico's puffy clouds drifting on their way to rain somewhere else and was content.

When Dante's sight returns at the end of the *Paradiso*, he happily rejoins the world:

> Sight appeared to me which held me so fast that of my condition I had no remembrance. As through smooth and transparent glass, the outlines of faces return.[1]

Well, I certainly remember. Notwithstanding, I checked out of the no-sight motel, muttered *sayonara* to defocus, and left behind that dark wood at the entrance to hell. The change happened effortlessly. Images were crystal clear.

Was this a function of my more relaxed eyes, or simply the way I saw before? No metric charted the change. I was so relieved to be myself that I was too impatient to devise objective measures of visual improvement. I could have been more scientific. I could report no grand discovery, nor whether my eyes actually saw better for their vacation. Ambivalence toward glasses, however, now seemed outmoded.

I would miss fighting temptation. Beating the impulse to pick up my glasses was each day a small achievement of self-control. I now knew two versions of sight: the standard one and my private one. And my "other sight," as I now called it, had advantages I wouldn't forget. I'd miss how sounds were magnified as I tuned into the grumbling of geese overhead or the faint "cheech" of bats at dusk. I'd miss the enhanced intensity of tastes, the way a breakfast burrito in New Mexico blended layers of potato, cheese, green chile, and eggs. Reviewing my week's journey, I wasn't finished exploring; perhaps I'll take a visual staycation every month or so. Maybe even try that crazy idea of inviting friends over for an unfocused fiesta. Would anyone come?

In the second part of this volume, I investigate why eyeglasses cost so much, and how the best ones are made. Then, I consider smart glasses and smart contacts, which may eventually offer wearers not just refraction but a brave new world of recording and streaming everything they see.

9

Glasses Today

Set aside all prudery, honestly confess that age is creeping on and without coquetry or apology, ask the optician for a pair of glasses.

—"THE DOCTOR," 1847[1]

I've always hoped to see better than nature provided. Despite the repeated deterioration in my vision, I stayed upbeat. I kept hoping a pair of glasses would show up that would finally let me see 20/20.

I'm still searching for that pair. Someday, maybe, through new surgical technologies, we will all see perfectly. Yet, as an old country song goes, we could still have "20/20 vision and be walking 'round blind."

In researching this book, I've heard of new hope for glassers: new ways of grinding lenses that open your field of vision, contacts with progressive lenses (multifocal) or that darken like sunglasses, glasses that automatically refocus according to where one looks.[2] My plan now is to travel to assemble the best pair of eyeglasses I can and, in doing so, learn about this vast industry and what glasses we'll wear in the future. This journey is overdue. Still, I'm apprehensive about the expense, the arrangements, and working in languages I don't understand. It's the small goals that will count: finding glasses that allow me to make out a smile across a room or notice mountains on the horizon. So here I go, a Don Quixote in specs. (Perhaps if he'd had them, he'd have avoided jousting at windmills.)

* * *

Now that I know a little about the history of glasses and their place in popular culture, I'm self-conscious about all I don't know: how they're designed, prescribed, and manufactured; and why they cost so much. If you've been wearing lenses for years, maybe you also wonder about these issues. To understand what's behind the making and pricing of glasses, a friend suggested I visit David Salk, owner of a high-end optical shop in Berkeley, California.

It's business as usual at Berkeley's Focal Point. Passersby buzz into the store like bees, hovering over displays of glasses until a pair catches their eye. A twenty-something squeals at her reflection in "granny" glasses, already retro back when John Lennon wore them.[3] A stooped academic carefully examines a black, square-rimmed pair exactly like the one he has on. We're not far from UC-Berkeley's campus; people look busy, serious, and smart. Undergraduates in cut-offs and designer tops walk by eyeing the graduate students, still tweedy in owlish glasses.

Salk comes over to me, wearing a charcoal-black sports coat and gunmetal-gray frames that match his swept-back hair. He's a good-looking guy in his sixties, with clean features. He sizes up my cherry-red frames and smiles. We walk past his attending desk, through two rooms of glossy frames, past his laboratory with on-site technicians, and into a windowless office that looks like the Bat Cave.

After being in the business for forty years, Salk's job has made him part technician, part salesman, part humanist. "The problem with glasses," he begins,

> is that some people believe they're all the same. And then when someone comes along and says, "Wait a minute, what about this issue you're having?" people say, "Well, I've just gotten used to it." They haven't had a first-hand experience of how much better their sight can be. If glasses aren't made properly, they'll tax someone's visual system. They're going to experience fatigue, headaches, dry eyes, muscle strain, neck and shoulder strain—and maybe a little bit of depression.

Some people can wear anything. They could wear six different categories of lenses and say, "I feel fine with all of them." It's kind of like people and restaurants: some don't distinguish between a three-star establishment and their neighborhood eatery; it all tastes good to them. As an optician, what you *don't* want to do is give somebody something that's not right and have them really experience stress with that pair.

A good optician, Salk says, goes beyond measurements to take into account a client's lifestyle and visual tasks.

Millions of Americans go through life without seeing well because they can't afford correction or don't have an accurate prescription. They can't read a laptop screen or the whiteboard at school and fall behind. How long will it be before we recognize visual correction as a basic human right? Flawed eyesight is the most prevalent untreated disability in the world; estimates of the visually untreated range around 2 billion people. So, you'd think the world would make correcting this a priority. And indeed, this vast unprescribed mass, the visually uncorrected, is addressed by many good-hearted organizations, though it's impossible to keep up with growing demand—particularly in places like Seoul, South Korea, where so many wear lenses (95 percent) that a low-bridge frame designed specifically for Asians is commonly used.[4]

The need for eyeglasses still runs up against twin barriers: avoidance and access. Avoidance is a legacy of all those tired old stereotypes. Many avoid wearing glasses, despite carrying pairs in their pockets, knapsacks, or purses, just in case. Access is a matter of resources and technology. Good glasses require effective exams, which in turn demand high-quality training for optometrists and opticians. Access to all this comes with a price tag.

Reading glasses, magnifiers, were the first pairs of glasses invented. You buy them today similarly to the way peddlers sold glasses in the fourteenth century: trying on pairs until you find one that lets you read small text. For these, no exam is needed (though everyone should have regular exams for eye health). These days, the cost of readers is not significant; you can find racks upon racks of them in your drugstore. For prescription eyewear, the story is much more complicated.

The cost of prescription eyewear has three parts: services, frames, and lenses. Services are the examination and the fitting that adjust a pair of glasses to their wearer. Better-trained and more experienced providers charge more. It's the near-monopoly of frame- and lens-makers that's exploding the price of eyewear. In the world today, 1.4 billion glasses wear a product that comes from one company, Essilor-Luxottica. Talk about concentration of ownership: the owner of that eyewear empire was Italy's second-richest man. (It's also the way Britain's first self-made woman billionaire built her wealth—on visual aids.)

It's thought that Essilor-Luxottica may own as much as 80 percent of the frame market.[5] The company produces 27,000 different frames; its brands include Prada, Versace, Channel, Armani, Burberry, Oakley, Oliver Peoples, and dozens more, including Ray-Bans, the most widely sold eyewear line in the world. Not only does Luxottica license or own all these brands, it owns stores that sell them: Lenscrafters, Sunglass Hut, Pearle Vision, Specsavers, John Lewis (in the UK), and Sears Optical are all part of this one vast Italian-French company.[6]

"The eyeglass industry is a small but potent symbol of what happens when you allow corporate consolidation to get out of control," said Professor Tim Wu on the podcast *Freakonomics*.[7] This conglomeration makes the industry a poster child for a larger trend: the steadily declining competition in major industries. Big Lens, meet Big Pharma—and Big Phone, Big Liquor, and Big Just About Everything Else. Fifteen years ago, the United States had ten major airlines; now four control 80 percent of the market. Five companies dominate book publishing. Similarly, banks, car-rental and train companies—and search engines like Google and mega-retailers like Amazon—have consolidated the world. In the same way, Essilor-Luxottica dominates the 150-billion-dollar eyewear industry, making everything from screws and hinges to frames with luxury names stamped on them. After its 2018 merger with Essilor, which already provided half the world's prescription lenses, Luxottica also swallowed Europe's largest chain optician, the Dutch company GrandVision, adding 7,000 stores to the 9,000 it previously owned. This is vertical monopoly, where supply chains and store are owned by the same company, with mark-ups between 100 percent and 1,000 percent.

I'm not the first to point out the problems with having a single company control this much of the market for glasses.[8] "Meet the Four-Eyed, Eight-tentacled Monopoly That's Making Your Glasses So Expensive," declares a 2014 article in *Forbes*. After quoting a Columbia professor on Luxottica's profits ("relatively obscene"), the writer wonders why laptops and screens are better and cheaper than ever—but not glasses, "a medical device you don't want and a fashion accessory you do."[9] The store owned by the same company that manufactures its products steers buyers through different price points for frames; this is known as "romancing the product." That's why consumers rarely find generic frames on the shelf—touted brands yield greater margins.

This loss of competition in the market goes beyond frames. The second-largest frame company is Marchon, owned by Vision Service Plan—the largest provider of vision insurance. When you buy a pair of Marchon frames, one division of the company simply charges another, and you get the bill after finding the frame that's "really you." For those not needing serious vision correction, frames are the expensive part of their eyewear. Profit margins can be eye-wateringly high: Even fancy frames often cost less than $60 to manufacture; a Dolce & Gabbana frame hand-painted in Sicily costs $4,500 to the consumer. In China, by contrast, manufacturers may mold a frame design and inject plastic into that mold over and over—a frame made for under $5.

"Does the $5 pair perform as well as one that wholesales for $150?" Salk asks. "If they both hold a pair of lenses and that's your criterion, there's no difference between them" (other than that the more expensive frame holds them better). But, he continues, take the ones I have on from Italy, made from a sheet of Zyl acetate [a mix of wood, cotton, and polyester]. The resin of cotton plants is made into a block, cured over 6 to 9 months, and colorized custom-to-order for frame designers. After they're aged, they go to the milling machines and to the manufacturer, where they basically use a jig to cut out the rough form. After that, there's lamination, polishing, bridges buffed, hinges inserted.

"But glass is glass," I can't resist saying. "It's not a precious stone."

"But that would be like saying, 'Cotton is cotton, so why should a shirt cost $200?' You're paying for design, patents, fabrication, R&D, and the tools that go into manufacturing those lenses." (You're also paying for the bricks-and-mortar retail operation that sells frames, an expense online firms don't face.)

For people with complicated prescriptions requiring strong correction, high-index materials, special centers, or base curves, lenses alone could run more than $800; the cost depends on the prescription and seller. Premium lenses, such as those sold at optical boutiques like Salk's, benefit from rigorous testing and research design. Proprietary software also raises the cost of lenses, sometimes causing sticker shock. High-tech lens makers like Zeiss own valuable patents to the software used to carve lenses; anyone using their design or technology must pay "click fees"—royalties—to Zeiss.

One way to minimize costs when buying glasses is to ask about generic frames; another is to scrutinize coatings, which add to the price: frames of CR-39 instead of polycarbonate, for example, are largely scratch-resistant; similarly, those made of poly are already UV-protected.[10] But none of these steps answers the fundamental question which everyone I talk to asks: "Why should a few dollars of plastic cost many hundreds of dollars?"

The answer is complicated. Eyeglasses are (or should be) precision goods. That plastic frame, for instance, goes through 180–230 steps in its manufacture. The authors of the algorithm used to grind lenses, like any author, need royalties. There are patents for the machines that cut those lenses, and patents for the rigs that make those machines. Designers from the humble to the famous create frames someone else manufactures and distributes. Add to this the cost of training expert opticians and optometrists to fit a pair properly, and one finds the invisible costs of eyeglasses. Does all this justify a 200 percent cost markup on frames, and even more on lenses and coatings?

As consumers balk at the soaring cost of glasses, inexpensive frame-and-lens packages are increasingly sold online. Warby Parker, for example, tripled its online sales in one year by offering free shipping and returns, though today their products are found in 300 stores.[11] Those needing mild, uncomplicated correction may be happy with this shopping experience. Similarly, if someone just needs reading glasses, over-the-counter ones work fine. But "Will those lenses necessarily have anti-reflective coatings and the best optics? No," Salk points out.

Nor will those glasses come with someone adjusting them for free. As the online glasses industry took off in the 2000s, Main Street optometrists worried. Their margins were shrinking. Online outfits were turning what used to be custom-made prescription glasses into, in effect, over-the-counter readers: adequate, but not excellent. Subsequently though, a lot of opticians' business became sorting out errors and misunderstandings from online purchases with inadequate customization. People coming into their shops needing adjustments showed surprise when asked to pay for this service, which had previously been baked into the price of their glasses.

Online opticians aren't even the last phase in the glasses-fitting process. To understand the coming revolution in how glasses will be prescribed and dispensed, meet Ralph, the friendly eyeglass robot. He'll someday reside in one of those photo kiosks where you used to sit for silly and fast-fading photos. Ralph will be unimpressed by such antics.

You will be asked to sit still. In front of you, a device will scan your face from different angles. Then the auto-refractor will power on. From its reflections, your eyeball will be mapped and your prescription written to 1/100 of a diopter.

But wait, there's more! Ralph's inventors wouldn't stint on convenience. Ralph is not just a set of lights and mirrors; he does eye exams too. Thus, the machine will bill you twice, once for the "exam," and then for the product or frames it dispenses. Ralph will be just like your local optometrist, only metal.

"Patience," Ralph will intone. "Your glasses will be done soon. Why not buy a cup of coffee next door at Starbucks?" Meanwhile, behind the curtain, widgets will dance. The plastic for the frame's mold will be microwaved hot. Once the prescription is entered, the scribing tool will roll into position. There will be a brief, ear-splitting noise as now-superchilled plastic meets the blade, and a soft thrush as polishers swirl about like tiny blades of a mixer. The selected frame will get a once-over from an electric eye; lenses will be positioned in frames; a case will slide over the finished product, and out she comes, dropping to the bottom of the chute like a candy bar. It's guaranteed! (If you have a problem, come back and talk to Ralph.)

The degree of market consolidation in an industry I depend on for sight unsettles me and many others preventing some from obtaining what they need. It reminds me of another talk I've had recently, with optician-inventor Dr. Mark Mattison-Shupnick in California, who has developed lenses to help the colorblind. "I personally don't agree with this monopolizing of the visual care business," Mattison-Shupnick says. "I think competition is better. They control much more of the industry than they should. Do I think they brought good things to the business? Absolutely."

"Why are consumers pissed off? Because they need glasses, goddammit. And don't want to spend $700. There's an opportunity for consumers to say to your government, 'This is a monopoly.' The government has turned a blind eye."

Listening to him, an optician joke comes to mind.

Patient: "How often should I wear my glasses?"
Optician: "Only when you want to see."

* * *

Hunting for glasses is nothing new, particularly for those who wear them only occasionally. Some people keep a dozen pairs scattered around the house and car, so as to always have them near to hand. For those who can't afford this, losing a pair may do more than frustrate; it reminds us of a deficiency we try to style away. That's what's ironic about those who wear spectacles "for shew," made as a fashion statement with clear glass: They have nothing to correct.

Glasses are a limitation in themselves. With or without corrective lenses installed, frames make a difference. They hang there, giving a square, rectangular, or round shape to our existence. When we turn, our frames turn. People often lower or raise them to look closely at something. We may lose consciousness of that frame much of the time; it may be subsumed into what is front and center—what we are looking at—but glassers carry this frame everywhere until the moment we remove it, and eyes are released from its grip.

What do we miss outside of frames? Glasses substitute a frame's shape for the 360° natural horizon; they force a choice of where to look. Thus, behind frames, many overlook what's above, below, and beside our lenses. No wonder the most common comment from those first wearing contacts is how the world suddenly surrounds them. So, like a camera's lens, frames limit what we see as they shape what's seen. If eyes are windows to the soul, frames are their window panes.

* * *

The frame I'm looking for is far away, in Sao Paulo, Brazil, in the shop of a guy who claims he's a magician. After learning about the business end of contacts and eyeglasses in Berkeley, I board a plane to Brazil.

On a gray winter day in June, seventy-six-year-old Miguel Giannini holds court, surrounded by men in white coats. His throne is a blue chair in his Victorian house, a simultaneously an up-to-date optical shop with a staff of thirty and an eyeglasses museum. Downstairs, Giannini's operation resembles the inside of a flying saucer, with red-and-white lights flashing and shiny metal scopes deployed by white-coated attendants. A crew of opticians bustle by like characters in a glasses opera awaiting a cue from Maestro; Brazil already has its first satirical song, "Óculos," and name for glasses, "bottle bottoms."

From the reception area, I walk through rooms of well-dressed customers, one with a small, elegant white dog on her lap (could the dog be here for specs?). The café staff is seriously disappointed I don't accept a "cafezinho," that tiny cup of fiendishly strong Brazilian coffee. Around me, hushed conversations suggest more than frames are being discussed. There's something political in the air, befitting an establishment that's made glasses for all the presidents of Brazil and some from Honduras, Panama, and Nicaragua. Giannini calls himself a glasses stylist, providing not just a frame but a "facial expression."

Under a cloud of white hair, Miguel Giannini's short body is like a wine bottle: narrow, straight, and pretty. His Italian designer clothes mask the mannerisms of an impish child. Giannini is a fifth-generation Italian-Brazilian, part of Sao Paulo's vast immigrant community.

"I can't help if I'm banging the mic," he apologizes to me in Portuguese. "I'm an Italian. I speak with my hands." Thus absolved, he continues. "My profession combines optics and magic. Yes, I'm a magician. My magic is in letting people see. The youngest child I worked with was a baby of four months. He had a problem. I was able to give him glasses that let that child know his father, see his grandparents. That's magic."

His assistant interrupts with a pair for his approval. He holds them up to the light, peers through them for defects, and plants a kiss, pinky in the air as if holding a teacup.

"There," he says. "Every pair gets a kiss." He shrugs, platinum hair touching his narrow shoulders. Ironically, Giannini doesn't wear glasses. His blue pupils pulse as if they, rather then he, drank that cafezinho. He suddenly stops, reaches over, and puts a finger on my frame. He's noticed a hairline fracture in the bridge.

"*Perigroso, isso!*" (Dangerous, wearing those!) He waves his hands. "You need a safe pair, right away. One tap on these, and they'd break in two, the sharp edges an inch from your eyeball. I'll make one for you. Gratis."

I refuse, pointing out I normally have one pair that works and a drawerful that don't. I never notice the crack; it doesn't bother me. But no, with the tenaciousness of Latin hospitality, Giannini is already signaling a technician, a tall, virile specialist whose mustache seems to smile independently of his mouth.

Though new glasses here are not part of my plan, avoiding danger to my eyes is. After the technician takes my details, Giannini pulls off his microphone, and we're off for a tour. On the wall there's a photo of Miguel at a vigorous, silvery fifty, smiling at the camera. In front of him is a line of men on a bench with jet-black hair in identical bowl haircuts; they're waiting for their first, free glasses, he tells me. Eyes flashing, he relates the story of working with these men, who are Xingu, a tribe in Brazil's state of Mato Grosso, a hot, wet corner far from airports.

Over at one side of the photo is an older man with a big grin. "So, this guy over here, he gets his first pair of glasses and he runs as fast as he can to his canoe. He immediately pushes off, leans over the side, and whap! He spears this long fish. His glasses fed his family." I bet *they* agree he's a magician.

Not everyone is as excited to receive glasses as those Xingu men. We discuss the challenges of offering pairs to kids who don't want them.

"We have to use psychology. We must prepare them carefully." Behind us, right on cue, a toddler is tipping back and forth with new, tiny red frames on his eyes. He stares into the mirror and howls. Papa can't comfort him. He'll have to learn to love his changed face.

"One time, a father brought in his daughter who didn't want glasses. I said, 'Okay, I'll talk to her. What's the name of her favorite doll?' So, then I start talking. Maybe her little doll was sad because she was not seeing much. The girl started to laugh."

"To work with children, I prepare the parents. I like to see people living with glasses not out of need, not as a consumable, but because they are magical. They let us see. I tell the kids, 'Will you want to play football? Do you want to fly an airplane? Will you be able?' Pretty soon, they get the idea: they need glasses."

Different customers, Giannini finds, require different psychological frames as well as physical ones. "As to women, I have to find a way to break down resistance, particularly for young ladies. So, I say, 'We're going to play with something really eccentric. What would you want to *happen* when you put on glasses? Who's watching? How can you be sassy, a little crazy?'

"Perhaps the woman is not receiving the attention she desires? Perhaps the man wants to wake up to fashion? I always have to pay close attention to who's with the client: Sometimes you have to persuade the escort rather than the wearer. Women are easier, because they show who they are. Men are harder; they don't always show themselves. To the lawyers and executives I work with, I am a joking child." Miguel leaves to seek out frames for my new glasses.

The little boy has gotten over his glasses panic; his father now rubs his arm gently. The serious, quiet technicians around them take little notice as they work on their large machines.

Miguel reappears with a tray holding a dozen frames. In his own shop, Giannini gets to pick the frames; you choose and he critiques, like the optical fashionista he is. There's a gray titanium pair so light I could toss them in the air with a pinky: trendy. A pair of horn-rims flickers between yellow and brown.

"I like this one. You know, in the old days, people seeking glasses went to the doctor, and he simply put a pair on their face. There was not the slightest concern in working with self-esteem, or how the glasses helped you look. Not right."

"I carry all of the fancy brands, but when we sit down here, eye to eye, it's how you see that's important. I don't even tell you the name of the frame or its cost," he says, hands shuffling through his frames like a Las Vegas croupier. "You can't buy glasses the way you buy onions and potatoes."

A frame selected, I sit before the first in Giannini's series of optical tools, like stations of the ocular cross. Back home, my old-school optometrist uses a ruler to measure pupillary distance, the distance between the centers of your eyes. In Sao Paulo, Giannini uses a machine the size of a small closet. It takes pictures of the person and the frame from multiple angles, to measure the pupil's precise center. Without a correct pupillary distance, eyes in glasses will not focus cleanly.

Then I'm on to the next station, a tall machine boasting wide, white metal arms with lights at their edges. This device measures the pantoscopic tilt, or how the lens is positioned in front of the patient's visual axis. For those with high correction, mistaking pantoscopic tilt can create blur or an eye ache, as uncomfortable as a couch without cushions. (This is particularly important in wearing progressive lenses.) I'm told to hold my head steady and move my eyeballs from side to side, following the timed lights as they blink. I find this exhilarating, like shooting at targets at a carnival.

Finally, Giannini and I sit at a desk with a magnifying mirror and go over the printout. "Glasses, we'll always be wearing them," Miguel insists as I leave a few minutes later. "For protection from the sun, after surgery. As we age, our eyes need help. After people wear glasses for 20 to 30 years, they become part of them. They'll be glasses, far into the future." Listening to this glasses-preacher, I believe him. I later send him a case of Bordeaux for the pair.

* * *

Leaving Sao Paulo, I gamely follow my new frame to Zeiss Glass Works in Germany, located near the Swiss border in the green, hilly state of Baden-Württemberg. A long way for a pair of glasses. Worth it? Tell me the price of sight.

My determination to come to this Alpine corner began with my interview with David Salk back in Berkeley. There, I quizzed Salk closely on where could I find the latest technology in lenses.

"Well, one newish technology (for progressive lenses) is called 'freeform' digital lenses. This means we're no longer locked into grinding the lens so it has the same prescription throughout."

In multi-focal, progressive lenses, Salk explains, the best sight is at the center of the lens, a sweet spot sometimes as small as a dime. Looking out toward the side of the lens, sharpness of focus declines. Inventors got together and said, "What if we could grind lenses so we could compensate for that?" Today's best glasses use these digital freeform lenses, ones ground so that no matter what direction you look, your vision is as good as at the center.

"Are these lenses expensive? Yes. Those lenses can cost upwards of $800 depending on the lens material, coatings, and whether they transition [turn dark]."

"Do freeform lenses really make a difference?" I ask.

"It depends on your prescription. With a very mild prescription, freeform lenses are not going to be a big 'wow.' But for people with high corrections, and astigmatics who've been plagued with limited peripheral vision their entire lives? Give them digitally compensated lenses, and they say, 'Whoa, this is amazing.'" Since that talk, I've tried looking out the edges of my lenses. Sight really does drop off when my eyes veer away from the center of the lens. He's convinced me. I want a pair and to watch some being made at Zeiss.

Arriving at the headquarters of one of the largest lens makers in the world sounds dramatic. Instead, visiting the hilly town of Oberkochen is more like walking onto the set of *The Sound of Music*. In the place of cowbells and the cherubic Trapp family, Zeiss's shiny high rise is the only peak. No lens-loving tourists arrive this mild spring day; only robins hopping along the grass near Zeiss's entrance, and they don't need glasses to find worms. After touring the 200-year-old business and a sit-down with the director, I'm sent off to Zeiss's Glass Works in nearby Aalen. Gerhard Kelch, the dapper-looking technical supervisor, takes me straight to their lab to double-check my prescription.

The Refraction Room, 20' × 14', is divided into two. In the back is Glasses Past: the traditional way of measuring vision, with eye charts and a machine holding test lenses. The front of the room has something more contemporary: an I-Profiler, or autorefractor, a gray box about 2' long and 2½' wide. One side is a terminal with a touch screen and a small joystick. On the other side sits the patient. He or she looks into the device. The machine sends a waveform to the eye and measures its reflection at different angles. The operator charts exactly how that light wave passes through the patient's eyeball, in less than thirty seconds.

On the sixteen-page color printout that results, my eyes shine like green marbles with glowing yellow centers at my pupils. Machine measurement offers serious advantages: when a patient can't speak at all, or speaks a different language from the optical provider, there's no other way to be precise. The optometrist here is a smartly dressed woman in her thirties. Marion Cookfell was trained to work old-style, with the Snellen eye chart, a process called subjective refraction. "This way is faster; but the old way's not wrong," she assures me. "We do it both ways and cross-check the results."

Anyone who's had an eye exam knows the drill: Sitting in a darkened room, you read letters off the chart, which diminish in size as you read down. You look at red and green slides to check for color blindness, and then the optometrist scans your retina with a too-bright light. Then comes the frightening-looking machine with the test lenses and dials. "Better or worse?" "A or B?" "This one, or *this* one?" Each time, the optometrist adjusts the correction by a quarter-diopter. (The I-Profiler, by contrast, measures refraction to one one-hundredth of a diopter.) This checking and rechecking should make my new pair of lenses more precise.

Next, we walk downstairs to the factory, an open, three-story assembly line without workers. Lens manufacturing has changed dramatically from the days when an artisan chipped away at a block of glass. Lenses used to be ground similarly to throwing a pot: The inside curve was carved from a glass block on a spinning wheel turned by a foot-operated treadle. Eventually, artisans figured out how to hold a lens blank against a rotating tool instead, and an operator would swing a metal arm along a piece of glass to grind the front or back surface of the lens; for astigmatism, they would take another tool.

That was long ago. Today, most lenses are made of acetate or polycarbonate rather than glass. Manual labor has largely disappeared, except in artisanal shops. Today's lenses are manufactured using tiny scribing tools that chatter away at a lens, using software to surface a lens precisely.

At Zeiss, hundreds of colored trays zip by us on a conveyor belt, each with a pair of lenses and a small computer chip whose prescription is then carved. The cutting tools sound like a giant sewing machine. Trays pass like model trains. Here, the trains run all night. Then, inside a closed vat the size of an industrial-strength popcorn popper, lenses are polished.

"If somebody wants something very rare, with a very high power or a very high cylinder [for astigmatism], we use this device," Kelch says, pointing to a metallic table. "It's old. The blank is put in here, and there's a grinding wheel that swivels along the backside of the lens. We want to help people. If modern devices reach their limit, we will try our best manually. And there are specially trained people around here who can operate this."

At the next stop, lenses are heat-tempered to 170 degrees. A few then continue to the tinting department—blue, green, brown, yellow. Their submersion in the dye vat is timed to the second. Opticians can specify an exact color and send a sample, which is then scanned and hand-dyed by women. "It's all women here because they have a very specific vision for that, better able to distinguish subtle colors," Kelch explains. The ladies dip the lenses like very expensive Easter eggs.

My day's done here, machines clanking behind me as I leave. While frames must be chosen subjectively, I've learned that lenses can be mass-produced with exactitude. I'm looking forward to mine.

* * *

Returning to the United States, I am carefully fitted for my new pair in Berkeley by David Salk, who double-checks Giannini's frame measurements with the prescription from Germany. The pair with my complex Rx has cost me $1,100, more than I've ever paid.

Despite inflation and large industry monopolies, there's good news about eyewear pricing. Alternatives exist: There's a sizable universe of independent frame and sunglasses manufacturers, plus Hoya, Younger, Zenni, and private-label lenses offered only to independent wholesalers and retailers. Consumers can now even create their own frames in 3D printers. With increased automation in manufacturing, auto-refractors, and visual exams done on smartphones, costs of producing and fitting eyewear will come down, and choice will increase. In 2020, *Consumer Reports* found that 57 percent of glasses wearers buy visual aids from big-box stores and optical chains; 26 percent from optometrists, and less than 20 percent online or from independent opticians. The magazine recommends buyers choose a priority: either convenience, service, selection, or rock-bottom prices. Consumers may also want to consider splitting an order (by, say, buying frames online, lenses at a chain store, and paying separately for a professional fitting). They suggest avoiding frames one can't try on.[12]

Complaints about eyewear prices rile some opticians. After all, people wear a pair of glasses, on average, for two and a half years, they say. At an optician, the average price for a pair of prescription glasses in the United States was $270 in 2020 (today it's closer to $350). Compare that to how much people pay for their smartphones, which most American consumers replace with roughly equal frequency.[13] Perhaps if they valued eyeglasses and clear vision the same way they value connectivity to social media, they would complain less.

"Goddammit, it's because people don't believe glasses are worth it," says optician Mark Mattison-Shupnick. "So, if they don't believe glasses are worth it, go buy them on the internet, or go buy them for $69 or $49, and you'll get some kind of glasses. You've made a choice, guy."

"For opticians, if you want to just make a profit without delivering on behalf of the patient, that customer? Then too bad. [That optician's] at risk. If you're not using the latest material and technology; if you're not going to every class, so you can to understand how to do your craft better; if you're not advocating for and proselytizing about how good eyewear is and all the magical things it can do, then don't complain that some giant company is eating your lunch. Because you're not doing your part."

"Now, you may find that it's impossible to compete, and I don't agree that that should happen. I don't like the monopolizing of the business by Essilor-Luxottica, and I've worked for both those companies at some point in my life. I don't agree with this, but it's business."

Buying glasses has become complicated, and both buyers and sellers have to keep up. New technologies promise a future when glasses will have way more bells and whistles; they may even be augmented with built-in computers capable of doing everything from displaying emails in a corner of your view to checking a bank balance (no ATMs on the frames, yet). "Apple, Meta, Microsoft, and Snap are steering toward a future in which we'll wear computers on our heads for interactions and fuse physical and digital life," wrote Shira Ovide in the *New York Times* in 2022.[14] Knowing what's around the corner for the next generation of visual aids is critical. For example, we now have glasses for the hard-of-hearing. At least two companies manufacture pairs with microphones to overlay real-time transcriptions of conversations on lenses.[15]

Back in Berkeley, I put on my new freeform glasses and step outside. Instantly, my field of vision opens. My sight at the edge of the lens is nearly the same as looking ahead. People who don't use bi- or trifocals won't see this difference, because their lens is the same all across its surface. But for someone in progressive lenses—where the lens is graded from top to bottom, far to near distances—the difference can be quietly dramatic, even startling. Rolling my eye left or right, up or down, I find everything is in focus.

Even though I know it's only optical glass (increasingly hard to find though said to produce sharper images), something's changed. It feels like my eyes have gone to the gym for toning and stretched my vision 20 percent wider. It's like the difference between watching a movie in my living room and watching one in a theater. In fact, I'm thinking about going to a movie theater right now.

Walking down the street, I try to see a panorama by moving my eyes instead of my neck. (Good thing no one's walking behind me.) Better, much better. I glance around, reading signs through the side of the lens. I've been given a visual bonus. I'm not sure if people are staring at me as my eyes slide from side to side, I don't care. It's my new fix.

* * *

Did I fulfill that hunger to see as well as possible? Yes, insofar as my vision can be corrected. Was the journey worth it? Yes, because sight is my second-most important sense. (I work in public radio.) Safety also comes into this. With sharper side vision, I might notice a cyclist beside me as I drive, or a car door opening as I cycle, thereby avoiding an accident. Still, taking a trip like this one certainly reveals my privilege.

What does it say about the world economy that we have promoted glasses to become a fashion and status symbol rather than a critical medical aid? Think of those Xingu tribesmen in the Amazon, for whom glasses brought home the catch. How many millions of the world's people could live improved lives if they could afford a well-made, customized pair of glasses?

What's next for visual aids, and what will glassers wear in the future? The answer is complicated. Fascinating, almost unimaginable, developments wait on the horizon, but at what cost to privacy? Smart glasses and smart contacts, discussed next, will allow streaming everything with cameras and microphones on faces. Whether that's worth it to have private lives on public display will be hard to sum.

10

Glasses Tomorrow
AR, VR, and Beyond

Now we see through a glass darkly, but then face to face . . . then shall I know even as I am known.

—1 CORINTHIANS 13:12

The impulse to immerse ourselves in another world visually is centuries old. In the next pages, I present what might happen next to eyeglasses. The short version is that most of us will likely be wearing a dramatically new version in the next decades—maybe even those not needing vision correction. We may, however, live to regret the change. "I'm a camera. A mechanical eye," wrote pioneering filmmaker Dziga Vertov a century ago. Could that be our future as a species?

In the 1700s, painters created theatrical backdrops and 360-degree murals to surround viewers. In 1838, the first stereoscope used tiny mirrors to simulate binocular vision. In the twentieth century, Virtual Reality (VR) surfaced first in print: *Pygmalion's Glasses* (1930), by Stanley Weinbaum, presented a virtual-reality concept. "Suppose I make it so you are in the story," the science-fiction author wrote. "You speak to the shadows, and the shadows reply, and instead of being on a screen, the story is all about you, and you are in it. Would that make real a dream?" An excellent question: but how? The hero of that prescient story, Professor Ludwig, manages this with a device vaguely reminiscent of a gas mask with goggles and a rubber mouthpiece.[1] In 1932, the "Feelies" of Aldous Huxley's *Brave New World* had moviegoers pressing their palms on a metal knob to add the illusion of touch to their visual perceptions. (Later novels, like *Counterfeit World* (1964), *Neuromancer* (1984), and *Snow Crash* (1992) would offer characters actual VR sets.)

1939 debuted the "View Master" stereo viewing system, which used images on slides to simulate 3D vision; it's still used today. Starting in the 1940s, simulators helped train pilots and soldiers; by 1956, one could sit in a cabinet to watch a film and simultaneously experience vibration, smell, and sound with a device called "Sensorama." (Sensorama was abandoned when the developers couldn't prevent the smell of one scene from blending disagreeably into the next. (Odors of the barnyard in one scene, for example, hovered over a virtual nightclub in the next.)

In the following decade, devices like the "Telesphere" (1960) or the "Headset" (1961) were first-generation head-mounted displays, a precursor to today's VR. Their goal was total viewer immersion, dissolving reality not through the creation of a trancelike state but by substituting one reality for another, dreamier one—a dream, we shall see, that could become a nightmare.

"See me, feel me, touch me" sang the Who in the rock opera *Tommy*, and young engineers were listening while designing products like 1968's Sword of Damocles (perhaps the first AR device connected to a computer), which hung above the user on thick cables. NASA's VIEW device, in the 1980s, added haptic (touch) feedback. Soon after, the computer scientist Jaron Lanier credited with coining the term "virtual reality," wielded "datagloves," for touch and arcades fired up multiplayer VR games. The development of Nintendo's Virtual Boy console and PlayStation VR in the mid-1990s suggested the primary audience for VR would be gamers. Popular science-fiction films of the era took up VR in *Star Trek* (1979), where the Geordie La Farge character wore VISOR smart glasses, *Lawnmower Man* (1992), *Johnny Mnemonic* (1995), and *Strange Days* (1995).

To create twenty-first-century VR glasses, mobile computing devices had to evolve to become faster, smaller, and more powerful, with dramatically larger memory. High-definition displays, facial-recognition software, and 3D graphics had to combine to create realistic images one could seemingly touch. Eye tracking and sensors with artificial intelligence then allowed tiny binocular cameras to capture surroundings, assess the user's location, and project all this back onto a pair of lenses. Combined laser and radar (LiDAR) allowed accurate measurement of the user's surrounding space. Advances in motion control added ring or hand-held controllers. Finally, humanity could sink completely into their fantasies.

Google Glass, the first widely distributed smart glasses, required users to touch the frame. However, later, voice-recognition software and gesture-controlled units became stand-alone, rather than tethered to phones. Finally, headsets developed from bearing a resemblance to Darth Vader's mask into futuristic ones undetectable except for slightly thicker-than-normal frames.

* * *

Smart glasses already offer incredible features: lenses which adjust manually or with an electric charge to change their refractive power; glasses that whisper messages or subtitle printed text; facial-recognition ones for use by police and the hard of sight; glasses to restore vision to those losing it from macular degeneration and glaucoma;[2] glasses with built-in hearing aids. Their future offers even more, as discussed in the next chapter. To learn how the optical profession anticipates its future, I visited Las Vegas for the Vision-Expo West, a bazaar for everything optical.

In the Capital City of Bad Conferences, tens of thousands of optical professionals ogle the newest frames and receive continuing education credit to keep up with industry changes. The consolidation of the largest frame maker and the world's largest lens maker has brought technical innovation and, with it, vast changes to the field. Auto-refractors are gradually de-skilling the optical professions, while phones permit at-home eye exams and measure pupillary distance. Optometrists and opticians worry such technology could undermine personal relationships with patients, which eyecare professionals cherish. Still, the technology hasn't been perfected yet, and until it is, human expertise matters. "When a client comes in who has been at garbagecanoptical.com," one speaker says, "I sit down with them. We talk about pantascopic tilt, face-forms definition [wrap angle, the distance between eye and lens], vertex, pupillary distance, the optical corridor needed for progressives—all the things we measure to give them the pair they need. They get it. None of this comes online." Old-fashioned, un-smart glasses will still be sold by many here; but they'll need to know what's around the corner by training those providing next-generation eyewear. For those providing glasses, it's hard enough today to find top optical labs and the best-trained opticians. In the near future, glasses providers will need computer training and a grounding in vision engineering. Otherwise, they may be great at fitting glasses and contacts but fail to understand (and explain) complex new functions.

Though not obvious at Vision Expo West, the future of eyewear is poking through like grass in cracks in the cement. The task for providers of multifocal contacts (like progressive lenses) is to help Boomers' aging eyes and suggest the next generation of contacts, with super-miniature cameras; and embedded circuits thinner than a human hair, which will gather energy to power them from blinking or eyeball movements. One manufacturer hopes to patent robotic contacts that zoom in or out with blinks of an eye.[3]

* * *

Let's break down this complex technological landscape from the beginning. Smart glasses are "smart" because they're computer- and phone-enabled. They mainly come in three kinds: Augmented Reality (AR), Mixed Reality (MR), and Virtual Reality (VR). (Collectively, these three constitute Extended Reality (XR), though the definition of these terms vary.)[4]

Augmented reality smart glasses overlay a transplant computer-generated hologram on your lenses or funnel images directly to the retina. They do this by using minicameras to survey surroundings and pea-sized projectors using "wave guides" to shoot these images to the inside of a glasses lens, which then uses tiny mirrors to reflect the images back to the eyes. The wide-angle lenses, processors, and holographic projectors increasingly fit into something like a standard-sized eyeglass temple, currently paired with a smartphone to enhance capabilities. A hologram on glasses could lay a schematic over an engine or overlay instructions to help assemble furniture. Once they are lighter and brighter, AR glasses can be worn all day; they don't block sight or interfere with movement. Because they don't block out light, there's less nausea (also less immersion) than with VR glasses.

Like augmented reality, Mixed Reality smart glasses also superimpose a hologram over your surroundings, but their crucial difference is in merging real and virtual worlds and allowing you to interact with what you see, rather than just having an image suspended in front of you. Like AR ones, MR glasses merge real and virtual worlds into hyperreality—the so-called metaverse, where physical and virtual worlds interact in real time. MR smart glasses let you not only see around you but interact with both real (physical) and created (digital) images. You could still look at that swing set in the backyard, but might overlay the image of an old friend sitting on it. Viewing a chessboard might offer an animation of a knight attacking a castle on the chess board. In theory, MR glasses could help you monitor calories by updating as your lunch plate empties. MR headsets, though, are less likely to be standalone (unattached to a computer or phone) than AR glasses, at least for now.

Virtual Reality glasses, unlike their AR and MR counterparts, transport you to a new, 360-degree-view, bringing immersive reality while largely obscuring physical sight. Inside a headset, new figures and landscapes, digitally created, surround you, allowing interaction using controllers. (Manufacturers are currently experimenting with blending what's real and what's digital in VR. Apple Vision Pro's "immersion control," for example, has a "reality dial" to allow users effective pass-through vision from front-facing cameras to see what's actually surrounding them.) To others, it looks like a brick of plastic swallowed your face.

Virtual Reality glasses plunge you into a fantasy, a video game, or a created scene. By being more immersive than AR or MR, Virtual Reality glasses have a significantly different aim. Instead of touring the neighborhood on a bike, it's like hopping on a tricked-out tour bus. Your VR set can bring you a video brochure from a travel agent or open a door to a place vastly different from your surroundings. Once in a headset, you arrive instantly—whether on a cruise or in a nightmare (or both). They're a vacation hanging on your nose, therapy without the couch. Wearing current models all day, though, might turn you into a dried-up radish and leave you feeling like you've been sitting in a prison cell on a pitching ship. In the future, VR may be embedded into normal-looking frames, but current VR headsets' weight become a pain in the neck.[5]

Many users first experimented with VR by sliding a smartphone into a frame, such as Google Cardboard or Samsung Gear. A video then opened around them in 3D. This is passive VR, in which you're simply along for the ride—observing a VR designers' fantasy world, where people appear to walk toward, by, or through you. By contrast, in interactive VR, this environment responds and reacts to you. As you navigate, virtual characters may react, such as stepping aside to let you pass. Managing interactive VR can be simple, such as staring at an icon to open an application. Or it can be complicated, with hand or ring controllers imitating touch and body tracking in your virtual environment.[6] AR glasses are like working with a hologrammed personal assistant. VR headsets are like walking into someone else's dream. AR is your friend walking you home after school. VR is his older brother sneaking you a beer to convince you that you can fly.

The number of applications for smart glasses of all kinds is exploding. Surgeons can operate while streaming images to a medical school classroom. Skiers can use head-mounted displays to monitor speed, elevation, and weather. Hunters can wear AR glasses to factor in wind speed when taking aim; soldiers with infrared glasses can find concealed attackers using a helmet display. These are current though not widespread uses, but before smart glasses widely appear in the workplace, engineers must debug them further. In a small 2019 study, not only didn't AR glasses assist wearers with precision tasks in a factory, but they made them so overconfident they didn't notice their errors.[7]

The smart glasses currently on sale are rudimentary compared to what's coming. AR devices may wait till 2030 before full functionality. "Making AR glasses is harder than VR pairs," said Mark Zuckerberg of Meta; "we need to fit a supercomputer into a pair of normal-looking glasses."[8] So far, batteries for smart glasses can't hold a long charge and projected images aren't necessarily sharp. Nonetheless, Meta's Ray-Ban smart glasses are hot consumer items, selling a million units in 2024.

At best, smart glasses may become a tool for social good, helping builders, firefighters, and others who need hands-free assistance. AI-compatible smart glasses could let travelers remember details of a trip or help an Alzheimer's patient find his way home. (They might even help find your keys.) At worst, smart glasses may someday reveal a lot more about you than you'd like.

The acceleration in human-computer interaction that led to smart glasses occurred as people got used to talking to computer assistant cylinders, like Google Nest or Amazon's Echo. In The Internet of Things (IOT), Wi-Fi has connected smart devices. The fridge might sigh that you're out of milk (again!). Or the Fitbit might bark, urging you out for a run. Now imagine having those same interactions with technology—but directly in your face. It's enough to make one take off glasses—or refuse to put them on in the first place.

In the *Atlantic*, James Fallows categorized smart glasses as the equivalent of the plow or the steam engine, "tools that freed people from routine chores."[9] But this raises the now-no-longer-science-fictional issue of how humans will withstand virtual assaults on our train of thought from all-seeing smart glasses. No one's tractor ever halted in the middle of a field to show them an ad. It's one thing to receive political ads on social media as we scroll through. It's quite another to have an ad for a fat tube of toothpaste fluttering before our eyes when we brush our teeth. "It's like writing on the brain with indelible ink," as one technology reporter commented.[10]

With smart glasses, businesses are ready to push ads not just toward your eyes but even *inside* your eyes, piped directly into your retina. Product placement is on the way. Consumer-viewers might soon walk into a virtual bar and be served the brand advertising there. In VR, wearers could sit on a chair with a price tag showing, turning smart glasses into a "buy-at-once" convenience store. Wearing smart glasses for shopping differs from using a computer-enhanced watch: removing a watch is easy; taking off prescription glasses, less so, and their bulky cases don't slip into a pocket. Meta, for one, has bet that the distance between smart glasses and traditional ones will collapse, taking a minority stake in Essilor-Luxottica.

Eyewear of the future may be a major step in human-computer interaction. For centuries, we have compensated for human frailty: we wear knee braces to shore up weak ligaments. We have slings for broken arms, crutches for walking—and, of course, contacts, eyeglasses, and smart glasses for sight. Eyeglasses are both an extension of the body—in the way Marshall McLuhan said the hammer is an extension of the hand—and a prothesis, replacing a non-working (or unsatisfactory) body part.

Health care will be a crucial part of smart eyewear. Already, a frame's been patented that would change from green to red in case of a retinal detachment and send an alert to an ophthalmologist via a smartphone. Glasses may be able to test for cataracts and glaucoma, like having a medical lab on your face. For those with limited sight, there's Vision and Ocutrx companies developing smart glasses to project an image onto the still-usable parts of a low-vision patient's retina.[11] A psychotherapist uses smart glasses to position someone virtually on the roof of a skyscraper to help them overcome their fear of heights. One researcher found that when people with a fear of flying were taken on a VR trip on a virtual plane, 90 percent of users recovered from their fear.[12] Or, consider the expression "your life flashing before your eyes." Smart glasses could, in the future, allow one to rewind images glasses recorded—a home movie of everything seen since you put them on (including the R-, and X-rated parts?) If you find all this preposterous, consider all the Extended Reality applications already in development, albeit some only as vaporware or patents. (Google and Verily, for example, patented a smart contact to measure glucose levels, but ultimately abandoned it due to challenges with accuracy.)

It could be that smart glasses, once perfected, become the first wearable computer most use: zooming in on objects with a finger tap; detecting blood vessels under the skin; tracking a home remodel remotely[13] Yet new technologies bring new dilemmas. Hi-tech smart eyewear could further divide the population along class lines: The poor will struggle to afford them, their add-ons, and subscriptions. The well-off will order theirs with extra features the way they added jewels to frames to stand out when glasses were first sold. It would be creepy if someone could check your credit or marital status on their smart glasses, and worse if this led to mistaken identity, as has already happened.[14] Since so much information about us is already available online, what's to prevent a company from aggregating and then displaying it on smart glasses? (As will be discussed later, a company already has, on a massive scale.)

Will smart glasses with cameras (not all models have them) reshape our public sphere into a goldfish bowl by introducing a world of crowdsourced surveillance? Wearable devices like smart glasses could create a society where every public moment can be shared, documented, and data-mined.[15] On phones today with earpieces in, people already seem to be talking to themselves. Soon, your glasses will do the listening, and record what you hear and see. In self-defense, we may end up buying smart glasses simply to learn who that guy is in the corner, eyeing us intently with his glasses.

I'm unsure if I'd walk around in these glasses. I am sure that I'm not looking forward to others wearing them around me, without an airtight guarantee of not being filmed and streamed. But how could society enforce such a ban? We can't even pry away people's AR-15 guns, despite the fact that in 2019, an Ohio man used one to kill nine people in 32 seconds. How much harder will it be to limit an innocent-looking pair of glasses from holding more information on you than your health insurer and credit-card company combined? The centuries-old antagonism to eyewear might continue in new forms as some resist using these "Inspectacles."

Many in the future will want only the visual correction their optometrists provide currently. Yet, smart glasses could reel in many converts. Consider entertainment: Today, we stream movies and videos on multiple devices. The screens sit before us, flat and bright. Images turn and dance. But what if instead of watching with VR glasses, we could step boldly into a dance scene in a movie and do-si-do? Such glasses might become like the "Holodeck" of *Star Trek*, with characters and sounds surrounding and interacting with us. Some of us may yearn to wander there forever.[16]

* * *

Over breakfast at a coffee shop at VisionExpo West, I again ran into David Salk, tired after nonstop meetings. He raised concerns about if VR glasses might harm the eyes. "When the light source is that close to your eyes," he asks, "will it bring macular degeneration?"

"We're gambling on what this smart-glass technology will do. To what extent will companies be responsible for potential health damages?" he asked. "We have the example of tobacco, of opioids. From tobacco companies we heard, 'It's okay to smoke now and then; don't smoke a whole pack at once.' We know where that led. Will these companies care about health effects [of smart contacts and smart glasses] when they are selling millions of units at once?"

Salk confessed he'd just bought a sweeping device: "I'm going to use it everywhere and ask the new question: 'Do you have another pair you could put on?' Someone is trying to record me with their glasses."

The world is dangerous enough now, with people driving or crossing streets glued to their cellphones. What if, in smart glasses, wearers accidentally step in front of cars while watching a movie? (Already people are rumored to have fallen off cliffs while taking a selfie.) Every technology has trade-offs, but it's unclear if consumer regulators will sound the alarm. Whether as a party game, training exercise, or the medium for everything visual from museum exhibits to pornography, smart glasses and smart contacts will play a role in our future—even for those not now wearing vision aids.

* * *

Mention "smart glasses," and people think of Google Glass. Whatever happened to that? They became a case study in resistance to adopting smart glasses.

In 2012, Glass put cameras on glasses and released them into the wild. Each had a touchpad on the frame, a microphone, and later, prescription options. It displayed and sent audio via a speaker that vibrated behind the ear. A small, cyclops-like camera squatted on a metal headband. With much fanfare, Google delivered prototypes to testers whom it dubbed "Glass Explorers." At first, Glass seemed wonderfully futuristic. Then trouble began.

It wasn't supposed to happen this way. Google cofounder Sergei Brin had overruled his engineers, who didn't want a public rollout, and leaned into heavy promotion. Instead of undergoing a quiet period of beta testing, the device appeared in fashion shows and on skydivers. *Time* touted it as "one of the best inventions of the year." Celebrities wore Glass. *The Simpsons* featured them as "Ogg Goggles."

Google expected Glass users to be heralded as ambassadors for technology's leading edge. Instead, they found themselves thrown out of bars. The way people (and the police) used Glass for surreptitious recording scared the public. Resistance spread; legal problems proliferated. The occasional bar fight broke out. Even the reviews were poor: *Consumer Reports* testers found Glass's display heavy, "goofy looking," and "more than a bit creepy."[17] CR's review panel asked the usual questions: Is the device comfortable? Does it take decent photos? Will it get our testers punched in the face? (Okay, that one's not so usual.) A *New Yorker* reporter experienced dizziness, visual confusion, and a wincing headache when starting on smart glasses.[18] (At least no one called him a "glasshole," a term later circulating.)

The more Google Glass went out in public, the worse things got. Countries declared them illegal under anti-spying laws. Movie theaters banned them to prevent bootlegging. University of Massachusetts scientists demonstrated how Glass could capture passwords by filming finger shadows as people tapped numbers on their phones. Worse, a hacker could potentially record passwords reflected in your glasses. Should this happen, wearers would become unwitting cameras and microphones, all trackable through GPS. (These privacy threats are not theoretical; only fourteen years after Glass's debut, Chinese police use similar pairs to scan crowds for fugitives.)[19]

People will have to outsmart their smart glasses. Widespread use may push the limits of what's public. What is a reasonable expectation of privacy in a public space where everyone is exposed to others? What about in a car? On a porch, facing the street? What about in spaces in the home where people interact, from activities in our kitchen to those in the bedroom? Though not illegal, one rarely sees people walking about in pajamas or underwear. We collectively abide by culturally determined norms of what's private, and that's what Google Glass violated. Like Martin Luther nailing his treatises to a church door, technology columnist Edward Champion came up with thirty-five arguments against Google Glass.[20] Among these was the threat that images uploaded from Glass risked being hacked, tagged, reviewed, indexed, and stored without the user knowing. And who owns images recorded by Glass or later devices—you or Google?[21] In the future, keeping *anything* private could prove difficult and costly.

Further, Champion pointed out that if someone left smart glasses by the bed and these were hacked, this might allow for online "sextortion," creating a situation similar to the way South Korean teenagers hesitate to date for fear of being videoed in an intimate moment.[22] Data collected by smart glasses could reveal hidden health conditions, imperiling one's health insurance. Finally, by overlaying information over what we see, smart glasses inevitably distract us. A stream of email and phone alerts will be harder to overlook when right before our eyes.

This analysis overlooked the device's potential advantages: reminders about when to take medicine, assistance to the differently abled, and much more. Such uses fell under the tree that hit Google Glass. In 2015, the initial model of Glass was withdrawn. To some, it was a monster who wouldn't die: When a new version appeared, it had software that snapped photos when you winked, disconcerting a *New York Times* reporter at a urinal. Surrounded by Glass wearers, he wondered if the guy next to him was "winking" at him or only blinking.[23]

In the end, Glass, the awkward godfather of wearable visual technology, "dampened customers' enthusiasm for smart eyewear," according to *20/20* magazine's new technology editor.[24] Google Glass almost set back smart glasses for a generation.

Despite this, since 2015, VR and AR headsets have arrived by the dozens on the consumer market, such as the Vive, Quest, Gear, Norm, N Real, Magic Leap, Go, PlayStation VR, Focals, Vusix, and many more.[25] Initially, customers were few: By the end of 2017, Oculus estimated sales of only several hundred thousand Rifts, disappointing analysts. (But a decade later, with Meta's low-priced Quest 3S and AR Ray-Bans, this number had risen to 10 million.)[26]

Before my glasses sabbatical, I already knew VR's advantages—the joyride into a different world, zooming around, fighting dramatic battles, dodging incoming objects. I'd watched testers staggering as they pulled off their headsets to reenter real reality. Hiding in this cardboard box was either danger or pleasure.

The first thing I noticed when I pried it open was, of course, another box. This held a forward-facing, white plastic headset through which you could see images in front of you with lens inserts. Alongside were two black-and-white hand controllers and a page of instructions.

The package also had disclosures: against using the Quest if pregnant, elderly, possessing mental disorders or a heart condition. Not for children, it proclaimed. If lack of balance and coordination persists, talk to your doctor. Don't wear with a pacemaker or hearing aid. Avoid collisions, trips, and falls, hazards like pets, stairs, and overhead objects or people. Flashes in the software may trigger seizures, severe dizziness, eye-twitching, or a complete blackout. (Was this device supposed to be *fun*?) Plastic covers removed, QR code scanned, I was finally ready—but no, first I had to charge the headset. I went to lie down in the hammock and lamented the end of printed instructions.

* * *

A far more upbeat experience was on offer at the Consumer Electronics Show, which brought me back to Las Vegas. You don't drift into CES: You are carried like a leaf in a current by crowds of more than 180,000 attendees. Here, entertainment is king. One booth advertised VR glasses that showed images equivalent in size to the display on a 200-foot screen. The demonstrators talked excitedly about new ways to watch films, but I kept imagining an email as wide as a plane from a mother-in-law.

A demonstrator saw me exiting a smart glasses booth and said, "Whoa, give this a try! After those heavy glasses, your neck needs a massage!" He pointed out an ordinary-looking recliner—only with this chair, a machine rolled padded bars of steel across your locked-in anatomy. I get why they call this a massage chair: After you sat there for a few minutes, you needed a massage. When I bailed on that, the salesman suggested I try the Wiggler instead. I stood on a metal device that rocks and rolls to its own rhythm, the idea being to wiggle pounds away. Instead, it felt like I was being rhythmically kicked from below my feet. In place of "shaking your way to weight loss," as the sign read, I watched stomachs shake like Jell-O™ fresh out of the mold.

Happily, the Wiggler wasn't the only physical exercise offered. The typical game player wearing Pico VR glasses (smaller in size than headsets) danced to an unheard tune and dodged invisible obstacles. No couch potatoes these: they looked like someone trying to break dance for the first time, throwing arms around, ducking and jumping as if an insect had climbed up their pants.

Nearby, the Mad Gaze booth demonstrated AR glasses. Their video showed potential uses: paired with a drone, one could look down at buildings and backyards (Peeping Toms will love this!) Calling up a 3D image and tossing off an email were a matter of simple hand gestures. Currently, this technology is used for video games; someday it might offer up a bordello with pink shades.

As I packed up, I noticed people stopping in front of the Hitachi Vision booth. A series of cameras and monitors captured your image, guessed your age (fairly accurately), and then added you to their database—a visual Venus flytrap, swallowing people's images. Behind me more people hunched over VR sets, leaning and punching or shooting at aliens. This begs the question: why are VR games so focused on destruction? Smart glasses were offering users the opportunity to do something new and exciting, never before seen in American culture: shoot people.

As I exited the hall, I was caught by the Hypervision demo: A life-size, holographic *maître d'* who could ask for your reservation, not find it, and ask you to wait while she shook (okay, wiggled) off to find her manager. In a corner, a pole dancer twerked, and nearby a pair of running shoes rotated slowly in a 3D holograph. I waved goodbye to the hostess, but she looked sightlessly past me to the unceasing crowd.

By the time you read this, manufacturers may well have found the elusive "killer app" that makes smart glasses and smart contacts useful, if not essential. Otherwise, as manufacturers have discovered, after a few weeks their glasses join other novelties gathering dust in closets.

* * *

Around the time of the CES, two business professors imagined how the widespread adoption of smart glasses technology might occur—what it would take to excite the public about Extended Reality. First, they decided, you'd rebrand smart glasses wearers: "Improve user image from 'glassholes' to fashionable and innovative consumers."[27] Next, society would have to solve privacy concerns—such as who owns what, and which data can be sold. Third, users will want a dash of hip design to shrink components.

* * *

One who helped me understand how current opticianry will fare in the smartglass era is Brian Wong, who chairs Opticianry at the Ben Franklin Institute of Technology in Boston. With twin master's degrees in optics and education and many professional honors, Wong has been called one of the most influential opticians in America. A short, curly-haired fellow who favors button-down shirts and speaks with a slight Boston brogue, might not stand out from hundreds of professors except in one way: he's blind.

He wasn't born that way. When Wong was twenty-six, and a trained optician, he went to meet friends at the movies. He arrived late, with the house lights down. And suddenly Wong realized he couldn't figure out where his friends had gone.

"How come you didn't follow us?" one asked later.

"I didn't see where you guys went."

"You couldn't see *anything* in there?"

Wong was diagnosed with *retinitis pigmentosa*, a progressive disease that starts by blocking vision at the periphery of the retina before encroaching on central vision. Today, he has no vision out of his left eye and only a speck, the diameter of a drinking straw, in the right. With this, he can read two or three letters at a time, no words. Wong's career as a clinical optician vanished with his sight. His mission now is to train students to help people see what he can't. His curriculum focuses on five critical responsibilities of opticians: to produce glasses that are safe, have the most comfortable fit, are aesthetically pleasing, meet the visual needs of the patient, and demonstrate optical precision. His students prompt him through his class outline.

Scientific innovation is already helping the blind dramatically. IRISVISION is a technology that uses smartphones, VR headsets, and algorithms to supplement visual function. The ORCAM My Eye Two uses AI to capture and voice digital text. It recognizes faces, gestures, and dollar bills. Vision aids like this would change Wong's work, but until then it remains a challenge: "You're sitting right across from me, and I have no idea what your face looks like, what you're wearing. I hope I'm looking at you the whole time. If I were advising someone like me, I would steer them in a different direction."

Wong said he doesn't see smart glasses technology and robotic dispensing as major threats to his profession. Portable autorefractors, for example, can correctly identify a patient's prescription, but they can't consider the use case for lens design: Is the patient on a computer all the time? Participate in outdoor activities? Play a musical instrument? Automated scanning devices will read a face's features but can't customize fit to a face, or check the appropriate curvature of the sidepieces and whether the frame is well-balanced to support its weight.

Such machines also lack the interpersonal skills of a Miguel Giannini helping a dubious six-year-old adjust to a new reality of a face with something hanging from it. The value of the emotional care opticians provide was brought home to Wong when, a month before our interview, Professor Wong discovered he was losing his hearing—the sense by which he navigated the sighted world.

* * *

The branding and hype at CES reminded me of two 2018 films that closely imagined virtual reality, *Ready Player One* and *Anon*. In the former, set in 2045, VR has definitely arrived. People dance by themselves in their apartment in VR glasses; a young girl's smart glasses let her play with an imaginary friend without taxing her imagination. In this film, VR has an all-purpose destination, the Oasis, where the limits of reality have dissolved. You can ski down the pyramids in Egypt, surf a fifty-foot wave in Hawaii, or climb Mount Everest with, for example, Bambi as a companion. "They come for all things they can do," the ads for the Oasis read, "but they stay for what they can be. And since we are all here, this is where we meet and make friends." It's VR all day long, except for eating, sleeping, and bathroom breaks. (Presumably, by 2045, no one has jobs.)

By contrast, Netflix's film *Anon* imagines life in the not-too-distant future when AR-like visual implants record everyone's lives, rewindable at will. Clothes show brand names and prices. People's name, age, and occupation appear above their heads; even more personal information floats nearby. Anonymity vanishes.

Naturally, in *Anon*, people want to edit what they've seen or lived through. They pay fixers to erase people and objects from their memories. It's not a pleasant world: People hack each other's eyes and must learn to move around with eyes closed. A brave few, the anonymous, show up on no one's radar. In the film's last line, one such person says: "It's not that I have something to hide. I have nothing I want you to see."

Such dystopian films have found a wide audience. Yet, just how plausible are these predictions of see-all, tell-all glasses? You could color these as wild-eyed fantasies, until you look closer.

On the afternoon of October 25, 2024, Kashif Hoda waited for a train at Harvard Square Station. A young man approached him for directions. Hoda noticed the man's "nerdy, thick-framed glasses," but thought little of it.[28] A few moments later, the man approached him again, to ask if he was the journalist who wrote about minority groups in India. Mr. Hoda was astonished. Only later did he learn he'd been an unwilling guinea pig in two Harvard engineering students' experiment. To rig up this scenario from *Anon* took the students only a month or so; their experiment combined existing smart glasses (Meta's AR Ray-Bans) which live-stream; added face-detection software: a face search engine that scans the internet for people's images; and an AI tool to collect data and cross-check it for occupation, address, phone number, and relatives.

Is this illegal? the students were asked. There's no federal law against it, apparently, though some states criminalize illicit recording. Mr. Hoda, it turns out, wouldn't have minded if asked. He later suggested that in the future, "privacy will be impossible."[29] But not everyone is so open to the idea. Having strangers pull your image away from your control is fundamentally dissociative. Disassociation is a disease—or, actually, several of them. The American Psychiatric Association recognizes dissociative amnesia; identity disorder; depersonalization disorder (when people experience their surroundings as unreal); and dissociative seizures triggered by, say, watching a violent video game in immersive technology.

When we disassociate, we forget who we are as individuals and as a society. With this disassociation comes a distrust of our experience and the inability to believe our eyes; we call this "seeing things." A person who reads a novel or watches a scene on a television or on a smartphone still has enough remove from the source to understand it as irreal. A two-hour session on VR, by contrast, may lodge us on a wholly different world. Even if we understand consciously that experience as artificially created, will our animal brains file it away in the same mental drawers as our genuine memories? Left behind in the real world could be the qualities that distinguish humanity as a species: concern for nature, empathy, mutual understanding. The tangibility and interactivity of VR surmount wearers, the way one mounts on a horse's back to ride. We hope we will be able to hop off at will, if only to tell if we're in someone else's dream or our own.

"Under your seats is a headset that will change the very nature of what it means to be human," chants a character in a VR experience from the company Wevr. "Under your seats is the end of your individuality. Put it on and you'll never want to take it off. Good luck."[30]

* * *

After considering such dire comments, I found something positive in the ways some used these technologies to connect during the pandemic with VR meet-ups. A doctoral student at the University of New Mexico assembled a network of friends, family, and colleagues who own VR headsets. They or their avatars socialized and shared virtual vacations to ease people's pandemic-driven anxiety and depression:

> We've been fishing, bowling, golfing, rock climbing, and traveling with people in VR. It's one thing to talk to a friend or family member over the phone, but another to be sitting near the base of El Capitan in Yosemite, experiencing the sights and sounds of a rolling river and gentle breeze, watching a black bear and her cubs walking on the opposite side of the river, and enjoying the tranquil setting with good company.[31]

One New Year's Eve, that graduate student explored VR social apps. That evening, he found himself at a large table with a selection of virtual hats, virtual foods (do they come with virtual calories?) and, virtual drinks (which may not get you drunk). He put on a virtual top hat, grabbed a digital martini and a sparkler, and walked over to a small, virtual bonfire. The creator of this virtual world clustered people along a virtual couch. As he was leaving, she addressed the guests. "She told us that she thought she was going to be alone for New Year's Eve and felt depressed. She thanked us for coming to her party; and that because of us and VR, she had stopped feeling alone."[32]

Epilogue
Three Years Later

"You have a choice: Which pair of eyes would you like?" the cataract surgeon asked.

Nobody ever offered me a choice like this. I was buying new eyes at the cost insurance would pay, but I had to choose how to see post-cataracts: nearsighted (one to two feet without glasses), at medium range (using bifocals for close or distance vision), or distance-only (for driving, also with bifocals). The newish, multifocal interocular lenses were not on offer. I chose to see close up, as I always did. I'm having a "combo," with two doctors working side by side: cataract surgery to clear my vision and a vitrectomy so floaters will disappear. Baby-boomer friends tell me they feel transformed, liberated, by the operation that frees them from wearing glasses. I'm less sure.

I began this book by addressing the sometimes-internalized negative experiences of glassers. I conclude it with the implications of wearing computers before our eyes and if attitudes toward glasses have changed.

As I imagined about seeing 20/20 for the first time in my life, I again considered the unfairness of unequal access to visual correction. Visual aids are essential; so how can humanity allow something as potentially life-changing as sight to be a matter of one's ability to pay? As Leo Tolstoy wrote, "If the arrangement of society is bad (as ours is), and a small number of people have power over the majority and oppress it, every victory over nature will inevitably serve only to increase that power and that oppression. This is what is actually happening."[1]

If we apply this quote to smart glasses as the next (visual) victory over nature, inequality becomes a reality for billions of people without universal access to basic visual care. And, if the dystopian projections of smart glasses as privacy-deniers become true, in the wrong hands bad actors could superimpose someone else's reality over ours—a risk especially for those who can't afford devices with the best available security measures. This calls to mind that line from George Orwell's *1984*: "The party told you to reject the evidence of your eyes and ears. It was their final, most essential command."

In 1819, Shelley wrote, "the pleasure of believing what we see is boundless, as we wish our souls to be." He also credited poets as the unacknowledged legislators of the world. Could we hope Shelley's poet-legislators—and those in Congress—will feel an obligation to educate people to the potential dangers of smart glasses and pass bills regulating health and privacy concerns before it's too late? Technology takes a long time to mature, but even longer to assess its effects or to change stereotypes. As we depend ever more on little-tested technology, we may find that a walk down a road paved with circuitry leads us to a path of no return.

* * *

The inside of a hospital is usually the soundtrack to nightmares with frequent beeps and alarms, but the cataract ward is eerily quiet. I'm rolled into the operating room on a trolley with padded wheels. Machinery buzzes faintly below the hushed conversations of nurses. Patients mumble quietly as their drugs kick in. In one corner, the doctor checks the lasers and sharpens instruments for a clean cut.

I'm slowly drifting off the shore of consciousness. Without my lenses, people look to me like they did in the hospital that night after the fire: white oblongs with blank faces.

There's something strange about trading the lens I was born with for another—the one I grew versus the one I bought. Will my birth lens be sucked down a tube into the trash? For a moment, I had the absurd thought that everything I'd seen would disappear with it. Then I giggled at a joke from comedian Joe E. Lewis: "They had me on the operating table all day. They looked into my stomach, my gallbladder; they examined everything inside of me. Know what they decided? I need glasses."

Lying here, I replay that risky week three years ago, in the Land of Blur.

* * *

Humans' hope for transformative vision is ancient. Through illuminated manuscripts, stained glass, brilliantly colored ornaments, prayer and fasting, meditation and mysticism, humanity has transported itself to alternate states of consciousness. In mystical transcendence, a yogi no longer senses his or her body and thus withstands pain and extreme heat. Such out-of-body experiences may be the true ancestry of AR and VR glasses.

"For most of us most of the time, the world of everyday experience seems rather dim and drab," Huxley asserts in his *Heaven and Hell*. "But for a few people often, and for a fair number occasionally, some of the brightness of visionary experience spills over, as it were, into common seeing, and the everyday universe is transfigured."[2] Yet, experience with psychedelic drugs like LSD, mescaline, or peyote, and meditation-induced trances—though resembling what VR could simulate—are more profound than anything smart glasses could offer. This is because meditation and psychedelic experiences are authentic and individualized, rather than something a video designer created. Our mental map of the world will always differ individually. If aping transcendence is all Extended Reality can provide, VR glasses might become the ultimate drug but not the "gratuitous grace" Huxley imagined humanity could achieve.[3] And if all VR glasses offer is the chance to buy exotic experiences, the smart glass era will have ushered in little more than escapism and new forms of cybercommerce.

* * *

In the operating room awaiting renewed vision, I am deeply grateful: for the surgeons who perform their delicate job. For the nurses comforting me. For the opticians who patiently ground lens after lens and put up with my complaints. For the optometrists who understood there was no point in showing me the big E as I sat in their chair. For the ophthalmologists who checked my macular area. For the entire optical industry, and of course, for friends and family who put up with me endlessly saying, "Would you move that a little closer?" "What does that say?" or "I'm sorry; I can't see that."

Andrew Leland, a writer slowly going blind from a genetic disorder, set out to discover how different his life would be without vision. By the end of *The Country of the Blind*, he had found comradeship in a community of those similarly afflicted. As a child, glasses allowed me entry into a world I could never otherwise visit. I became a devoted, even compulsive reader, an activity often suited for the nearsighted (and as a child best done outdoors). Books took me across time and place. In college and after, reading became my currency, trading books with friends and students. Later, as floaters shadowed my eye and my prescription steadily increased, scrutiny of the apparatus that let me see began.

As we age, we look harder at physical limitations. Some fight their limits; some accept them with grace. Not having to hide visual frailty is a prize of adulthood, salving wounds for those who were told early in life that they're ugly in glasses or incapable (or too capable). We are so much more than the stereotypes others pin on us.

* * *

For 750 years, people who wore eyeglasses felt pressured to hide them. Monks and nuns stowed them out of sight. No one dared admit being their inventor. Women and men were shamed for wearing them. So, has that changed? Perhaps, though the glasses stigma has continued into the modern era. In the fall of 2025 before a Canadian election, the conservative candidate for prime minister, Pierre Poilievre, felt the need for a glasses make-over: "he jettisoned his squarish glasses for contacts and Aviator Sunglasses. He's transferred his own image from a nerdy little guy with the glasses," wrote *The New York Times*.[4]

Glasses-shaming remains in Japan, where public-facing workplaces still discourage glasses for females. According to *Business Insider Japan* in 2019 and the Japanese broadcaster NHK, those working on airplanes, in childcare, and in hospitality industries are sometimes forbidden them. Reasons vary: "glasses are dangerous because they could fall on customers." "Glasses don't go well with Kimonos." "They create a gloomy atmosphere." "It's for safety reasons as glasses could fall and break."[5] Some workers likened this nonsense to Japanese "black school rules," which in some schools regulate hair length, skirt length, and even underwear color.[6]

Not until 2022 did Japanese legislators pass a law prohibiting employers from denying female employees the right to wear glasses on the job.[7] In East Asia, male TV announcers routinely wear glasses on the set, though in South Korea, women haven't. Women allergic to contact lenses had to have surgeries or find other jobs. Then one newscaster, Lim Hyeom-ju, shocked viewers by wearing hers on camera.[8]

Next, smartphone abuse: before the New Orleans bombing on January 1, 2025, the terrorist used smart glasses to reconnoiter Bourbon Street, where his bombing would take place: "he rode through the area on a bicycle, recording videos of his target."[9]

And that fantasy of a company using smart glasses to feed facial recognition to a smart phone? It's already here, from Clearview AI which vacuumed up 20 billion photos online and created code that links data to the display of AR glasses display like those Harvard students' experiment, only on a massive scale.[10] We need regulation of this technology.

As far back as 1893, a doctor with the British Medical Association looked forward to a day when almost everyone would be a glasser: "A man who goes about with his eyes naked," he ventured, "will be so rare that the sight of him will almost raise a blush."[11]

That day may still be distant, though attitudes toward glasses continue to evolve. If one day, nearly everyone wears some sort of glasses, glasses-shaming could finally cease, and "Four Eyes" could no longer be a taunt.

* * *

Looking back on my week without glasses, I remember the dented toes, the wrists wet from spilled food or tea, the memories of bullying, the dreams, the bruises—but also the quiet moments of visual peace when I demanded nothing of my eyes. Over the course of that week, something changed for me. Now, I glance down the hall and take a moment to decide how much clarity I need. One of the things that week gave me was the understanding that vision is relative; not every detail must be sharp all the time. Though I now recognize eye correction as a bridge to the world, that doesn't mean I have to cross it every minute. I'll take the best science can offer and, with that clarity, find insight, empathy, and connectedness (newly appreciated).

ACKNOWLEDGMENTS

As authors often remember when they finish a book, volumes are not the product of one person alone. I would like to thank all those who read and commented on drafts of the book: Molly Beer, Laura Brandt, Bob Elwood, Eda Gordon, Nancy Guinn, Dr. Neil Handley, Andrew Karp, Steve Mayer, Juliette Cunico, James McGrath Morris, Molly Pisani, Barry Santini, and members of a writing group in Albuquerque. John Berger contributed excellent editing. I also recognize the valuable assistance of my University of New Mexico students and assistants, Abby Campbell, August Edwards, Emma Featherman, Nora Hickey, Jillian Kovach, Katherine Lies, Steve Mandrogoc, Lizbeth Torres Quinoz, Kelsa Mendoza, and Claire Wheeler.

I thank the organizations who provided research support on the meaning of glasses in personal experience and popular culture: British Optical Association Museum, Museum of the Eye, and the German Optical Museum; and Carl Zeiss.

To the many interviewees, too numerous to list here, go my heartfelt thanks, and particularly to David Salk of Focal Point, who explains optical issues masterfully.

I also must acknowledge the young people whose lives were tragically lost to severe bullying over having to wear glasses; it saddens me. We've had too much suffering for this to continue.

To Deni Remsberg and Jenna Dutton, my editors at Bloomsbury; and particularly to my agent, Peter Rubie, at Fineprint Literary, my thanks for assistance in thinking through and placing the manuscript. Last but not least, I thank Dr. Nina Wallerstein, our son Alexei, and granddaughter Mirabel, who, if she eventually wears glasses, may enjoy this book.

NOTES

Preface: Glassers

1. Sandra Aamodt and Sam Wang, "The Sun the Best Optometrist," *New York Times*, June 20, 2011, op-ed page.

Introduction

1. "37 Best Earth Quotes by Astronauts, Scientists, and Authors," Space Quotations, https://spacequotations.com/quotes-about-earth-by-astronauts (accessed May 4, 2023).
2. "37 Best Earth Quotes by Astronauts, Scientists, and Authors."
3. James Gregg, *The Story of Optometry* (New York: Ronald Press, 1965), 27.
4. John Berger, *Ways of Seeing* (New York: Penguin Books, 1997), 7.
5. Berger, *Ways of Seeing*, 60.
6. Nicolas Wade, *A Natural History of Vision* (Cambridge, MA: MIT Press, 1998), 99.
7. Wade, *A Natural History of Vision*, 40.
8. Wade, *A Natural History of Vision*, 120.
9. Brian Clegg, *The First Scientist: A Life of Roger Bacon* (New York: Carroll & Graf, 2003).
10. Attributed to Oliver Sacks.
11. Berger, *Ways of Seeing*, 93.
12. Michael F. Marmor and James G. Ravin, *The Artist's Eyes: Vision and the History of Art* (New York: Harry N. Abrams, 2009), introduction.
13. Michael F. Marmor, PhD, interview with the author on November 13, 2015.
14. Marmor and Ravin, *The Artist's Eyes*, 6.
15. Berger, *Ways of Seeing*, 11.

Sunday

1. Roni Caryn Rabin, "Ask Well: Floaters in the Eye," *New York Times*, February 5, 2016, D4.

2. Quoted in David Dunaway, *Huxley in Hollywood* (New York: Harper, 1989), 350.

3. Katharyn Schulz, "The Moral Judgements of Henry Thoreau," *New Yorker*, October 12, 2015, 41.

Chapter 1

1. Steven Johnson, *How We Got to Now* (New York: Nutopia/pbs, 2014), Disc 1clean/time/glass.

2. Alan MacFarlane and Gerry Martin, *Glass: A World History* (Chicago, IL: The University of Chicago Press, 2002), 12.

3. James Gregg, *The Story of Optometry* (New York: Ronald Press, 1965), 17.

4. Sarah Dowhower, "Painted Literacy: Lens and Light Celebrating the Tools That Help Us See Text," *American Reading Forum Arrival Yearbook* 2011 Vol. 31, 6.

5. Macforlane and Martin, *Glass: A World History*, 104.

6. Kerry Segrave, *Vision Aids in America: A Social History of Eyewear and Sight Correction Since 1900* (Jefferson, NC: McFarland & Company, Inc., 2011).

7. Dowhower, "Painted Literacy: Lens and Light."

8. Guy Turner, "Allume Catina and the Aesthetics of Venetian Cristallo," *Journal of Design Research* 12, no. 2 (1999): 111–12.

9. Dr. David Baker, *How Glasses Caught a Killer* (self-published, FeedARead.com, 2016), 220.

10. Baker, *How Glasses Caught a Killer*, 207–9.

11. Richard Corson, *Fashions in Eyeglasses from the Fourteenth Century to the Present Day* (London: Peter Owen Publishers, 2011), 122.

12. Baker, *How Glasses Caught a Killer*, 145.

13. Alberta Kelley, *Lenses, Spectacles, Eyeglasses, and Contacts: The Story of Vision Aids* (Nashville, TN: Thomas Nelson, 1978), 16.

14. Kelley, *Lenses, Spectacles, Eyeglasses, and Contacts*, 170.

15 Corson, *Fashions in Eyeglasses*, 18.

16 Brian Clegg, *The First Scientist: A Life of Roger Bacon* (New York: Carroll & Graf, 2003), 76.

17 Clegg, *The First Scientist*, 76.

18 Quoted in Stuart Easton, *Roger Bacon and His Search for a Universal Science* (Oxford: Blackwell, 1952), 21.

19 Clegg, *The First Scientist*, 80.

20 Christened Clement IV, the new pope probably wanted to avoid a confrontation with the powerful heads of the Franciscans, some anointed by St. Francis himself.

21 James Blish, *Doctor Mirabilis* (New York: Dodd, Mead, 1964), 151. This source is a novel about Bacon that was heavily researched in the period.

22 Clegg, *The First Scientist*, 135.

23 Clegg, *The First Scientist*, 48.

24 Clegg, *The First Scientist*, 135.

25 David Lindberg, *Roger Bacon and the Origin of Perspectiva in the Middle Ages* (Oxford: Clarendon Press, 1996). There is a scholarly debate about Bacon's imprisonment; David Lindberg calls this "questionable"; yet during this time, Bacon uncharacteristically published nothing.

26 Amanda Power, "A Mirror for Every Age: The Reputation of Roger Bacon," *English Historical Review* 1.121, no. 492 (June 2006): 660.

27 Clegg, *The First Scientist*, 6.

28 Richard Drewery, "What Man Devised that He Might See," http://www.teagleoptometry.com/history.htm (accessed November 18, 2016).

29 George Ripley, *The Online Museum and Encyclopedia of Vision Aids*, http://www.antiquespectacles.com/ (accessed April 12, 2018).

30 J. W. Rosenthal, *Spectacles and Other Vision Aids* (Novato, CA: Norman Publishing, 1916), 196. The definitive investigation of the Armati claim is Edward Rosen, "The Invention of Eyeglasses," *Journal of the History of Medicine* Volume 11, Issue 2 (January 1956) 183–218.

31 Gregg, *The Story of Optometry*, 48.

32 C. S. Flick, *A Gross of Green Spectacles* (London: The Hatton Press, 1951), 3.

33 Corson, *Fashions in Eyeglasses*, 20.

34 Rosen, "The Invention of Eyeglasses," 198.

35 Rosen, "The Invention of Eyeglasses," 192.

36 "The Holy Family with John the Baptist," sixteenth century, Museum and Encyclopedia of Vision Aids, http://www.antiquespectacles.com/ (accessed April 21, 2017).

37 Corson, *Fashions in Eyeglasses*, 18.

38 Segrave, *Vision Aids in America*, 21.

39 Drewery, "What Man Devised that He Might See."

40 Corson, *Fashions in Eyeglasses*, 52–4.

41 National Library for the Study of George Washington, Mt.vernon.org/library/digitalhistory/quotes (accessed June 18, 2021).

42 Corson, *Fashions in Eyeglasses*, 140.

43 Georg Bier, *The Art of Preserving the Sight Unimpaired to an Extremely Old Age* (London: Henry Coburn, 1815), 121–2.

44 Gregg, *The Story of Optometry*, 147.

45 Corson, *Fashions in Eyeglasses*, 77. A few in England and Germany had already been experimenting earlier with bifocals; see the Online Encyclopedia of Antique Spectacles.

46 Walter Isaacson, *Benjamin Franklin* (New York: Simon & Schuster, 2003).

47 Stanley Finger, *Doctor Franklin's Medicine* (Philadelphia, PA: University of Pennsylvania Press, 2005), 256–7.

Monday

1 Peggy Wood, "Glasses Aren't So Bad," *American Magazine*, 1932, 51–2.

2 Sarah Dowhauer, "Painted Literacy: Lens and Light," *American Reading Forum Annual Yearbook* [online] 31, no. 6 (August 8, 2022).

3 The editors, "Letters/Bad Translations," Commonweal Magazine, May 2, 2018, 5.

Chapter 2

1 Jane Brody, "The Cognitive Effects of Poor Vision and Hearing," *New York Times*, September 26, 2017, D5.

2. Laura Barnett, "Why Is There an Epidemic of Short-Sightedness?," *The Guardian*, November 11, 2009.

3. Atli Arnarson, "20 Foods High in Vitamin A," *Healthline*, April 1, 2024, https://www.healthline.com/nutrition/foods-high-in-vitamin-a.

4. K. Annabell Smith, "A WWII Propaganda Campaign Popularized the Myth That Carrots Help You See in the Dark," *Smithsonian*, August 13, 2013.

5. Barry Santini "The Real Details of Vortex, Tilt, and Wrap," *20/20 Magazine*, March 15, 2015, https://www.2020mag.com/ce/the-real-details-of-vertex-5E16F (accessed June 19, 2021). Also, letter to the author, July 4, 2021.

6. Dr. Joshua Ehrlich, quoted in Kevin Loria, "How to Keep your Vision Sharp," *Consumer Reports*, November 2024, 52.

7. Walter J. Zinn and Herbert Solomon, *Complete Guide to Eyecare, Eyeglasses and Contact Lenses*, 4th ed. (Hollywood, FL: Lifetime Books, 1996), 46.

8. Barnett, "Why Is There an Epidemic of Short-Sightedness?"

9. Yu-Meng Wang et al., "Myopia Genetics and Heredity," *Children* 9, no. 3 (March 2022): 382, https://www.ncbi.nlm.nih.gov/pmc/articles/PMC8947159/.

10. Elie Dolgin, "The Myopia Boom," *Nature* 519 (March 2015): 275–6; Shuyu Xiong, Padmaja Sankaridurg, Thomas Naduvilath, et al., "Time Spent in Outdoor Activities in Relation to Myopia Prevention and Control: A Meta-analysis and Systematic Review," *Acta Opthalmologica* 95 (September 2017): 551–6.

11. David Fleishman, *Sight: The Story of Vision*, Koenig Films, 2016.

12. Xiong et al., "Time Spent in Outdoor Activities."

13. Barry Santini, "Understanding Myopia in the New Millenium," *Rxpertise*, June 2019, 6.

14. Claudia Hammond, "Is Reading in the Dark Bad for Your Eyesight?," *BBC*, October 2, 2012, https://www.bbc.com/future/article/20121001-should-you-read-in-the-dark.

15. Ian Morgan and Kathryn Rose, "How Genetic Is School Myopia?," *Progress in Retinal and Eye Research* 241 (2005): 22. See also Young, F. A. et al., *American Journal of Optometry Archives of American Academy of Optometry*, Vol. 46, 1969: 675–85

16. CBC Radio, "Gene Tied to Short-Sightedness Found," September 13, 2010, https://www.cbc.ca/news/science/gene-tied-to-short-sightedness-found-1.917383.

17. Stephen Dubner, *Freakonomics Radio*, July 17, 2024.

18. Dolgin, "The Myopia Boom."

19. C. S. Flick, *A Gross of Green Spectacles* (London: The Halton Press, 1951), 34.

20. Heidi Mitchell, "Does Reading in Dim Light Hurt Your Eyes?," *Wall Street Journal*, December 12, 2016, http://www.wsj.com/articles/SB10001424127887323646604578404581544768850.

21 *CNN*, https://www.cnn.com/ (accessed July 25, 2016). The report did not distinguish between screen sizes.

22 Azi Paybarah and John Yoon, "Study Suggests Children's Eyesight Got Worse in Pandemic," *New York Times*, September 18, 2021.

23 Anahad O'Connor, "The Claim: Reading in the Dark Will Damage Your Eyes," *New York Times*, July 4, 2006, http://www.nytimes.com/2006/07/04/health/04real.html.

24 Jones et al., "Parental History of Myopia, Sports, and Outdoor Activities, and Future Myopia," *Investigative Ophthalmology & Visual Science* 48 (2007): 3524.

25 Claudia Hammond, "Myopia," *BBC*, December 12, 2016, https://www.bbc.com/future/article/20140513-do-glasses-weaken-your-eyesight.

26 Sara McCullough and Kathryn Saunders, "Childhood Myopia in the 21st Century," *Optometry Today*, May 28, 2016.

27 Aamodt and Wang, "The Sun Is the Best Optometrist," *New York Times*, June 20, 2011; Erica G. Landis et al., "Dim Light Exposure and Myopia in Children," *Investigative Ophthalmology and Visual Science* 59, no. 12 (October 2018) 4804–11.

28 Ian G. Morgan and Kathryn Rose, "Yunnan Minority Eye Study Suggests That Ethnic Differences in Myopia Are Due to Different Environmental Exposures," *Investigative Ophthalmology & Visual Science* 56 (July 2015): 4430.

29 Xiong et al., "Time Spent in Outdoor Activities."

30 Anders Ericson and Robert Pool, *Peak: Secrets from the New Science of Expertise* (New York: Houghton Mifflin Harcourt, 2016), 36–7.

31 *CNN*, https://www.cnn.com/ (accessed July 25, 2016).

32 Sara Zhang, "The Myopia Generation," *The Atlantic*, September 13, 2022, 1.

33 Lisa A. Jordan, et al., "Myopia and Ambient Night-Time Lighting. CLEERE Study Group. Collaborative Longitudinal Evaluation of Ethnicity and Refractive Error," *Nature*, April 2000: 143

34 Kathryn A. Rose et al., "Outdoor Activity Reduces the Prevalence of Myopia in Children," *Ophthalmology* 115 (2008): 1279.

35 Seo Wei Leo, "Current Approaches to Myopia Control," *Current Opinion in Ophthalmology* 28, no. 3 (May 2017): 3.

36 Nicholas Bakalar, "Contact Lenses May Slow Nearsightedness in Children," *New York Times*, August 25, 2020, consulted Novemeber 31, 2021.

37 Barry Santini, "Myopia Management," *Review of Myopia Management*, February 10, 2020.

38 Leo, "Current Approaches to Myopia Control."

39 Santini, "Myopia Management."

40 Sinday Bhanoo, "A Debatable Fix for Your Eyes," *New York Times*, November 3, 2014.

41 Center for Disease Control, "Fast Facts: Contact Lenses," http://medbox.iiab.me/modules/en-cdc/www.cdc.gov/contactlenses/fast-facts.html. (accessed August 13, 2018).

42 Thomas Chassine, Max Villain, Christian P. Hamel, and Vincent Daien, "How Can We Prevent Myopia Progression?," *European Journal of Ophthalmology* 25, no. 4 (2015): 284.

43 Chassine, Villain, Hamel, and Daien, "How Can We Prevent Myopia Progression?"

44 O'Connor, "The Claim: Reading in the Dark Will Damage Your Eyes."

45 Chassine, Villain, Hamel, and Daien, "How Can We Prevent Myopia Progression?"

46 Barry Santini, letter to the author, September 20, 2020.

47 American Academy of Ophthalmology (San Francisco), "Refractive Surgery," Basic Clinical and Science Course, 2007, 6.

48 Tommaso Rossi et al., "Cataract Surgery Practice Patterns Worldwide: A Survey," *BMJ Open Ophthalmology* 6, no. 1 (January 13, 2021): e000464, https://pmc.ncbi.nlm.nih.gov/articles/PMC7812090/.

49 American Academy of Ophthalmology, "Refractive Surgery," 6.

Tuesday

1 Clark Night, "Ophthalmologist William Bates & The Bates Method History (South San Francisco: Clearsight, 2011) 8.

2 Quoted by Anthony Attenborough, Huxley Workshop on Bates, Aldous Huxley Society, Riga, 2004, 4.

3 Samuel Berne, *I Sense: At Play in the Fields of Healing* (Tesuque, NM: Color Stone Press, 2014), 21.

4 Dr. Michael Marmor, interview with the author, November 13, 2015.

5 Melissa Kirsch, "Tired of Being Pushed around by Your Devices?" *New York Times*, January 16, 2024, D5.

6 Adam Phillips, "What we talk about when we talk about giving up," *The Guardian*, January 2, 2024.

7 Claire Murushima, "I Avoided Plastic for a Week," *Morning Edition*, NPR, July 26, 2024.

8   Kirsch, "Tired of Being Pushed around by Your Devices?"

9   See, for example, Cal Newport, *Digital Minimalism: Choosing a Focused Life in a Noisy World* (New York: Portfolio, 2019).

10 Simar Bajaj, "All Hung Up," *The Guardian*, Weekly, January 5, 2024, 42; Jan Hoffman, "Rethinking Addiction as a Chronic Brain Disease," *New York Times*, September 3, 2024, D4.

Chapter 3

1   Georg Bier, *The Art of Preserving the Sight Unimpaired to an Extremely Old Age* (London: Henry Coburn, 1815), 121–2, quoted in Brandt, "Boys Don't Make Passes at Girls Who Wear Glasses: Gender, Vision Aids and Persona in Early American Republic," 18.

2   Corson, *Fashions in Eyeglasses*, 21.

3   Ted Goia, *A Subversive History of Music* (New York: Basic Books, 2019), 135.

4   Mark Mattison-Shupnick, interview with the author, July 2019.

5   Natalie Jacewicz, "Shots," NPR, July 7, 2016.

6   Segrave, *Vision Aids in America*, 9.

7   Baker, *How Glasses Caught a Killer*, 221.

8   Kerry Segrave, *Vision Aids in America: A Social History of Eyewear* (Jefferson, NC: McFarland, 2011), 29.

9   Quoted in Brandt, "Boys Don't Make Passes at Girls Who Wear Glasses: Gender, Vision Aids and Persona in Early American Republic," 18.

10 J. Woodforde and D. Hughes (eds.), *Diary of A Country Parson* (London: The Folio Society, 2015).

11 Neil Handley, "To Wear or Not to Wear: Changing Social Norms with Regard to Eyewear," Lecture, Gresham College, London, March 21, 2012.

12 Laura Brandt, "Boys Don't Make Passes at Girls Who Wear Glasses: Gender, Vision Aids and Persona in Early American Republic," Senior thesis, 16, William and Mary College, 2009.

13 National Library for the Study of George Washington, Mt.vernon.org/library/digitalhistory/quotes

14 Sarah Dowhower, "Painted Literacy: Lens and Light," American Reading Forum Arrival Yearbook 31, no. 6 (2011): 41.

15 Handley, "To Wear or Not to Wear."

16 Richard Corson, *Fashions in Eyeglasses from the Fourteenth Century to the Present Day* (London: Peter Owen Publishers, 2011), 199.

17 C. S. Flick, *A Gross of Green Spectacles* (London: The Halton Press, 1951), 87.

18 Flick, *A Gross of Green Spectacles*, 87.

19 Quoted in Kelly Segrave, *Vision Aids in America: A Social History of Eyewear and Sight Correction Since 1900* (Jefferson, NC: McFarland & Company Inc., 2011), 69.

20 Kathryn Hughes, "Through the Looking Glasses by Travis Elborough Review—The Spectacular Life of Spectacles," *The Guardian*, https://www.theguardian.com/books/2021/jul/24/through-the-looking-glasses-by-travis-elborough-review-the-spectacular-life-of-spectacles. (accessed February 3, 2024).

21 Ted Goia, *A Subversive History of Music* (New York: Basic Books, 2019), 135.

22 Rhie Thomas, "Men Never Make Passes," *Atlantic Monthly*, No. 185, January 1950, 94.

23 Len Snowden, "Specs and the Single Girl," *Mademoiselle*, May 1990, 82.

24 Snowden, "Specs and the Single Girl," 82.

25 Peggy Wood, "Glasses Aren't So Bad," *American Magazine*, 1932, 51.

26 Johann Peter Eckerman, *Conversations with Goethe in the Last Years of His Life* (Boston, MA: Hillard, Gray, and Company, 1839), quoted in Flick, *A Gross of Green Spectacles*, 44.

27 Alberta Kelley, *Lenses, Spectacles, Eyeglasses, and Contacts: The Story of Vision Aids* (Nashville, TN: Thomas Nelson, 1978), 20.

28 Aldous Huxley, "Spectacles," in *Along the Road* (New York: Harper, 1925), 55–60.

29 David King Dunaway, *Huxley in Hollywood* (New York: Harper, 1989), 131–3.

30 Edward Rosen, "The Invention of Eyeglasses," *Journal of the History of Medicine* 2 (January 1956): 218.

31 Wood, "Glasses Aren't So Bad," 53.

32 Segrave, *Vision Aids in America*, 72.

33 George Gould, "A Warning Against Eyeglasses," *Literary Digest*, December 24, 1921, 20.

34 Hiroko Washizu, "The Optics of Green Spectacles," *Edgar Allen Poe Review* 12, no. 2 (2011): 48–57.

35 Segrave, *Vision Aids in America*, 25.

36 [No author listed], *New York Times*, November 26, 2019.

37 [No author listed], *New York Times*, March 18, 1929.

38 Segrave, *Vision Aids in America*, 25.

39 Segrave, *Vision Aids in America*, 134. Note that in 1845, Sr John Hershel had suggested "a spherical capsule of glass" could help those with irregular corneas.

40 Timothy Bowden, *Contact Lenses: The Story* (Kent: Bower House, 2009) 7, 536.

41 Segrave, *Vision Aids in America*, 125.

42 Bowden, *Contact Lenses*, 537.

43 Clara Hemphill, "A Quest for Better Vision: Spectacles Over the Centuries," *New York Times*, August 8, 2000, 3.

44 Walter J. Zinn and Herbert Solomon, *Complete Guide to Eyecare, Eyeglasses, and Contact Lenses*, 4th ed. (Hollywood, FL: Lifetime Books, 1996), 107.

45 Andrew Karp, letter to the author, September 2019.

46 "Google Contact Lenses Will Have a Camera Built In," *YouTube*, uploaded by The Rubin Report, April 16, 2014, https://www.youtube.com/watch?v=yleGVK_oeWg.

Wednesday

1 Megan Gannon, lovescience.com-like-mystery, April 14, 2019, 3.

Chapter 4

1 Barry Santini, "The War Between Optics and Cosmetics," *20/20*, February 2019.

2 Richard Corson, *Fashions in Glasses* (London: Peter Owen, [1967] 2011); Neil Handley, *Cult Eyewear: The World's Enduring Classics* (London: Merrell, 2011); Vanessa Brown, *Cool Shades: The History and Meaning of Sunglasses* (London: Bloomsbury, 2015).

3 John Bunyan, *The Pilgrim's Progress* (1678), https://www.gutenberg.org/files/39452/39452-h/39452-h.htm (accessed August 6, 2019).

4 Samuel Mazza, *Spectacles* (San Francisco, CA: Chronicle Books, 1996), 24.

5 Mazza, *Spectacles*, 14.

6   Richard Corson, *Fashions in Eyeglasses: From the Fourteenth Century to the Present Day* (London: Peter Owen, 2011), 209.

7   Gladwell, *The Tipping Point*.

8   Corson, *Fashions in Eyeglasses*, 135.

9   Vanessa Brown, *Cool Shades* (London: Bloomsbury Academic, 2015).

10 Corson, *Fashions in Eyeglasses*, 225.

11 Kristin Cole, "Some Sunglasses Are Cheap in Price Only," WEBS-TV, April 11, 2006.

12 Simon Murray and Nicky Albrechtsen, *Fashion Spectacles: Spectacular Fashion* (New York: Thames and Hudson, 2012) 7, 72.

13 Corson, *Fashions in Eyeglasses*, 7.

14 Interview with the author, July 2019.

15 Corson, *Fashions in Eyeglasses*, 215.

16 Corson, *Fashions in Eyeglasses*, 206.

17 Corson, *Fashions in Eyeglasses*, 220–1.

18 Jessica Glasscock, *Making a Spectacle: A Fashionable History of Glasses* (New York: Black Dog & Leventhal, 2021), 113.

19 Corson, *Fashions in Eyeglasses*, 208.

20 P. G. Wodehouse, "In Defense of Astigmatism: A Brief in Favor of Specs, Pince-nez, and Goggles," *Vanity Fair*, 1930.

21 Neil Handley, letter to the author, April 28, 2020.

22 Murray and Albrechtsen, *Fashion Spectacles*, 86.

23 Murray and Albrechtsen, *Fashion Spectacles*, 2.

24 Glasscock, *Making a Spectacle*, 153.

25 Elborough, *Through the Looking Glasses*, 237.

26 Michael Braunn in Elborough, *Through the Looking Glasses*, 242.

27 Elborough, *Through the Looking Glasses*, 242–3.

28 Corson, *Fashions in Eyeglasses*, 194.

29 Mazza, *Spectacles*, 99.

30 Elborough, *Through the Looking Glasses*, 183.

31 Patricia Marx, "Four Eyes: Looking for Glasses," *New Yorker*, March 22, 2010, 50.

32. Elisa Anniss, "Luxury Brands, from Tiffany to 3.1 Phillip Lim, Are Entering Luxury Eyewear Market," *New York Times*, September 27, 2007.
33. Marx, "Four Eyes," 51.
34. "Fashion vs. Function," *Vision Expo Daily*, 2019, 52–3.
35. Barry Santini, interview with the author, July 2019.
36. Vanessa Friedman, "Open Thread," *New York Times*, November 11, 2019, A3.
37. Eliza Cline, "Wear Clothes? That's a Problem," *New York Times*, November 4, 2019, A27.

Thursday

1. Andy Warhol, *Mean, Eye, Thinking* (N.Y: Houghton Mifflin, 2014), 82.
2. Kathryn Hughes, "Through the Looking Glasses by Travis Elborough review—the spectacular life of spectacles," https://www.theguardian.com/books/2021/jul/24/through-the-looking-glasses-by-travis-elborough-review-the-spectacular-life-of-spectacles.
3. Jan Myrdal, *Confessions of a Disloyal European* (New York: Vintage, 1964), 191.
4. Neil Handley, interview with the author, November 21, 2017.
5. NT Vision Centers, "What Did People Do Before Glasses," https://www.nvisioncenters.com/glasses/do-before-glasses/ (December 2, 2022).
6. George Orwell, "In Front of Your Nose," *Tribune*, March 22, 1946.
7. Aldous Huxley, *The Cicadas and Other Poems* (New York: Doubleday, Doran, 1931), 62.

Chapter 5

1. Edgar Allan Poe, "The Spectacles," *Poe Stories*, 1850, https://poestories.com/read/spectacles. (accessed October 2, 2023).
2. Poe, "The Spectacles," 1–2.
3. Poe, "The Spectacles," 5.
4. Poe, "The Spectacles," 7.

5   Sinclair Lewis, *Main Street and Babbitt* (New York: Library of America, 1992), 4.

6   Quoted in Elborough, *Through the Looking Glasses*, 185.

7   Conan Doyle, "The Adventure of the Golden Pince-nez," 222.

8   Conan Doyle, "The Adventure of the Golden Pince-nez," 223.

9   C. S. Flick, *A Gross of Green Spectacles* (London: The Hutton Press, 1950), 5.

10 David Baker, *How Glasses Caught a Killer and other Stories of how Optics Changed the World* (self-published: FeedARead.com, 2016), 54.

11 Flick, *A Gross of Green Spectacles*, 10.

12 Flick, *A Gross of Green Spectacles*, 23.

13 Flick, *A Gross of Green Spectacles*, 32.

14 Charles Dickens, *Pickwick Papers*, "The Second Meeting of Mudfog," *The Literature Network*, https://www.online-literature.com/dickens/mudfog/3/ (accessed July 8, 2024).

15 Henry James, "Glasses," ProQuest Ebook Central, 1896.

16 James, "Glasses," 12–14.

17 James, "Glasses," 41–2.

18 James, "Glasses," 51.

19 James, "Glasses," 17.

20 Dan Abitz, "Beauty and Blindness," *Henry James Review* 37, no. 3 (Fall 2016): 47.

21 Abitz, "Beauty and Blindness," 51, 290.

22 The heroine's device may be "an astigmatic pince-nez of the sort that had the lens rims suspended beneath a telescopic spring bridge," according to Neil Handley, curator of the British College of Optometrists Museum.

23 Wilkie Collins, "The Devil's Spectacles," eBooks@Adelaide, 1879.

24 Collins, "The Devil's Spectacles," 10.

25 Collins, "The Devil's Spectacles," 25.

26 Max Pemberton, *The Iron Pirate* (England: Forgotten Books, 1893), 16.

27 Arthur Anderson, *A Touch of Fantasy: A Romance for Those Lucky Enough to Wear Glasses* (Sydney: John Lane, 1912), 1.

28 Anderson, *A Touch of Fantasy*, 26.

29 Anderson, *A Touch of Fantasy*, 283.

30 Anderson, *A Touch of Fantasy*, 303.

31 Marivus Hentea, "Monocles on Modernity," *Modernism/Modernity* 20, no. 2 (April 2013): 230.

32 Aldous Huxley, "The Monocle," in *Two or Three Graces: Four Stories* (London: Chatto & Windus, 1949), 224–5.

33 Huxley, "The Monocle," 225.

34 Arthur Miller, *Focus* (New York: J. J. Little & Ives Company, 1945), 17.

35 Miller, *Focus*, 24.

36 Miller, *Focus*, 39.

37 Miller, *Focus*, 217.

38 Raymond Chandler, *The Little Sister* (New York: Vintage Books, 1949), 4, 8.

39 Chandler, *The Little Sister*, 6.

40 William Goldman, *Lord of the Flies* (New York: Penguin Books, 1999), 160.

41 Ned Delaney, *Two Strikes Four Eyes* (Boston, MA: Houghton Mifflin, 1976).

42 Peter Cohen and Olof Landstrom, *Boris's Glasses*, trans. Joan Sandin (Stockholm: Raben & Sjogren, 2003).

43 Marilyn Levinson, *The Fourth-Grade Four* (New York: The Trumpet Club, 1989), 2.

44 Kate McMullen, *Pearl and Wagner: Four Eyes* (New York: Penguin Books, 2009).

45 Lyn Marinello, *Franky Four Eyes* (Mustang, OK: Tate Publishing & Enterprises, 2007).

46 J. K. Rowling, "Talons and Tea Leaves," in *Harry Potter and the Prisoner of Azkaban* ed. Steven Weisberg (New York: Scholastic, 1999), 102–103.

47 "Spectacles," Harry Potter Wiki, https://harrypotter.fandom.com/wiki/Spectacles. (accessed July 4, 2024).

48 Camille Bordas, "The State of Nature," *The New Yorker*, April 9, 2018, 65.

49 Bordas, "The State of Nature," 61.

Friday

1 James Ravin, "James Thurber and the Problems of Sympathetic Ophthalmia," *JAMA Ophthalmology*, May 2002 (May. 1, 2019).

Chapter 6

1. Isaac Asimov, "The Cult of Ignorance," in *Is Anyone There?* (New York: Doubleday, 1967), 19.

2. Colette Smith, "We Need to Kill the 'Ugly Girl in Glasses' Trope," *Fandom*, November 10, 2016, https://www.fandom.com/articles/kill-ugly-girl-glasses-trope. Danielle Wolfe, "30 Bespectacled Characters on Film," *Shortlist*, November 10, 2016, https://www.shortlist.com/news/30-bespectacled-characters-on-film.

3. The film inspired a knock off, *The Glasses*, with a similar theme.

4. Interview with John Carpenter on Wikipedia, https://www.wikipedia.org/ (accessed September 10, 2024).

5. Jim Burrows, "The Origin of the Nerd," *Eldacur*, November 5, 2004, https://www.eldacur.com/~brons/NerdCorner/nerd.html.

6. Joseph L. Burneni, *Looking Back: An Illustrated History of the American Ophthalmic Industry* (Alexandria, VA: Optical Laboratories Association, 1994); Annette D'Agustino, "Harold Lloyd: The Glasses," June 4, 2018, https://silentsaregolden.com/lloydglassesarticle.

7. Wikipedia, "Harold Lloyd," January 2, 2018, https://en.wikipedia.org/wiki/Harold_Lloyd.

8. Virginia Lyon, "Harold Lloyd Collection." King Video, 2004.

9. Lyon, "Harold Lloyd Collection." In early television, the most prominent character in glasses was Mr. Peepers (Wally Cox), a shy, precise schoolteacher in a bad suit and transparent frames, the sort who folds napkins double in his lap. Like Mr. Magoo, poor vision keeps getting Mr. Peepers in trouble.

10. Miss Cellania, "Why Do Nerds So Often Wear Glasses?," *Neatorama*, January 11, 2012, https://www.neatorama.com/2012/01/11/why-do-nerds-so-often-wear-glasses/.

11. Optical professionals appear in The *Secret of Dr. Kildare* (1939), *Shadowed Eyes* (1939), *This Woman is Dangerous* (1952), *Magnificent Obsession* (1954), *Crimes and Misdemeanors* (1989), *Blink* (1994), and *Secrets and Lies* (1996).

12. See *Kommandant Kramm* (1964), *Marathon Man* (1976), and *Bent* (1997); the neo-Nazis include those in *American History X* (1998) and the Gestapo leader Arnold Tohtr in *Raiders of the Lost Ark* (1981). "Four Eyes, Zero Soul," TV Tropes, https://tvtropes.org/pmwiki/pmwiki.php/Main/FourEyesZeroSoul. (accessed June 6, 2024).

13. Not all scientists in specs are harmful: There's Dr. Spengler, in *Ghostbusters* (1984); Agents J and K sporting sunglasses in *Men in Black* (1997); Dr. Jung, in *A Dangerous Method* (2011); even the bookish Sean Connery in *Indiana Jones and the Last Crusade*

(1989) and its sequels. Bespectacled scientists can even be figures of enlightenment, like Dr. Bilderbeck in *War of the Worlds* (1953).

14 These range from sadistic gangsters (the villain in photo-gray aviators in the James Bond film *A View to a Kill*, in 1985) to arrogant CEOs (Gary Winston in *Antitrust*, 2001) or crooks (the dapper Michael Caine in *The Ipcress File*, 1965).

15 Patrick McGilligan, *Alfred Hitchcock: A Life in Darkness and Light* (New York: Harper Perennial, 2004), 242.

16 Monique L. Threatt, "Bad to the Bone, Librarians in Motion Pictures: Is it an Accurate Portrayal," *Indiana Libraries* Vol. 24 Num. 2(2005), 6–9.

17 Jen Snoek-Brown, "My Super Ex-Girlfriend Is Not a Librarian," *Reel Librarians*, November 13, 2012, https://reel-librarians.com/2012/11/13/my-super-ex-girlfriend-is-not-a-librarian/.

18 *How to Marry a Millionaire* trailer.

19 "The Joy of Specs: Eyewear's Starring Role in Cinematic History," *2luxury2*, September 14, 2017, https://www.2luxury2.com/the-joy-of-specs-eyewears-starring-role-in-cinematic-history/.

20 Smith, "We Need to Kill the 'Ugly Girl in Glasses' Trope."

21 Smith, "We Need to Kill the 'Ugly Girl in Glasses' Trope."

22 Amanda Hess, "The Framing of Meryl Strep," *New York Times*, July 25, 2002, C1.

23 Dun Roman, "Magoo by Huxley: A Tale of Movie Myopia," *Los Angeles Times*, January 30, 1977, 3.

24 Roman, "Magoo by Huxley."

25 Rob Wishart, "A Word to Disney: Pass Up Rights to 'Mr. Magoo,'" *Los Angeles Times*, October 16, 1995, https://articles.latimes.com/1995-10-166/entertainment/ca-5749.

26 YouTube, the 1997 film *Mr. Magoo* URL (accessed September 9, 2024).

27 Wishart, "A Word to Disney."

28 "Mr. Magoo An Insult, Blind Say," *Tulsa World*, July 3, 1997, https://tulsaworld.com/archive/mr-magoo-an-insult-blind-say/article_0f540836-0e82-502d-8835-9028d3ca9adf.html.

29 Barbara Pierce, "Let the Old Creep Die," *Braille Monitor*, October 1997, 5.

30 Kathi Wolfe, "Memories of Mr. Magoo," *Washington Post*, July 22, 1997, https://www.washingtonpost.com/archive/opinions/1997/07/23/memories-of-mr-magoo/e9d37bb5-256a-4087-b298-fac151ba0fcd/.

31 Jeremy Horwood et al., "Common Visual Defects and Peer Victimization in Children," *Investigative Ophthalmology and Visual Science* 46 (2005): 1180.

32 [no author listed] "Do Children with Glasses Get Bullied More?," *Insight Vision Center Optometry*, August 9, 2016, 1. https://www.insightvisionoc.com/glasses/children-glasses-bullied/ (accessed January 22, 2025).

33 Lucy Johnson, "Spectacles Relinked to School Bullying," *Bullying Express*, June 9, 2019. Here a researcher asked kids to write stories about vision. Half wrote about being bullied for their glasses.

34 Emily Crane, "Indiana Boy, 10, Kills Himself After Suffering Horrific Bullying – Parents Say They Complained to School 20 Times," *New York Post*, May 15, 2024, https://nypost.com/2024/05/15/us-news/indiana-boy-10-kills-himself-after-suffering-horrific-bullying/

35 Mike McDaniel, "Mother Mourns the Death of Daughter Gone to Suicide after Being Bullied," *4WWL*, November 18, 2021, https://www.wwltv.com/article/news/crime/mother-mourns-the-death-of-daughter-gone-to-suicide/289-4dd7fddc-b1e9-48ee-8128-a3db0a5b77a4.

36 Wendy Kantor, "10-Year-Old Killed Himself After Relentlessly Bullied," *People*, September 9, 2024, https://people.com/sammy-teusch-suicide-after-bullying-leads-family-fight-for-change-8651107.

37 Emily Crane, "Indiana Boy, 10, Kills Himself After Suffering Horrific Bullying – Parents Say They Complained to School 20 Times," *New York Post*, May 15, 2024, https://nypost.com/2024/05/15/us-news/indiana-boy-10-kills-himself-after-suffering-horrific-bullying/.

38 Steven Oppenheimer, interview with the author, December 2021.

39 Lowri Moore, "The Adventure," January 2, 2018, https://www.lowrimoore.com/the-adventure.

40 "Encanto Ticks Another Box: Disney Film Makes Girl's Glasses Wearing Heroine Wish Come True," Trends Desk, *The Indian Express*, February 9, 2022, https://indianexpress.com/article/trending/trending-globally/disney-film-makes-girls-glasses-wearing-heroine-wish-come-true-7761290/. (accessed February 14, 2021).

41 Magoo's ghost returns: A film, *Magoo* (2024), has been released in yet-another version in France.

Chapter 7

1 Stephen J. Taylor, "The Black Stork: Eugenics Goes to the Movies," *Hoosier State Chronicles*, February 4, 2016, https://blog.newspapers.library.in.gov/the-black-stork-eugenics-goes-to-the-movies/.

2   T. C. Boyle, *The Inner Circle* (New York: Viking, 2004), 98.

3   Thurman B. Rice, "Physical Defects and Character Part I: Farsightedness," *Hygeia*, June 1930, 536–8.

4   Thurman B. Rice, "Physical Defects and Character Part II: Nearsightedness and Astigmatism," *Hygeia*, July 1930, 644–6.

5   Rice, "Physical Defects and Character Part II," 644.

6   Advertisement in *The Elvia Ohio Chronilel-Telegraph*, December 17, 1917.

7   G. R. Thornton, "The Effect of Wearing Glasses upon Judgments of Personality Traits of Person Seen Briefly," *Journal of Applied Psychology* 28 (1943): 203–7; Wolfgang Manz and Helmut E. Lueck, "Influence of Wearing Glasses on Personality Ratings: Crosscultural Validation of an Old Experiment," *Perceptual and Motor Skills* 27 (1968): 704; "Perspectives: Glasses Research Confirms Stereotypes," *Inside UW*, April 30, 2013.

8   Lesley A. Stockton and Roger L. Terry, "Eyeglasses and Children's Schemata," *The Journal of Social Psychology* 133 (1993): 435.

9   Rita Handrich, "The Glasses Create a Kind of Unspoken Nerd Defense," *Keene Trial*, March 7, 2011.

10 Åke Hellström and Joseph Tekle, "Person Perception through Facial Photographs: Effects of Glasses, Hair, and Beard on Judgments of Occupation and Personal Qualities," *European Journal of Social Psychology* 24 (1994): 693–705.

11 Max Schapero, and Monroe J. Hirsch, "The Relationship of Refractive Error and Guilford – Martin Temperament Test Scores," *Clinical and Experimental Optometry* 35, no. 4 (1952): 162–4.

12 Mary B. Harris, Richard J. Harris, and Stephen Bochner. "Fat, Four-Eyed, and Female: Stereotypes of Obesity, Glasses, and Gender," *Journal of Applied Social Psychology* 12 (1982): 503–16. When this study was redone twenty years later in Germany, with three times as many students; ratings of those with glasses changed very little.

13 David, "I Hate My Glasses," *Thought Catalog*, June 3, 2006, https://thoughtcataloge.com/.

14 Kerry Segrave, *Vision Aids in America: A Social History of Eyewear and Sight Correction Since 1900* (Jefferson, NC: McFarland, 1988), 81.

15 Roger L. Terry, "Eyeglasses and Gender Stereotypes," *Optometry and Vision Science* 66 (1989): 697.

16 Terry, "Eyeglasses and Gender Stereotypes," 410.

17 Nita Odedra et al., "Barriers to Spectacle Use in Tanzanian Secondary School Students," *Ophthalmic Epidemiology* 15 (2008): 412.

18 Odedra et al., "Barriers to Spectacle Use," 414.

19 H. Leder, P. T. Tinio, I. Fuchs, and I. Bohrn, "When Attractiveness Demands Longer Looks: The Effects of Situation and Gender," *Quarterly Journal of Experimental Psychology* 63 (2010): 1858–71.

20 Michael Argyle and Robert McHenry, "Do Spectacles Really Affect Judgments of Intelligence?," *British Journal of Social Clinical Psychology* 10 (1971): 27.

21 Segrave, *Vision Aids in America*, 82.

22 Flora Hui, "Shortsightedness Is on the Rise in Children: There's More We Can Do Than Limit Screen Time," *The Conversation*, The University of Melbourne, November 12, 2024.

23 Hellström and Tekle, "Person Perception through Facial Photographs," 698.

24 Michael J. Brown, "Is Justice Blind or Just Visually Impaired? The Effects of Eyeglasses on Mock Juror Decisions," *The Jury Expert* 23, no. 2 (March 2011): 1–4.

25 Brown, "Is Justice Blind or Just Visually Impaired?," 3.

26 Francine C. Jellesma, "Do Glasses Change Children's Perceptions? Effects of Eyeglasses on Peer- and Self-perception," *European Journal of Developmental Psychology* 10 (2013): 449–60.

27 Jellesma, "Do Glasses Change Children's Perceptions?," 457.

28 Lynne Speaker, "Making Glasses Cool," *NEA Today*, February 2006, 46.

29 Réta Nemesszeghy, "Blinding Stereotypes of People with Glasses," *The Watchdog*, April 19, 2016.

30 Rick Paulas, "The Hidden Psychology of Wearing Glasses," *Pacific Standard Magazine*, January 27, 2015.

31 Segrave, *Vision Aids in America*, 74.

32 Abigail [last name withheld], interview with the author, January 2023.

Sunday

1 Dante *Paradiso*, Canto XXVI, 373.

2 David Dunaway, foreword, *Barbara Kingsolver*, Linda Wagner-Martin, ed. (Philadelphia: Chelsea House, 2004), xi-xiii; Barbara Kingsolver, "*Writing the Southwest*," Albuquerque: University of New Mexico Press, 1995, 98–113.

Chapter 8

1. Jane St. Clair, letter to the author, August 12, 2018; Ben Schott, "Brillenbrillanz," in *Schottenfreude: German Words for the Human Condition* (New York: Blue Rider Press, 2013).

2. Dr. Stephen Oppenheimer, interview with the author, April 4, 2021.

3. Chrissy Baclagan, email to the author, April 4, 2016.

4. Lesley A. Stockton and Roger L. Terry, "Eyeglasses and Children's Schemata," *The Journal of Social Psychology* 133 (1993): 435.

5. Jacob Kaplan, "Eyeglasses as a Social Status Symbol," in *The Trinity [College] Papers* (Hartford, CT: Trinity College, 2023), 5.

6. Dr. Steven Oppenheimer, interview with the author, 4 April 4, 2021.

7. Phil [last name withheld], letter to the author, July 16, 2018.

8. Dr. Mark Mattison-Shupnick, interview with the author, September 9, 2016.

9. "Purple Is the New Black: Mom Sticks Up for Son Wanting Bright-coloured Glasses," *CBC News*, January 28, 2016, https://www.cbc.ca/news/canada/toronto/programs/metromorning/purple-glasses-1.3423367.

10. Francine C. Jellesma, "Do Glasses Change Children's Perceptions? Effects of Eyeglasses on Peer- and Self-perception," *European Journal of Developmental Psychology* 10 (2013): 449–60.

11. Lynnette Davis, Ruth Manny, Erick Weissberg, and Karen Fern, "Myopia, Contact Lens Use, and Self-esteem," *Ophthalmic & Physiologic Optics* 33 (2013): 573–80.

12. M. J. Rah, J. J. Walline, L. A. Jones-Jordan, et al., "Vision Specific Quality of Life of Pediatric Contact Lens Wearers," *Optometry and Vision Science* 87 (2010): 560–6. Yet, in 1997, researchers in Sweden measured this idea with ethnically diverse subjects at least eight years old (thought to be the earliest possible age for using contacts conscientiously). Improvement in self-esteem in that study was not statistically significant, though girls showed slightly more improvement than boys.

13. Mary Ann [last name withheld], letter to the author, May 14, 2016.

14. Mary B. Harris, "Sex Differences in Stereotypes of Spectacles," *Journal of Applied Social Psychology* 21, no. 20 (1991): 1659–80.

15. R. L. Terry, A. J. Berg, and P. E. Phillips, "The Effect of Eyeglasses on Self-Esteem," *Journal of the American Optometric Association* 54 (1983): 949.

16. Richard Key, "Four Eyes," email sent to the author August 15, 2018.

17 Brad, "I Hate My Glasses," November 2011, https://thoughtcatalog.com/.

18 Ulinvisiber, "I Hate My Glasses, They Make Me Ugly, What Do You Think about Them?," *Yahoo Answers*, 2013.

19 Ulinvisiber, "I Hate My Glasses."

20 Nancy Gustafson, "Last Date," letter to the author, July 19, 2016.

21 Dunnerhead, "I Have Glasses: I Hate Wearing Glasses!" July 29, 2012.

22 Gustafson, "Last Date."

23 Julie [last name withheld], letter to the author, July 22, 2022.

24 Ulinvisiber, "I Hate My Glasses."

25 Helin Jung, "Here's What 10 People Look Like with and without Their Glasses," *Cosmopolitan*, September 29, 2015, https://www.cosmopolitan.com/style-beauty/a46959/glasses-on-and-off-photos/.

26 Leslie Sittner, "Better Up than Down the Stairs," essay sent to the author. July 21, 2016.

27 Janet Davey, Chloe King, and Mary Fitzpatrick, "Perceptions of Glasses as a Health Care Product: A Pilot Study of New Zealand Baby Boomers," *Health Marketing Quarterly* 29 (2012): 353–5.

28 Kerry Segrave, *Vision Aids in America: A Social History of Eyewear and Sight Correction Since 1900* (Jefferson, NC: McFarland & Company, 2011), 74.

29 Evan Osnos, "Doomsday Prep for the Super-Rich," *New Yorker*, January 30, 2017, 36.

30 Betty [last name withheld], email to the author. July 28, 2016.

31 Segrave, *Vision Aids in America*, 84.

32 David, [last name withheld] "I Hate My Glasses," June 3, 2006.

33 Sreeparna Mazumder, "Nerdy, Boring, and Depressed: How Bollywood Stereotypes Women Who Wear Glasses," *Idiva*, 2017, https://www.idiva.com/fashion/celebrity-style/bollywood-stereotypes-wearing-glasses/18010863.

34 Mamamia, August 8, 2024, Mamamia.comav/i-love-my-glasses.

35 Laura Ruof, "Confession: I Wear Glasses to Look Cooler," *Refinery29*, 2014.

36 Rashmi et al., "Challenges Faced by Spectacle Wearers: A Cross Sectional Questionnaire Survey among Urban Youth," *Journal of Dental and Medical Sciences* 15, no. 2 (2016): 102–5.

37 Tchiakpe Michel Pascal, Nhyira Samaa Ansah, and Andrew Nartey, "Awareness and Response of Undergraduate Spectacle Wearers to Contact Lens Usage," *Journal of Clinical Ophthalmology and Optometry* 1, no. 1 (2017) 103–9.

38 Jellesma, "Do Glasses Change Children's Perceptions?," 449–60.

39 M. K. Biaggio and E. Bittner, "Psychology and Optometry International Collaboration," *American Psychology* 45, no. 12 (December 1980): 1313–5.

Monday

1 Dante Alighieri, *Paradiso*, Canto III, 49.

Chapter 9

1 C. S. Flick, *A Gross of Green Spectacles* (London: The Harton Press, 1951), 43.

2 Jordana Cepelewicz, "Eyeglasses, No Prescription Needed," June 2016, *Scientific American*, Vol. 314, No. 6.

3 Neil Handley, *Cult Eyewear* (London: Merrell, 2006), 61.

4 Ree Jackson, "Discovering Race Bias while Shopping for Glasses," *Medium*, July 22, 2019.

5 *Myopia-nopoly*, www.snopes.com. (accessed October 14, 2016).

6 Ana Swanson, "Meet the Four-Eyed, Eight-Tentacled Monopoly That's Making Your Glasses So Expensive," *Forbes*, September 10, 2014, 1.

7 Quoted in *Freakonomics* Radio, Episode 598, July 24, 2024.

8 Sam Knight, "The Spectacular Power of Big Lens," *The Guardian*, May 10, 2018, https://www.theguardian.com/news/2018/may/10/the-invisible-power-of-big-glasses-eyewear-industry-essilor-luxottica (accessed May 10, 2018).

9 Swanson, "Meet the Four-Eyed, Eight-Tentacled Monopoly," 2.

10 "A Clear New Look at Coating Costs," *Consumer Reports*, September 2020, 29.

11 Diane Estes, "Warby-Parker's CEO on How to Thrive in Retail," *PBS News Hour*, August 17, 2017, 4.

12 Anthony Giorgianni, "The Joy of Specs," *Consumer Reports*, February 2017, 8.

13 Statista, "Average Lifespan (Replacement Cycle Length) of Smartphones in the United States from 2013 to 2027," https://www.statista.com/statistics/619788/average-smartphone-life/. (accessed December 28, 2024).

14 Shira Ovide, "Waiting to Be Wowed by Virtual Reality," *New York Times*, June 8, 2022, B5.

15 David Owens, "Subtitling Your Life," *New Yorker*, April 21, 2025.

Chapter 10

1 Stanley Grauman Weinbaum, "Pygmalion's Spectacles," in *A Martian Odyssey and Other Science Fiction Tales: The Collected Short Stories of Stanley G. Weinbaum* (Westport, CT: Hyperion Press, 1974), 5.

2 Anabel Sosa, "Spotlight," *California Magazine*, March 22, 2022, https://alumni.berkeley.edu/california-magazine/2022-spring/spotlight-2/ (accessed April 7, 2022).

3 Chris Davies, "Mojo Vision Smart Contact Lens Is Straight out of Sci-Fi," Slashgear, November 11, 2024, https://www.slashgear.com/mojo-vision-smart-contact-lens-night-vision-augmented-reality-medical-wearable-16606978/; Tejasri Gururaj, "Eyes of Tomorrow: Smart Contact Lenses Lead the Way for Human-Machine Interaction," *Techxplore*, May 13, 2024, https://techxplore.com/news/2024-05-eyes-tomorrow-smart-contact-lenses.html. (accessed December 12, 2024).

4 Nick Zuidhof, Somaya Ben Allouch, Oscar Peters, Peter-Paul Verbeek, "Defining Smart Glasses: A Rapid Review of State-of-the-Art Perspectives and Future Challenges From a Social Sciences' Perspective," *Augmented Human Research* (6) 1, Consulted August 27, 2025.

5 Stephanie Pappas, "Why Does VR Make You Sick?," *Live Science*, https://www.livescience.com/54478-why-vr-makes-you-sick.html. (accessed April 16, 2022).

6 Andrew Marantz, "Studio 360," *New Yorker*, April 25, 2016, 86–94.

7 "Warning over Using Augmented Reality in Precision Tasks," *BBC News*, May 20, 2019, https://www.bbc.com/news/technology-48334457. (accessed June 22, 2019).

8 TechAltar.com, https://www.youtube.com/watch?v=VhFKKvKO6sU (accessed January 12, 2025).

9 James Fallows, "Artificial Intelligentsia," *Atlantic*, October 1, 2006, 149.

10 Robert Hoff, "Brands Look Far and Wide for Niche in Virtual Reality," New York Times, November 16, 2015, B6.

11 Jennifer Jolly, "Doctors are Saving Lives with VR," *USA Today*, July 28, 2017, https://www.usatoday.com/story/tech/columnist/2017/07/28/doctors-using-virtual-reality-breathe-new-life-into-technology/506437001/.

12 Cade Metz, "A New Way for Therapists to Get Inside Heads: Virtual Reality," *New York Times*, July 31, 2017, https://www.nytimes.com/2017/07/30/technology/virtual-reality-limbix-mental-health.html. (accessed September 4, 2018).

13 Nora Young, "The Tech World Is After Your Eyes," *CBC Radio*, November 25, 2016.

14 Maria Cramer and Kashimir Hill, "False Arrest Shows P.T. Fails at Facial Recognition, *The New Yorker*, August 28, 2025, 1.

15 Nick Bilton, "Why Google Glass Broke," *New York Times*, February 2, 2015, https://www.nytimes.com/2015/02/05/style/why-google-glass-broke.html. (accessed March 8, 2020).

16 Ray Bradbury, "The Veldt," in *The Vintage Bradbury* (New York: Vintage Books, 1965), 13–39.

17 "That Computer Looks Good on You," *Consumer Reports*, October 2014, 24.

18 Edward Champion, "Thirty-Five Arguments Against Google Glass," *Reluctant Habits*, March 14, 2013.

19 Paul Mozer, "Inside China's Dystopian Dreams: A.I., Shame, and Lots of Cameras," *New York Times*, July 8, 2018, https://www.nytimes.com/2018/07/08/business/china-surveillance-technology.html.

20 Champion, "Thirty-Five Arguments Against Google Glass," *Reluctant Habits*, March 14, 2013.

21 This is the same company that claimed ownership of the email addresses and texts scanned by Google camera vehicles.

22 Sophie Jeong, "For Many Young South Koreans, Dating Is Too Expensive, or Too Dangerous," *CNN*, May 11, 2019, https://www.cnn.com/2019/05/11/asia/south-korea-dating-intl/index.html. (accessed February 8, 2019).

23 Champion, "Thirty-Five Arguments Against Google Glass," *Reluctant Habits*, March 14, 2013.

24 Andrew Karp, "Smartglasses: The Apple of Our Eyes?," *20/20*, August 2019, https://www.2020mag.com/article/smartglasses-the-apple-of-our-eyes. (accessed March 30, 2022).

25 "39 Smart glasses of the Future," *The Optical Vision Site*, March 25, 2022, https://theopticalvisionsite.com/39-smart-eyeglasses-of-the-future/. (accessed April 8, 2022).

26. Deniz Ergürel, "How Virtual Reality Will Revolutionize Multiple Industries," *Media Shift*, April 2016, 3–10.

27. Philip A. Rauschnabel, Alexander Brem, and Young K. Ro, "Augmented Reality Smart Glasses: Definition, Conceptual Insights, and Managerial Importance," *ResearchGate*, July 2015, 16, https://www.researchgate.net/publication/279942768_Augmented_Reality_Smart_Glasses_Definition_Conceptual_Insights_and_Managerial_Importance. (accessed April 8, 2022).

28. Kashmir Hill, "Two Students Created Face Recognition Glasses. It Wasn't Hard," *New York Times*, November 11, 2024, https://www.nytimes.com/2024/10/24/technology/facial-recognition-glasses-privacy-harvard.html. (accessed November 11, 2024).

29. Hill, "Two Students Created Face Recognition Glasses."

30. Marantz, "Studio 360," *New Yorker*, April 25, 2016, 24.

31. Jageson Diviant, interview with the author, January 22, 2024.

32. Jageson Diviant, January 22, 2024.

Epilogue

1. This quote opens Aldous Huxley's most pacifist work, *Science, Liberty, and Peace* (New York: Harper, 1946), 1.

2. Aldous Huxley, *Heaven and Hell* (New York: Harper and Row, 1963), 93.

3. Joshua Rothman, "Are We Already Living in Virtual Reality?" *New Yorker*, April 2, 2018, 4–22.

4. Norimitsu Onishi, "Canada May Soon Install A Combative Populist Leader," *The New York Times*, January 10, 2025, 8.

5. Ruqayyah Moynihan, "Women in Japan are being told not to wear glasses at work to avoid looking 'cold' and 'unfeminine,'" *Business Insider*, November 9, 2019.

6. Naima Niemand, "10 School Rules in Japan: Bizarre but Common," *Japanalyze*, September 3, 2020, Japanalyze.com/10-school-rules-in-Japan/ (January 13, 2025).

7. Macro, Margetioff, "Japanese Business are telling women not to wear glasses to be more 'Appealing,'" ATI (April 24, 2000), 1.

8. [No author listed], "It gives a cold impression: Why Japanese companies can ban female staff from wearing glasses," Quartz.com, September 11, 2023, 3 (January 5, 2025).

9   Rick Rojas, "Before Attack, Driver Visited New Orleans Twice," *The New York Times*, January 7, 2025.

10 Kashmir Hill, "Unmasking Those Unmasking Us All," *New York Times*, January 21, 2020.

11 Richard Corson, *Fashions in Eyeglasses from the Fourteenth Century to the Present Day* (London: Peter Owen Publishers, 2011), 140.

INDEX

Note: Page range *130–1* refers to illustration section.

3-D printing   201
4 Eyes (song)   176
8½ (film)   100
20/20 (magazine)   217

acetate   102, 103, 190, 200
Adams, Arthur   121–2
addiction   64–6
"*Adventures of the Golden Pince-Nez, The*"
   (Doyle)   115
Africa   161, 162
African-Americans, vision problems
   among   50, 52
age-related defects   29, 34, 49, 108, 179
alcoholism   32
Alexandrian glass   20
Alighieri, Dante   10, 167, 168, 183
Allen, Woody   135
American Graffiti (film)   139
American Optical   96, 100
American Optometric Association   47–8
Amos 'n' Andy   148
Anon (film)   221, 222
Antic Hay (Huxley)   73
Apollo 11   1
Arab scholars   21, 23
Archimedes   20
Aristotle   2, 3
Armani   103, 188
art and artists   6–8, 31, 109; *see also*
   Literature, glasses in, glasses in;
   Movies
Art of Seeing, The (Huxley)   43
artificial intelligence (AI)   3, 207, 221
Artist's Eyes, The (Marmor and Ravin)   6
Asimov, Isaac   136

astigmatism   6, 49, 108
atropine   57, 78
augmented reality smart glasses   208–11,
   217, 219, 222–3
Austin, Jane   118

Bacall, Lauren   143–4
Backus, Jim   146
Bacon, Roger   2, 21, 23–7, 30, 72, *130–1*
Balzac, Honorè de   78
Bartisch, Georg   19, 79
Bates Method for Better Eyesight, The
   (Bates)   43, 62–3
Bates, William   62
Bausch & Lomb   100
Beattie, Ann   126
beauty pageants   79, 100
Beecher, William   33
Beer, Georg   71
behavioral optometry   63
Berger, John   3, 6
Berne, Samuel   63
bifocals   27, 34–5, 82, 179
Big Sleep, The (film)   143
binocular vision   7, 28
Blake, William   6, 85
Bleak House (Dickens)   118
Blues Brothers, The (film)   100
Bogart, Humphrey   135, 143
Bond, James   136
Book of Kells   109
Botticelli   6
   (Huxley)   42–3, 206
Brazil   193, 195
Brillenbrillanz   13
Brin, Sergei   215

INDEX

Bringing Up Baby (film)   140
British Medical Journal   80
British Optical Association Museum   72
Brosnan, Pierce   136
Bunyan, John   94–5, 97
burning glass   20, 27
Burns, Robert   171
Business Insider Japan (magazine)   229

Cage, Nicholas   140
Caine, Michael   100
camera obscura   4
Candide (Voltaire)   117
Cardboard, Google   210
Carlyle, Thomas   78
carrots   47
Carson, Richard   71–2
cataracts   7, 59, 212, 225–7
Cavell, Stanley   44
Cézanne, Paul   7
Chandler, Raymond   124–5, 142, 163
Channel   188
Chaucer, Geoffrey   116
China   20, 31, 50–1, 53–4, 73, 96, 189
ciliary muscles   5, 34, 49
Cinema Isolation: A History of Physical Disability in The Movies   148
Citizen Kane (film)   143
clear lensectomy   59
Clearview AI   229
Clegg, Brian   24, 26
Clement IV, Pope   24–5
collagen injections   58
Collins, Michael   1
Collins, Wilkie   120–1, 160–1
color
    effects of corrective lenses   49
    in scientific concepts of vision   3, 5, 7
colorblindness   192
Columbus, Christopher   26
community of glassers   vii, 14, 167–8
conductive keratoplasty (CK)   59
Confessions of a Disloyal European (Myrdal)   39–40

Consumer Electronics Show   218, 221
Consumer Reports (magazine)   201, 215–16
contact lenses   175–8, 180
    benefits and drawbacks   49–50
    design and function   49, 81
    fears of   47
    gas-permeable   49, 82
    for myopia management   57–8
    technical development   80–2, 102, 208
Cookfell, Marion   199
cornea   4, 5, 48
    contact lenses and   81
    laser surgery   59–60
Counterfeit World   206
Country of the Blind, The (Leland)   228
CR-39 lenses   102, 190
Crooks, William   96
Cruise, Tom   102
Curtis, Tony   145

Da Vinci, Leonardo   27, 80–1
D'Armati, Salvino   30–1
Darwin, Charles   41, 78
Dean, James   100
Degas, Edgar   6
Depth perception   7
Descartes, Réné   4–5, 27, 81
Devil Wears Prada, The (film)   142
"Devil's Spectacles, The" (Collins)   120–1
Dickens, Charles   118
Dickinson, Emily   74
Disney corporation   147–8
Dissociative disorders   223
Dolce & Gabbana   189
Dombey and Son (Dickens)   118
Don Quixote (film)   146
Donne, John   117
Doors of Perception, The (Huxley)   43
Doyle, Arthur Conan   95, 115
Dr. Caligari (film)   141
Dr. Terror's House of Horrors (film)   141

Ebert, Roger 148
Echo, Amazon 211
Edward II, King 72–3
Eisenstein, S. 151–2
El Greco 6
Elborough, Travis 101
Elizabeth I 22
Emerson, Ralph Waldo 34
Emma (Austen) 118
Encanto (film) 151
Essilor-Luxottica 103, 188–9, 202, 212
Eugenics 87, 157–9
Eulenspiegel, Till 116
European Journal of Ophthalmology 58
European Journal of Social Psychology 161
Eurovision 101
evolutionary science 41
Extended Reality (XR) 208, 213
eye; *see also* science of sight; *specific anatomical element*
  accommodation system 5
  ASA surgery 59
  infant development 53
  scientific understanding of 4–5
eyeglasses; *see also* Fashion, eyewear; Frames, eyeglass; lenses, man-made; Social and historical contexts of eyewear; Stigma and opposition to glasses
  to alter eye growth in children 53–4
  author's childhood experience with vii, 12–14, 54–6, 104–5, 135, 177–8, 228
  average price 201
  benefits and drawbacks 45–7
  computer-augmented 202, 208–9
  cristallo 21–2
  early development 2, 3, 6, 10, 20, 23, 25, 27–36, *130–1*
  emerging technologies 185
  fitting to wearer 48–9, 191–2, 196–7
  future 102, 185, 191–2, 207–8
  health benefits attributed to 31–2
  inequities in access 225
  invention of 27–31
  with no correction 97, 151, 177, 193
  oldest surviving 74
  online market 93–4, 190, 191, 207–8
  problems of poor design 32, 34, 186–7
  sale and manufacture 31, 33, 73, 93, 94, 96–7, 99, 102–3, 186–91, 201–2
  strategies for avoiding 62–3, 80
  studies of popular attitudes toward 159–64
  worldwide need for vii, 187
  worldwide use of 36, 50–1
eyestrain 22, 47–8, 52, 78

Fallows, James 211
farsightedness 8, 21, 133–4; *see also* vision problems
  age-related 29, 34, 49, 108, 179
  cause 49
  corrective lenses 48, 49, 108
  invention of bifocals for 34–5
  scientific understanding of 5
  surgical interventions 59
fashion, eyewear
  aviator sunglasses 98, 102
  browline frames 100, *130–1*, 139
  cateye glasses *130–1*, 144
  current trends 103–4
  eyeglass stigma and 96, 101
  functionality and 94–5, 98, 103–5
  harlequin frames 100
  historical evolution 95, 98–103
  horn-rimmed glasses 80, 139, 164
  Huxley satire on 73
  library frames 100, *130–1*
  marketing 79, 99, 100, 102–3
  self-image and 93–4, 98–105, 181, 193
  sunglasses 96–8
Fight Club (film) 141
Flaubert, Gustave 117
floaters 11, 17, 68–9, 225, 228
Focal Point eyeglass store 186
Focus (Miller) 123–4

INDEX

focus; *see also* farsightedness; Nearsightedness
Fonda, Henry   139
Food and Drug Administration   102
For Your Eyes Only (film)   141
Forbes (magazine)   189
Fortune (magazine)   81-2
Foul Play (film)   143
Four Eyes and Six Guns (film)   140-1
Four Eyes epithet   14, 88-90, 121
Fourth-Grade Four (Levinson)   127
Frames, eyeglass   193
  early development   32-3
  fashion in   93-6, 100-4, *130-1*
  fit   48-9
  high-end provider   193-7
  industry characteristics   188-91
Franciscans, Order of   23, 24
Franklin, Ben   27, 34-5, *130-1*
Franky Four-Eyes   127
Freakonomics   51, 188
Freeform digital lenses   197-8, 202-3
freeform lenses   197-8, 202-3
  scientific understanding of   4-5
Freud, Sigmund   160
"Full Court Seduction" (Williams)   129

Galen   4, 22
Galileo Galilei   2, 3
Garbo, Greta   97
Gear, Samsung   210
Geek(s)   139-40
Gender differences   35-6, 74-9, 180
  depictions of glassers in movies   135-7, 142-5
  frame selection   196
  popular perception of glasses   161, 176
Germany   28, 31, 35
Ghana   182
Giannini, Miguel   193-7, 221
Givenchy   98
Glass history   19-22, 82
Glassaholic   13, 65-6

Glassers, defined   vii, 14
Glasses defense   160, 163
"Glasses" (James short story)   118-20
Glaucoma   53, 212
Godey's Lady's Book   74
Goethe, Johann Wolfgang von   5, 78, 117, 157
Goia, Ted   72
Golding, William   125
Google Glass   207, 215-17
Google Nest   211
Gould, George   80
Graduate, The (film)   82
Grandvision   189
Grant, Cary   140
Guardian, The (news resource)   52, 66, 108
Gulliver's Travels (Swift)   117
Gutenberg   21, 108
Guy de Foulques, Cardinal   24

Handley, Neil   72, 109, 164
Hari, Johann   64
Harper's Bazaar (magazine)   100
Harrelson, Woody   105
Harry Potter and The Prisoner of Azkaban (Rowling)   128
Harry Potter movies and books   128, 150, 164
Hatachi corporation   219
Hawn, Goldie   143
Hawthorne, Nathaniel   34
Headset technology   206
Heaven and Hell (Huxley)   227
"Heidelberg Ballad"   117
Henry IV, Part II (Shakespeare)   116
Hepburn, Audrey   101-2
Hepburn, Katherine   140
Highsmith, Patricia   142
Hitchcock, Alfred   142
Hitler, Adolf   74
Hoda, Kashif   222-3
Hoffman, Dustin   82
Holly, Buddy   100

Holmes, Sherlock   115
Holographic projections on
    eyeglasses   208–9
Horse Feathers (film)   140
How to Marry a Millionaire (film)   143–5
Hoya corporation   201
Huxley, Aldous   16, 37, 42–3, 63, 73, 78–9, 111, 122–3, *130–1*, 146, 206, 227
Hyeom-ju, Lim   229
Hygeia (journal)   158
hypermetropia   48; *see also* farsightedness
hyperopia; *see* farsightedness
Hypervision   219

I Don't Want to Go to Bed (Lindgren)   126
I-Profiler   198–9
Ibn Al-Hayem   21
Ibn Al-Hazen   21
Ibn-Firnas, Abbas   21
If I Ran the Zoo (Seuss)   138
Infant and childhood development
    hiding from glasses   161–2
    myopia prevention and management   53–4, 56–8
    myopia risk   51–4
    puberty and teen years   176–8
    self-image of glassers   161–2, 164–5, 173–8
Inner Circle, The (Boyle)   157
Insurance, vision   189
Intellectualism, glasses and   76, 100, 160, 162–3, 178
Internet of Things   211
Inuit   51, 96, *130–1*
Investigative Ophthalmology Visual Science   149
Ipcress File, The (film)   100
IRISVISION   221
Iron Pirate, The (Pemberton)   121
Irwin, James   1
Italy   21–2, 28–31
It's a Wonderful Life (film)   143

Jackson, Andrew   33
James, Henry   34, 118–20, 129
Japan   28, 229
Jefferson, Thomas   33
Jellesma, Francinea   163
Jerk, The (film)   136, 140
John, Elton   102
Johnny Mnemonic (film)   206

Kansas City Star   99
Karp, Andrew   82
Kaye, Danny   *130–1*
Kennedy, John F.   1
Kent, Clark ("Superman")   139
Kepler, Johannes   4, 5, 27, 51–2, 78
Keratitis punctata   42
King Lear (Shakespeare)   116–17
Kingsolver, Barbara   167
Kinsey, Alfred   157
Kitchener, William   52, 96

Lacan, Jacques   65
Lady in the Lake, The (Chandler)   163
Lanier, Jaron   206
laser-assisted in situ keratomileusis (LASIK)   59
Laser surgery   59–60
Lawnmower Man (film)   206
Leland, Andrew   228
Lennon, John   101, 186
Lens of the eye   48
    age-related problems   49
    scientific understanding of   4–5
Lenscrafters   188
lenses, man-made; *see also* Eyeglasses
    bifocals   27, 34–5, 82, 179
    early development   2, 20–1, 27, 34, 35, 199
    impact-resistant   46
    intraocular   59
    low-index   82
    magnifying lenses   20, 21, 25, 87, 187
    manufacturing and sale   31, 33, 190–1, 197–201

INDEX

materials   19–21, 28, 102
  polycarbonate   102, 190, 200
  problems of   46
  progressive   197–8, 202, 208
  quizzers   35–6, 76, *130–1*
  scratch resistance   190
  tinted   31, 96–8, 200
  tools for making   *130–1*
  vision correction with   48–50
lentils   21
Léon (film)   141
Lewis, Jerry   140
Lewis, John   188
Librarians   136, 142–5
LIDAR   207
light
  for reading, nearsightedness and   47–8, 51–3, 58
  in scientific concepts of vision   3–5, 21
Lindgren, Astrid   126
Linus Gets Glasses   127–8
literacy   27–8, 33–5, 108
literature, glasses in
  historical development   115–25
  stigma and shame in depictions of   118–21, 126–8
  uses of   113–16
  for young readers   125–9
Little Sister, The (Chandler)   124–5
Lloyd, Harold   99, 138–9
Lord of the Flies (Golding)   125
Lorgnette   36, 95, *130–1*
Los Angeles Times   147
Lovin' Spoonful (rock band)   176
Luce, De (Al-Hayem)   21
Lucite   82
luminance   7
Luther, Martin   73, 216
Luxottica; *see* Essilor-Luxottica

McAllister, John   33
McLuhan, Marshall   212
Mad Gaze   219

Madame Bovary (Flaubert)   117
Magoo, Mr.   119, 145–8, 151, 171
Magnus, Albertus   24
Major League (film)   143
Makeup and glasses   101
Male Animal, The (film)   139
Malone, Dorothy   143
Mann, Thomas   63
Marchon company   189
Marco Polo   20
Marie Antoinette   95
Marmor, Michael   6
Martin, Steve   136, 140
Marx, Groucho   140
Marx, Patricia   102, 103
Mastroianni, Marcello   100
Matisse, Henri   6
Matrix Reloaded (film)   103
Mattison-Shupnick, Mark   192, 201
Meditation   227
Meredith, Burgess   129
Mesopotamia   20
META   211, 212, 217
Metaphors for sight   1–2
Metaverse   209
Migliore, Leopoldo Del   30–1
Miller, Arthur   123
Mirage (film)   141
Mitchum, Robert   135
Mixed reality smart glasses   208, 209
Modigliani, Amedeo   6
Monk, Thelonious   100
Monocles   99, *130–1*
Monroe, James   33
Monroe, Marilyn   143–5
Moore, Lowri   150–1
Motion perception   4, 7
Mouskouri, Nina   101
Movie Gen   3
Movies, glasses in
  as actors' props   145
  effect on viewers   147–52
  evil characters   141–2
  female characters   142–5

Mr. Magoo   119, 145–8, 151, 171
nerdy/geeky professors   139–40
notable examples   136–48
optician characters   140–1
smart glasses   221–2
stereotypes   135–6, 148
stigma-reducing effects   138–9, 150–2, 164
studies of   136–7
"Mr. Magoo" (cartoon and film)   119, 145–8, 151, 171
Multifocal lenses; *see* Progressive lenses
Mummy, The (film)   143
Myopia; *see* Nearsightedness
Myrdal, Jan   39–40, 110, 153

NASA   206
National Eye Institute   50
National Foundation for the Blind   147
National Health Service of Britain   101
National Treasure (film)   140
Nearsightedness   21; *see also* Vision problems
  in artists   6–8
  associated vision problems   53
  cause   47–8, 51–3, 58
  corrective lenses   48, 108
  incidence and trends   viii, 50–1, 108
  invention of bifocals for   34–5
  in pre-modern times   87, 108–9, 116
  prevention and management   53–4, 56–8, 116
  refractive laser surgery for   59–60
  scientific understanding of   5
  social attitudes toward   87
Neatorama   139
Nerd(s)   80, 138–9
Nero   20
Neuromancer   206
New York Times   53, 77, 98, 105, 228
New Yorker   102, 103, 180
Newton, Isaac   5, 27
Nielsen, Leslie   147
Night vision   47

Nintendo corporation   206
Nutty Professor, The (film)   140

Oakley   188
Oculus corporation   217
Ocutrx corporation   212
Oliver Peoples Company   103, 188
Onassis, Jacqueline   101–2
Online Encyclopedia of Antique Spectacles   74
Opera glasses   95
Ophthalmologists   50, 57, 62–3, 129–30, 140–1, 212, 228
Oppenheimer, Stephen   150, 172, 174
Optic nerve   4, 48
Optica, De (Al-Hayem)   21
Optical Journal   76
opticians   201–2, 207–8, 220–1
  access   187
  eyeglass sales   201
  future   191–2, 207–8
  on-line   93, 191
  role of   50, 208, 220–1
Optometrists
  access   187
  education and licensing   50, 99
  examination procedure   198–9
  eyeglass sales   201
  future   191–2, 207–8
  in movies   140–1
  resistance to glasses from   79–80
  role of   50, 208
Opus Majus (Bacon)   25
ORCAM My Eye Too   221
orthokeratology   57–8
Orwell, George   12, 111
Outdoor activity, myopia and   53–4, 108
Ovide, Shira   202
Oxford University   162

Pangaia   98
pantascopic tilt   48–9, 197
Paradiso (Dante)   167, 183

Parker, Dorothy   76, 165, 230
Peanuts (comic strip)   127–8
Pearl and Wagner: Four Eyes (McMullan)   127
Pearle Vision   188
Pemberton, Max   121
Pepys, Samuel   116
percepts   4
Persian scholars   21, 23
Personals (film)   143
Phillips, Adam   64
Phoenicia   20
Pico VR glasses   219
Pierre Cardin   98
Pilgrim's Progress (Bunyan)   94–5
Pince-nez   95, 98, 99, 115, *130–1*
pinhole spectacles   *130–1*
Pirenzepine   57
Pitt, Brad   141
Pius II, Pope   160
Pixie glasses   164
Plano (clear) lenses   97, 151, 177
Play It Again Sam (film)   135
PlayStation   206
Plexiglass   82
Pliny the Elder   4
Poe, Edgar Allen   113–14
Pope, Alexander   113
Popular Science Monthly   97
posterior-vitreous detachments (PVD)   11; *see also* Floaters
Potemkin (film)   151–2
Potter, Harry   128, 150, 164
Prada   188
Predestination (film)   150
Prentiss, Elizabeth Payson   75
presbyopia   29, 34, 49, 108, 179
Presley, Elvis   102
Princess Rose and the Golden Glasses (Moore)   151
photorefractive keratectomy (PRK) surgery   59
progressive lenses   197–8, 202, 208
prospect glasses   95

pseudo myopia   47–8
psychedelic experience   227
psycho-optometry   182
Ptolemy   4
Publilius Syrus   135
punk scene of 1980s   102
Pygmalion's Glasses (Weinbaum)   205–6

Queensland University   58
Quest 3S device   217–18

Rabelais   116
Racial Hygiene (Rice)   157–9
Ramones, The (rock band)   102
Ravin, James   6
Ray Bans   100, 102, 188
reading glasses   34, 49, 187–8
Reading stones   20–1, 27, *130–1*
Ready Player One (film)   221–2
Reason for Marriage, The (Lauren)   129
Rebel Without a Cause (film)   100
Reed, Donna   143
refractive surgery   59–60
Reiner, Carl   140
Reinhold, Judge   141
Religion, eyeglass stigma and   28–30, 71–4, 160
Retina   4–6, 11, 47–9, 53, 57–9, 68, 199, 208, 212, 220
retinal detachment   53, 212
retinitis pigmentosa   220
Revenge of the Nerds (film)   139
Rice, Thurman   87, 157–9, 163
Rift device   217
Rihanna   146
rimless glasses   124–5, 162
Rivalto, Giordano da   29
Robot, optician/optometrist services by   191–2, 221
Rock crystal   20, 21, 28, 29
rods and cones   4, 48
Roosevelt, Theodore   98, *130–1*
Rosen, Edward   30–1

Rudolph the Red-Nosed Reindeer (TV show)   174
Ruskin, John   1

Sacks, Oliver   6
Safety Last (film)   138
St. Clair, Jane   171
Saint Francis   23
Saint Jerome   160
Salk, David   186–7, 189–91, 197, 200, 214
Santini, Barry   58, 93–4
Saturday Evening Post   76–7
Scarlett, Edward   33
science of sight; *see also* eye; vision problems
   depth perception   7
   diopter   9, 49, 74, 191, 199
   elements of   4, 48
   evolution of   2–5, 8, 21, 24–5
   fovea   48
   night vision   47
   perspective   7
   retinal dopamine   53, 57
Scientific American (magazine)   81
screen time   8, 52–3, 58, 64–5
scrimshaw   109
self-image of glassers   9, 14, 39, 171–82
   avoidance behaviors   39, 75–8, 81–2, 114, 118–20, 128–9, 132, 161–2, 175, 180–1, 187
   children   46–7, 77, 125–8, 173–4, 176
   contact lenses and   175
   effects of fictional portrayals   151–2
   fashion-consciousness   93–4, 101, 105
   gender differences   180
   global comparison   181–2
   hiding from glasses   161–2
   literary depictions   113, 125–8
   meta-study   163
   others' perceptions *versus*   182
   strategies for improving   164–5
Seneca the Younger   20
Sensorama   206
Sessions, Jeff   147
Seuss, Dr.   138
Shakespeare, William   74, 116–17
Shelby, Jim   52
Shelley, Percy   226
Sight (PBS documentary)   51
Simpsons, The (TV show)   215
Simulators, training   206
Single Man, A (film)   140
Smart glasses   3, 203, 207, 218–19
   applications   210–13
   early technology   215–17
   future of   211–17, 220–3, 226, 227, 229
   types of   208–9
Smith, Addison   33
Snellen eye chart   199
Snow Crash   206
Snowden, Len   77
social and historical contexts of eyewear   viii, 14–15, 27–8, 60; *see ALSO* Literature, glasses in; movies, glasses in; Stigma and opposition to glasses
   in early United States   33–5
   first appearances in artworks   6, 31
   future of smart glasses   210–14, 216–17, 220–4, 226, 227, 229
   intellectualism and glasses   160, 162
   literacy   27–8, 33–5
   modern era   8, 165
   perceived cost   201
   pursuit of better vision   1–3, 41
   studies of popular attitudes   159–64
   technological advancement   21, 27–8, 31, 221
Some Like It Hot (film)   145
Sora   3
South Korea   51, 187, 216–17, 229
Spain   31
Speaker, Lynne   164
Specsavers   188
Spectacle Maker, The (film)   141
Spectacles (Beattie)   126

"Spectacles" (Huxley)   78
"Spectacles" (Poe)   113–14
Spina, Alessandro Della   29–30
Spinoza   27
spiritual/mystical vision   4, 227
spy glasses   95
squinting   4
Star Trek (film)   206
"State of Nature, The" (Bordas)   128
Stellist lenses   53
stereopsis   4
stereoscope   205
stereotypes of glassers   163–4; *see also* Stigma and opposition to glasses
   as aging or infirm   74–7
   as bad guys   141–2
   in early U. S.   33
   eyewear fashions and   96, 97, 99–100
   gender differences   135–6, 142–5
   as intellectual or bookish   76, 142–3, 160, 162–3, 178
   media efforts to undo   150–2, 164
   as mentally deficient   80
   as nerds and geeks   80, 138–40
   research on   159–63
Stevenson, Robert Louis   63
stigma and opposition to glasses   3, 12, 14, 29, 30, 34–6, 46–7, 73, 132, 229–30; *see also* stereotypes of glassers
   celebrity eyewear and   100–2
   eugenicist proposals   157–9
   eyewear fashion and   96, 101
   in literary fiction   117–21, 126–8
   as markers of weakness and aging   74–7
   on medical grounds   62–3, 79–80
   in movies   135–7, 139–40
   persistence of   82–3, 228–9
   from religious institutions   28–30, 71–4, 160
   as social control   72–3
   strategies for overcoming   79, 164–5
   studies of popular attitudes   159–64

sunglasses   97
   types of   71
   as unattractive   76–9, 81–2
Stolen Focus (Hari)   65
strabismus   47
Strange Days (film)   206
Strangers on a Train (film)   142
Stravinsky, Igor   63
Streep, Meryl   142, 145
suicide   149–50
Summer Lightning (Wodehouse)   99–100
Sunglass Hut   188
sunglasses   2, 20, 78, 96–8, 100–3, *130–1*, 137, 144, 185, 201, 228
sunlight   53–4
Superman (film)   139
Surgery, eye   179–80
   author's experience   225–8
   laser   59–60
   myopia intervention   58
Swift, Jonathan   39, 78, 117
Sword of Damocles device   206
Sydney Myopia Study   53

Tanzania   161, 162
tea shades   101
Tears   81
Teasing and bullying   12, 14, 174–7, 229–30
   author's experience   86, 88–91, 147
   in children's literature   126
   effects   149–50, 162
   movies and   147–9
   risk of, for glassers   149, 164–5
telescope(s)   3
telesphere   206
Temples, eyeglass frame   33
Ten Things I Hate About Me (Abdel-Fatteh)   129
Teusch, Sammy   149–50
"The Boy" (film)   138
They Live (film)   137–8
Thoreau, Henry David   17
Thornton, G. R.   160

INDEX

Thurber, James 43, 133
Time (magazine) 215
tinted lenses 31
titanium 103
Titian 6
Tommy 206
Top Gun (film) 102
Touch of Fantasy, or Romance for Those Lucky Enough to Wear Glasses (Adams) 121–2
traffic accidents, vision and 45, 80
Travelers' glasses 96, *130–1*
Trumbull, John 45
Turner, J. M. W. 6–7
twelve corporation 98
Twilight Zone (TV series) 129
Two Strikes, Four Eyes 126

Ultraviolet rays 96, 190
University of Massachusetts 216
University of Melbourne 162–3
University of Vienna 162

vacation from eyeglasses
   author's decision regarding viii, 8–14
   author's experience 37–41, 43–4, 61–4, 68–70, 85, 87, 91, 107, 110–11, 131–4, 153–6, 167–9, 230
   author's termination of 183–4
   preparation for 17–18
   purpose 18, 36, 169
vacation from technology 64–6
Van Gogh, Vincent 6
Venetian glass 21–2, 31
Versace 188
Vertov, Dziga 8, 205
VIEW device 206
View Master 206
Villon, François 116
Virtual Boy console 206
Virtual reality 36, *130–1*, 205–10, 212, 217–19, 221–4, 227
vision corporation 212
Vision Council 104

Vision-Expo West 207–8, 214
vision problems; *see also* astigmatism; eyeglasses; farsightedness; nearsightedness
   age-related 29, 34, 49, 108, 179
   artistic expression and 6–8
   associated problems 45
   author's experience of 9, 12, 43, 228
   crossed eyes 47
   early interventions 2, 22–3
   eugenics proposal 157–9
   Huxley's experience 42
   individual differences in experience of 38–40, 228
   invention of bifocals 34–5
   medical professions dealing with 50
   misinformation about 47–8, 51–2
   patterns and trends 50–1, 187
   refractive surgeries for 59–60
   role of corrective lenses 48–50
   smart glasses and 212, 214
Vision Protechnology 209–10
Vision service Plan 189
visual cortex 4, 48
Vitamin A 47
Vitamin D 53
vitrectomy 225
vitreous humor 11
Vogue (magazine) 100
Voltaire 117

Wallace, W. C. 80
Warby Parker 103, 191
Warhol, Andy 107–8
Washington, George 33
Weinbaum, Stanley 205–6
Weisz, Rachel 143
Wheeler, John M. 80
Who, The (rock band) 206
Wiggler 218
Wilhelm Meister's Apprentice (Goethe) 117
Wilhide, Jenny 165, 230
Williams, Cynthia 129

wire-rim glasses 32, 101, 128, 136, 141, 164
Wodehouse, P. G. 99–100, 115
Wolfe, Kathi 148
Women's Wear Daily 100
Wong, Brian 220-1
Wood, Peggy 77, 79, 93
World Is Not Enough, The (film) 136
World War II 100
Worshipful Company of Spectacle Makers 32
Writing the Southwest (Dunaway) 167
www.glassers.us 172

X-Ray Spex 102
Xingu people, vision correction and 195, 203

Yamini, Musa 149
Yamini, Sabrina 149
Younger corporation 201
Yves St. Laurent 98

Zeiss corporation 81, 122, 190, 197–200
Zenni corporation 201
Zuckerberg, Mark 211

ABOUT THE AUTHOR

David King Dunaway has written extensively about American culture since earning the first PhD in American Studies from UC-Berkeley. Author and editor of ten volumes of history, including prize-winning biographies of Pete Seeger and Aldous Huxley, his articles have appeared in publications ranging from the *Virginia Quarterly* to *The New York Times*. He has taught in Denmark, England, Colombia, Kenya, and at the University of North Carolina-Chapel Hill and the University of New Mexico. He is currently Visiting Professor of Broadcasting at the University of Sao Paulo. He has worked as a consultant to UNESCO, the National Park Service, and the Library of Congress. His oral history documentaries have aired on National Public Radio and internationally. www.davidkdunaway.com